MOMS IN LABOR

An Employment Lawyer's Secrets to
Protect Your Baby and Your Career
(That HR Won't Tell You)

Daphne Delvaux, Esq.

HarperCollins
Leadership
An Imprint of HarperCollins

For all the mothers,

May this book center all the unseen labor that keeps the world turning
and celebrate your devotion, which forms the fabric of all of life.
For it is through mothers that life itself dares to begin again.
May we remember that every story, and every breath, starts with the Mother.

Published by HarperCollins Leadership, an imprint of HarperCollins Focus LLC, 501
Nelson Place, Nashville, TN 37214, USA.

Any internet addresses, phone numbers, or company or product information printed in
this book are offered as a resource and are not intended in any way to be or to imply an
endorsement by HarperCollins Leadership, nor does HarperCollins Leadership vouch for
the existence, content, or services of these sites, phone numbers, companies, or products
beyond the life of this book.

ISBN 978-1-4002-5260-2 (ePub)
ISBN 978-1-4002-5259-6 (HC)

HarperCollins Publishers, Macken House, 39/40 Mayor Street Upper, Dublin 1,
D01 C9W8, Ireland (https://www.harpercollins.com)

Library of Congress Control Number: 2025947558

Art direction: Ron Huizinga
Cover design and illustration: Mel Judson
Interior Design: Neuwirth & Associates, Inc.

Printed in the United States of America
25 26 27 28 29 LBC 5 4 3 2 1

Contents

Foreword

As a ballerina, I've spent my whole life stretching my body to its limits. My body has been my instrument, the way I tell stories and share art. And when I became the first Black woman promoted to principal dancer at American Ballet Theatre, my body itself became part of the story. It was more than just dancing. It was a statement. A revolution in motion.

I've worked hard to take care of it. I've pushed through injuries, trusted physical therapists and coaches, and found ways to heal so I could always return *en pointe*. Bodies change. They adapt. They hold our struggles. And yet, they keep showing up for us. That's one of the most humbling lessons dance has given me.

Ballet taught me discipline and strength in ways I could never have imagined. But nothing prepared me for the transformation of motherhood. Suddenly, it wasn't just my body anymore.

Even with all my training and experience, pregnancy humbled me. The idea that my body could create both life and art at the same time? That was the ultimate advanced class.

While I was pregnant, I produced and starred in the short film *Flower*. It was such an ambitious project to take on at that time, but I felt pulled to do it. I was often sick during shoots, worried if I could perform at the level I demanded of myself and others expected from me. But pregnancy didn't hold me back. It expanded me. Even through nausea and exhaustion, I felt my dancing deepen. Carrying life inside me gave every step, every gesture, a new layer of meaning.

That's why *Flower* is so important to me. It wasn't just another project, it was a snapshot of who I was in that moment: standing at the threshold of motherhood, creating art and life at the same time. Dancing with Jackson inside me, I could feel two rhythms woven together: the rhythm of my body as a dancer, and the rhythm of new life growing within me.

I'm proud that *Flower* has been recognized and celebrated, but its true power, for me, is personal. It captures me in transition, an artist becoming a mother.

In April 2022, my husband and I welcomed our son, Jackson. He is the love of my life. He is the masterpiece I am most proud of.

Motherhood tested every ounce of strength I thought I had built in the studio, as well as my stamina, focus, and persistence, but in ways I had never known before. It wasn't just about caring for my son. It was about reimagining myself, reshuffling priorities, and finding a resilience I didn't know existed.

Returning to the stage after Jackson's birth was one of the hardest challenges I've ever faced. Ballet is unforgiving. There's an unspoken expectation that you stay in peak form at all times, because this art is a team effort; others depend on your presence. But pregnancy, childbirth, and the early months of caring for a newborn don't fit neatly into that mold.

The pressure was real. But I've never been new to breaking molds. I kept dancing, even while nurturing a child. It was heavy, yes, but also deeply magical.

Motherhood also shifted the way I see my own mother and the realities she faced. It gave me a deeper understanding of how unsupported mothers are in America, especially Black mothers. And in the dance world, like so many industries, we still have so far to go.

This isn't just about maternity leave or time off. It's about changing the culture so that no parent has to choose between being an artist and being a caregiver.

Like all working parents, we deserve the chance to be present for both our craft and our family without impossible trade-offs. Sharing these stories out loud is one way we begin to change the culture.

That's how I came to connect with Daphne Delvaux. I'll never forget her words to me:

I loved your performances while pregnant the most. Full of strength and regenerative creation, weaving beauty and life at once, like only you can.

Deep bow to the power of your womb, and *révérence*,

Daphne

Her words landed so deeply for me. It was the first time I felt fully seen in both parts of myself: the artist and the mother.

Daphne's work is all about that. She centers motherhood as the superpower it is, instead of something we're expected to minimize or push aside. Through her legal practice, the first in the nation devoted to mothers' rights at work, and her platform, The Mamattorney, she gives mothers the tools, knowledge, and language to advocate for themselves in workplaces that were never designed with us in mind. And she does it as a dancer too.

What I love about her work is that it's not just about laws, it's about a cultural shift. She reminds us that advocating for ourselves and our families isn't only our right, it's necessary.

In my career, I've always had access to coaches, teachers, mentors, and physical therapists to support me. In motherhood, you must search for those guides on your own. That's why I'm so grateful for Daphne. She is exactly that—a guide and an advocate.

Motherhood is work that often happens behind closed doors, without applause, without acknowledgment. And that's where we need support the most. Integrating motherhood and work is an act of advocacy, and like any practice, you need a coach. Daphne is that coach.

When I read her work, I felt an immediate connection. Ballet taught me that visibility matters. My presence on stage tells young dancers that they belong. Daphne does the same for mothers. She makes us visible. She equips us to ask for what we need, set boundaries, and build our careers and families with confidence and without apology.

Her work is a movement. It's transformative.

Motherhood redefined strength for me. It's no longer just about physical stamina or technique. It's about patience, adaptability, emotional resilience, and the courage to advocate not only for yourself, but for your family. It's about the sacrifices and the small, everyday choices: leaving earlier, saying no sooner, holding space for what matters most. It's about living in that in-between, pulled in every direction but still showing up.

That's what Daphne's work reflects: that being a mother and being a professional aren't opposites, they're both part of a full and powerful life.

I'll never forget the week I returned to rehearsals postpartum. My body felt different. My energy was scattered. But I walked into the studio and kept going. I thought about mothers everywhere, navigating offices, classrooms, and boardrooms while balancing sleepless nights and endless responsibilities at home.

Daphne's voice is for them too. She's saying: You don't have to choose between your family and your career. You can ask for support. You can set boundaries. You can have both, and you deserve both.

To the mothers reading this book: Your journey is real. Your struggles are valid. Your dreams are worth it.

Daphne gives you a road map, not just to survive, but to thrive. And for those who work with mothers—employers, colleagues, partners—this book is a call to see us, respect us, and support us.

As a mother, a dancer, and an advocate, I can say this with certainty: This book is more than a guide. It's a call to action. It's proof that mothers don't have to compromise their ambition, creativity, or professional dreams. And it's a reminder that when we support mothers, we uplift entire communities, including the next generation.

My hope is that this work empowers mothers to claim their rightful place in any space, whether that's a stage, a boardroom, or a seat at the negotiating table. And my hope is that by continuing to share our stories—the hard ones, the triumphant ones—we keep moving closer to a culture where mothers never have to choose between passion and family.

Daphne is leading that charge with courage and compassion. And it's an honor to stand with her, in art, in advocacy, and in motherhood.

—Misty Copeland,
American ballet dancer

Opening Argument

I stood in front of the fridge in disbelief. I was in the middle of a trial, I had only a few minutes left during our lunch break, and I'd gotten special permission to go into the judge's chambers' kitchen, where only the judge, clerks, and bailiffs are authorized to be. Staring back at me was a sandwich, soggy with breastmilk. My breastmilk. The *judge's* sandwich. And I didn't know whether to laugh or to cry.

I was trying a difficult case—and not just because the facts were challenging or the law was complex. It was difficult because I was also a new mom, and I was learning very quickly how much I would have to (sometimes literally) juggle to make it all work.

Just a few days earlier, while I was giving an opening statement, I'd had a letdown. I don't mean that I let my *client* down: I mean my milk came pouring down because I was not able to take a pump break. Luckily, I was wearing breast pads (a.k.a. boobie diapers), but I was acutely aware that while I was orating about justice, my mother body was Niagara Falls'ing horchata. Uncomfortable, to say the least.

As the trial continued, the only time I was able to pump ended up being during our short breaks. Usually, these breaks are reserved to review exhibits and strategize with the client. Instead, I found myself topless in the judge's chambers (does not help the letdown), stress-rushing to set up my pump (does not help the letdown), and with the AC permanently cranked high (*definitely* does not help the letdown). I was alternating between swiping through photos of my baby, trying to will my body into releasing the traffic jam on the milky way, and reviewing screenshots of new exhibits.

Meanwhile, the judge would not wait for me to get back before resuming the trial (which was so uncool), so the proceedings continued without me there until I finally rushed back into the courtroom with a big ol' pump bag. (And yes, I had to hustle: The judge had actually gone so far as to have my witnesses be cross-examined *without me present*.)

Toggling between being a badass attorney standing up for my client and the exclusive food source for another human was already getting sitcom-level absurd. But then came the sandwich.

After my pumping breaks in the chambers, I would store my milk in that special kitchen reserved for the judge and authorized court staff. That day had been particularly chaotic, and I had been in such a hurry after pumping that I didn't fully close one of my bottles.

When I returned to the fridge on our lunch break, I realized with horror that my open bottle had poured all over the interior. And I also realized that one of the sandwiches in the fridge was soaked with Daphne's daily dairy.

Not just any sandwich, either.

Oh my God. The judge's sandwich.

Without even thinking, I grabbed it and tossed it.

But now the judge had no sandwich. With mere minutes to spare, I ran to the deli in a blind panic to order a replacement sandwich. (What kind of sandwich? I'd totally forgotten. What would a judge eat? Pastrami with mustard? Sure, fine.)

Sandwich in hand, I ran back upstairs and was relieved to discover that the judge was still reviewing briefs, her glasses still on for Work Mode. (Yes, *her*—did you assume she was a man this whole time? Ha! Welcome to your implicit bias.) I darted into her chambers, replaced the sandwich, cleaned the fridge, and barely caught my breath.

In the end, no one ever said anything. (Although, to this day, I still imagine the judge taking a bite of her sandwich and being surprised that it was pastrami—because she was *so sure* she'd bought a Reuben that day.) We won the case, too, which was incredible for our client. But when I look back on the soggy sandwich saga of 2018—and my desire never to repeat the logistical craziness of those few days—I realize that it was one of many moments that ultimately motivated me to become a fierce advocate for other mothers, something I'd secretly been working toward my whole life as the daughter of a single mom.

Even though it was darkly humorous at the time, that fateful sandwich made me wake up to the reality that what us moms go through in the workplace is *quidam de armento cacas.* That's lawyer Latin for "some bullshit."

I know this because I'm a mom, one who's navigated pregnancy and motherhood while working a demanding job.

But I also know this because, well, I'm a lawyer—an award-winning trial attorney in employment law. My law firm is dedicated to championing women's rights in the workplace, and with a practice focused on representing mothers in cases of discrimination, retaliation, and harassment, we are the nationwide leader on issues of motherhood discrimination. Over the course of my career, I've recovered countless six- and seven-figure settlements and verdicts, not just securing the monetary justice my clients deserve but also helping restore their dignity and sense of self-worth. I was named Outstanding Trial Lawyer by my peers for winning an equal pay trial, and I've taken on all the big corporate players: Walmart, Amazon, Fox News, Target, and thousands more. I've been featured in news outlets like *The New York Times*, *The Wall Street Journal*, Bloomberg, *Forbes*, and Vox, sharing my story and my clients' victories.

Beyond the courtroom, I'm also a mother to two boys and a passionate advocate for women and mothers. I cofounded the Chamber of Mothers, a grassroots movement devoted to mothers' rights in America. Together with my colleagues, I've worked to advance federal paid leave, affordable childcare, and healthcare for families—a mission that has taken us to both the White House and Congress.

I'm also the creator of The Mamattorney, a platform designed to educate women about their workplace rights and teach them how to advocate for themselves and their babies. My goal is to empower mothers to achieve financial and time freedom without sacrificing their career ambitions. With thousands of followers across platforms, I've become a trusted expert on pregnancy and postpartum protections as well as maternity leave regulations.

So I know, in precise and exhaustive detail, how pregnancy, mother-hood, career paths, and employment laws interact and intertwine. And I can tell you that it is shocking how many people—how many *employment attorneys*, even—don't know the first thing about these rights.

For example, when I was pregnant for the first time, I researched state and federal laws and learned about my own employment situation. As a California employee, I could take five and a half to seven months off, *paid by the state*, depending on the conditions of my postpartum experience, with a potential extension to a one-year paid leave. Even I was a bit surprised—if only because absolutely *no one* I knew was taking these long paid maternity leaves; the most I'd ever heard of a new mom taking was twelve weeks. At the *employment law* firm where I worked, no one knew the specifics of these obscure maternity laws and benefits.

I ended up drafting a maternity leave policy for the firm, setting terms for both time off and financial benefits. After that, whenever newer associates became pregnant, they were sent to me.

But I didn't stop there.

When my friends got pregnant, I started sharing my template with them to help their negotiations with their employers, and they all got way more time off and more benefits than they imagined possible. I started sharing it with my community, and each woman left more flabbergasted than the one before her at just how much she was legally entitled to. My template helped them back their employers into a corner because it simply laid out the regulations, and employers had no choice but to follow the law.

Through building my niche, I started litigating more and more maternity rights cases: pregnancy discrimination, leave retaliation, and postpartum and pumping accommodations, which eventually led to me starting my own law firm entirely devoted to mothers' rights at work.

As a mother, it felt so nourishing and purposeful to do these cases. I felt like I was the mother's (my client's) attorney, but also her baby's attorney, and, Mama, let me tell you: *Your baby needs a good lawyer.*

But as an expert in maternity law in the context of the workplace, I was operating in a part of the law that was (relatively) niche and new. Despite being an employment trial attorney for many years, I was actually alone in this field. I became more and more in demand not just for clients, but to educate other attorneys. And the more I shared this information about maternal rights, the more and more I was confronted with the fact that *no one knows this.*

As a speaker at a prestigious trial attorneys conference, I was invited to lecture about maternal rights. I got up onstage in front of dozens of seasoned trial lawyers, *the best* in the country, many of them employment lawyers, and quizzed them.

"How long is paid maternity leave in California? What about New Jersey? Massachusetts?"

No one knew. (The few people who thought they did know got it wrong.) This was a roomful of my expert peers, attorneys who were practicing at well-heeled firms, who'd passed the nightmare of the bar exam, who were smart and empathetic and some of them even mothers themselves, and they didn't know this (relatively) basic fact.

A few weeks later, at an employment law seminar, I did the same thing. "How long is maternity leave in this state?"

This time, I got a lot more (and more confident) answers. But they were wrong too.

I have a pending case against the City of Los Angeles, in which we alleged the city misapplied leave laws. The local government can get it wrong, too, and so does the federal government. When we advocate for paid leave in Congress, representatives are usually surprised to learn they already have access to paid leave and generally (wrongly) assume the private sector pays for paid leave entirely out of pocket. This was one of the questions at the VP debate, "How long should employers be required to pay for workers while they are home taking care of their newborns?" completely ignoring that paid leave systems are funded through payroll deductions and that it's actually employees paying for their own leaves.

What I know for certain, after doing this work for many years, is that mothers' rights are not general knowledge and that, yes, everyone is getting it wrong. This lack of knowledge is everywhere. In small companies, in employment law firms, in the government.

Unlike other concepts like equal pay for women (pretty self-explanatory) or sexual harassment (don't be a perv at work), maternal rights are this obscure field: mysterious, inconsistent, disorienting, chaotic, kind of like motherhood itself. Over and over, I heard, "I had *no idea* this is how it is."

Which is, again—kind of like motherhood itself.

As I established myself to the public as a maternity rights expert, I could not keep up with demand. The questions were endless, and there was always an undertone of deep desperation. Most of the time, the questions started with "HR is giving me wrong information," or "HR is giving me no information," or "HR is not responding to my emails," or "HR gave me information but I'm still confused."

So, once I had started working exclusively with clients on maternity cases, I also started sharing the information through my online community. Because, at that time, what I found online was a hot mess: blogs and accounts replete with inaccurate legal advice related to maternal rights, resulting in many moms resigning out of confusion or desperation. When I would point out that there *were* options available, I was often accused of "well, you're in California," even though many regulations apply in the other forty-nine states. I wanted to help women across the nation with their leave plans, based on the *actual* laws and regulations, not the urban myths. Namely: (1) Maternity leave does not exist in America (not true), (2) Your maternity leave depends on your employer's policies in the handbook (also not true), (3) Maternity leave separates mother from baby at six weeks, while newborn *puppies* get eight weeks before they can be sold to new owners (sensational, but not true), (4) Your doctor decides how long you can take off (also not true).

In all likelihood, you *do* have some options. The options may not be ideal, but they're more than nothing. What they almost certainly are is *confusing*. And the reason why leave laws are so confusing is because your rights to take time off will depend on winning the zip code lottery, how long you've worked at your current employer, and how big your employer is. In addition, a lot of company handbooks are based on the wrong set of laws, especially if the company has staff in different states (which has become quite common since the pandemic). It's easy to get confused, frustrated, or give up entirely—but please, don't.

Make no mistake: This is not a book intended to celebrate the state of American maternity leave, which categorically remains abysmal compared to other nations. In fact, part of my work is advocating in DC for paid leave laws for *all* American mothers. Maternal discrimination is everywhere, in so many forms. But while I strongly believe in righteous rage, and I curse daily about how we shortchange mothers, I also know that indignation and long-game activism is not helpful when you're trying to figure out how to get accommodated at work *now*.

The focus of this book is to take a deep look at the options that are right in front of us that we didn't know we had. Not in a future, speculative time when we all get along, but today. What can we do right now?

So, while we must advocate for paid leave for all, we also have to work with what we do have. Yes, the legal protections are a bit barren, but with some creativity and savviness, you may have more options than you think you do. One of the things I like to tell mothers is that pregnancy and post-partum are covered by disability protections, and while the United States does not have a comprehensive framework protecting the parenting experience, it actually has a fairly robust disability rights system. The American disability system offers a multidimensional landscape of rights and protections that most mothers miss because they are looking for the wrong things (usually maternity or parental rights). It is true that American motherhood and parenting is bone-chilling and backbreaking unsupported and unseen labor. I don't need to explain to you that most American mothers don't have enough time with their newborns and are routinely punished for having children through the motherhood tax or the mommy track. I trust you've seen the data, and other than activating our nervous systems and making us feel desperate and hopeless, I don't see the point in rehashing all of it. So excuse me if I skip all the depressing facts and figures. While important, they contribute to hopelessness and the sense that things will never change and we have no control or power. I'm also certain that many mothers are rushing back to work because they have not exhausted their disability rights. I know this because I've had this conversation thousands of times.

This is a both/and situation where nuance is important, because it's in the nuance that we find the gems: more months of time off, more payment, more peace of mind in our motherhood and our careers.

So, with this book, I'm here to do two things: inform you of the truth *and* empower you to take advantage of every legal right you have.

When we do this, it works. I've seen it happen for so many moms.

When I share my teachings, I am met with two responses: *I am so happy I met you*, or *I wish I'd known this when I had my babies.* In fact, I have a folder on my phone titled "You saved my leave" to hold the many stories I received from parents, thanking me for the time off with their babies they took because of me. That folder has thousands of screenshots and counting. That's thousands of babies! I have another folder called "Flexin' Mamas" with stories from many mothers I've helped with flex or remote work accommodations. Another folder is called "Mama Got Paid" because so many women shared how I helped them get a raise or negotiate a severance while protecting their reputation.

Here are just some of their stories:

- *I just returned to work today after 10 months of benefits. HR didn't tell me about them—you did.*
- *I got my leave extended by five weeks thanks to you. I never would have known and my employer never offered. Had no idea that this was my right.*
- *I am now working from home three days a week with my reasonable accommodation. So very thankful!*
- *I was about to quit breastfeeding because pumping was impossible. Then you taught me how to work with my employer on getting my needs met, and now we are back on track! Nursing my baby is my favorite moment after coming home from work and it's all because of you. You are truly an angel on earth.*
- *You're doing God's work! I was about to quit my job and was experiencing so much stress that my doctor was telling me it was impacting my pregnancy and baby. Because of you, I was able to calmly request my needs in a way they couldn't say no to, and now I am able to work from my bed. I'm so, so relaxed, all while knowing my job will be there when I return. Thank you on behalf of me and thank you on behalf of my baby for giving her a relaxed mommy.*
- *I am kind of dumbfounded that I had options I didn't know about. Now I know that the law has my back and I should not be fucked with. The world is a better place because of you.*
- *I shared my story with my state representative. They voted for paid leave in our state, and the bill passed! Thank you for giving me the courage to use my voice, to not be scared, and to fight for change.*

These stories represent my proudest achievements, because allowing babies to come into the world to parents who can enjoy a stress-free and supported bonding experience prevents generational trauma.

So that's what we will do in this book. I promise that you will learn something you did not know, which will make you feel less powerless and less hopeless. Because if we feel disempowered, we act accordingly. Instead, this book is the consolidation of my secrets as a trial lawyer protecting employees at work from exploitative and demanding expectations. I will share a lot of stories about my cases and trials—and I will be sure to share plenty of positive stories as well, because the good truly does outweigh the bad. No matter what the outcome, however, these stories will show you the bravery of my former clients. I hope you let their courage inspire you. What I will *not* do is teach you how to sue your employer, but rather, how to prevent legal conflicts entirely: how to be a powerhouse at work, some-one to be respected, even feared a little, because you know your rights and you know how to advocate for what's right. I will be that protective shield between the forces of capitalism and you and your baby. Think of me as Arya Stark just back from Braavos, crazy skilled and able to fight in the dark. My goal here is to protect your pregnancy and baby bubble, and I will do that through a combination of education, step-by-step road maps, hot takes, and snackable success stories.

One final note before we get started is that I'm a lawyer, but not your lawyer. This means that you will use this information as a source of inspi-ration, not as a strict constitution. As the law is nuanced and complex, it is always wise to consult with a local attorney if you are unsure of the particulars of your personal issue.

So come here, my dear friend. Grab a warm beverage. Put your phone in another room. Let me teach you my secrets. Let us outsmart them, together. It can be done, and I know that because I've done it a thousand times. The patterns are the same, there is a method, and you can learn it. You will never regret advocating for your rights, and you will never regret advocating for your baby.

Because you are not "lucky to have a job"—that's some bullshit. No, your *job* is lucky to have *you*. And so is your baby.

Let's get started.

1

Motherhood

The Best Thing That Will Ever
Happen to Your Career

Motherhood is the best thing that will ever happen to your career. Seriously.

As someone who is deep in storytelling related to motherhood and work, I notice that we tend to focus on the inflammatory stories more than the success stories. And because we are so inundated with horror stories, we assume that is reality, but it is more likely that everything turns out fine. Not wonderful, but just fine, and in the context of motherhood and work, "just fine" is a great goal, at least during the baby years. We don't want to put too much pressure on ourselves, after all. Motherhood transitions do not have to be the time to reach for the stars or gain a competitive edge. We have a lot of time to do that.

What is most vital with my work is that we tell well-balanced stories. You will read stories in this book that will make your blood boil, but for every one of those stories, there are a hundred stories of mothers who were supported at work, and a handful of truly remarkable success stories. What I want to inundate you with is not more data or terrible stories, but the joy of motherhood and work. These are the stories we should be telling to pregnant mothers.

When I was pregnant for the first time, I dutifully attended the hospital birth prep classes. Let me tell you, I wish I never did that. One week after another, the nurse gave us horror stories on how everything could go wrong, including long lists of complications and medical traumas. It was terrifying. During my second pregnancy, I took an online course filled with loving and respectful teachings. My first birth ended in a painful forceps extraction. My second baby was a flash birth, born in the car. (I do actually recommend a car birth. It's like being in a private cave, the movement helps shake the baby loose, and it is over before you realize it started.) My first birth left me feeling confused, scared, traumatized, and numb, just as the hospital classes prepared me for. My second birth left me feeling powerful, fierce, and Divine, just like the second birthing classes prepared me for.

What if I told you: It is so, so, so much more likely things will go right. When we hear that, our nervous system releases. We can exhale a little deeper and relax our jaws and shoulders. This is what I intend to do in this book.

So: Motherhood is awesome. I love it. It's my favorite thing in life. I mean, I created humans—the ultimate act of creation! We mothers are incredible!

And, yes: Motherhood will be *amazing* for your career. I promise. It may just take some time.

We'll be talking a lot about the challenges that mothers face in the workplace and in their careers. I won't shy away from making sure you know the reality of what some mothers experience. However, these stories, more than anything, will demonstrate what you already know: You need to be prepared. Just like we prepare for the impact of birth on our bodies and our family life, we need to prepare for the impact of birth on our careers and workplace lives.

But it's just important to highlight the joy of motherhood amid all the challenges. I don't want to read another book about the draining narrative. Yes, motherhood is hard, but it's also magical. It's like preparing for an Ironman Triathlon—you might be nervous, but afterward, you'll feel invincible. You'll experience a love like never before and tap into parts of yourself you never knew existed. You'll get clarity and insight on yourself and your career like you never would have imagined. You'll get to know yourself, your irreplaceable value, your motivations, and your purpose deeper and more meaningfully than ever before.

You are going on a thrilling adventure. LFG.

"Yes Girls" Anonymous:
No to the Grind. It's Time to Glide.

I don't know about you, but I have been a "yes girl" my entire career. Most women have.

When I came into the workforce, my expectations for support were low and my tolerance for stress was high. Young, eager, an immigrant, ambitious, and with a deep longing for belonging, I could always be counted on for the hardest case, the most pressing brief, or the most challenging client. Colleagues and managers told me I was extremely hardworking, diligent, and reliable. I took pride in this feedback, and it became my identity. In those first few years as a junior attorney, I never complained about the low pay or the long hours because I was used to being broke and felt "grateful to have a job."

And for those first five years, it paid off. From the outside, I was a success: I won my first jury trial at just age twenty-six—an equal pay case against a female business owner, the first reported equal pay case tried in California—and then won an Outstanding Trial Lawyer award for my work on the case, elected by more seasoned trial attorneys. Over the years, I became a senior attorney and started managing a team. I was a rising star.

Then came motherhood. During my first pregnancy, I essentially acted like I was not pregnant, terrified of the impact on my career, scared that all this hard work and sacrifice would go to waste. This star was still on the rise, after all!

So I worked through nausea and from hospital beds. I spent most of my time driving to depositions instead of decorating a nursery. In the days before deadlines, I sometimes slept under my desk. After maternity leave, I pumped in cold, sterile offices during the day and nursed a baby all night, reading transcripts with a flashlight.

When we won the trial, I was called Wonder Woman. That felt good. Look at me, doing it all!

Yet at the same time, I was just so exhausted, and felt like I was failing everyone.

When the presiding juror shared that they had ruled in our favor, I remember feeling completely numb. I didn't actually *want* to be Wonder

Woman. Wonder Woman is lonely, and she has to sacrifice love and belonging for her destiny of saving everything and everybody.

The irony of this chapter of my life was that despite being an all-star lawyer, despite being a fierce advocate for my clients, I couldn't *self*-advocate effectively. Not because I didn't know what I needed, or because I didn't know my legal rights—I was working on equal pay and gender discrimination lawsuits, after all!—but because I was stuck in my "yes girl" mentality.

If you're a recovering "yes girl" or "Wonder Woman" like me, you may have struggled with these feelings of guilt, anxiety, and fear around your work as well. So often, we're told to be grateful to have a job, that we should feel lucky to work where we do. We have been conditioned to keep our heads down and work without complaining. We don't want to be perceived as difficult, needy, demanding. We don't want to be "that person." Over time, we become our own toxic boss. We don't let ourselves rest. We ignore our bodies. We suppress our needs. We even hold our pee. And when we're pregnant, we pretend it's no big deal. We're just the same. We won't skip a beat, promise! We smile and work through our bodies' alarm signals because a real #girlboss pushes through and shatters those glass ceilings!

But at the same time, pregnancy *is* demanding. And shattering glass ceilings actually hurts your head! And you have to clean up the pieces of glass and pull them out of your skin yourself too. As a habitual ceiling-shatterer, I can say this: Ceiling-shattering left me exhausted, and it gave me a headache.

For many of us who are otherwise able-bodied and healthy, pregnancy is the first confrontation we'll have with the limits of our body. Whether we encounter fatigue and mild nausea or more serious side effects like high blood pressure or gestational diabetes, we will not be operating at our peak performance while nurturing and growing a new person. And because we're starting with much less energy, we end up facing a gap between who we were and who we've become—especially for recovering "yes girls" like me.

This can spark feelings of grief and anger. We feel like we're failing to meet our *own* standards, and yet the pace of work keeps zipping around us. Suddenly not knowing what's next can be unsettling, especially if we've been pushing hard and climbing the ladder. It's like riding a bike at a steady pace and having your feet slip off the pedals: The momentum persists and keeps spinning, and you're scrambling to get back in control.

At that point, you have two choices: push through it, which can be unhealthy (for you *and* your baby), or strengthen your advocacy muscle.

That's not always easy for us yes girls. It can be scary to figure out what you truly need and how to ask for it. We might not even be familiar with our own needs.

Remember, though: Advocacy is a skill, and it can be learned.

First, I want you to acknowledge that it's okay not to keep up sometimes. In fact, expecting yourself to keep up 24/7, even when your body is screaming at you for rest, is setting an unreasonable and unhealthy standard. In a culture of pushing through, I want you to take a step back. Don't be complicit in your own exploitation.

In my hometown in Belgium, there is a little shop that is open only Wednesdays from 2:00 p.m. to 5:00 p.m. It's been in business for thirty years. *How?!* I have no idea, but apparently, working three hours a week is *also* a sustainable business model. I offer this as a study in contrast and to drive this point home: There is enough time. To do all the things you want, but not all at the same time. Save some things for later and trust that what is yours to achieve will be there, waiting for you to arrive when you are ready.

Second, remember that pregnancy is its own full-time job. It's an extremely demanding, physical job. When you see animals in the wild, the pregnant and nursing ones just rest, nurse, nothing else. They're not expected to hunt or find shelter or fight over territory. Professional athletes are encouraged to rest and have teams taking excellent care of their bodies. Meanwhile, mothers end up juggling two high-priority tasks: growing a baby and keeping up at our work. And there are no breaks from the baby-growing. It will take a lot out of you, day in and day out.

Third, know that *this* is why you have rights. Fortunately, in today's workplace, most women don't have to think about things like accessibility, accommodations, or discrimination until they embark upon motherhood. But when you're pregnant, it's no longer a choice: You *must* know your rights, and exercise them, to keep yourself and your baby healthy. It might feel scary to know that you'll be leaning on legal terms, setting boundaries, and drawing lines in the sand, but remember, the law has your back.

While it's far from perfect, the law *does* recognize that pregnancy, child-birth, recovery, bonding, and breastfeeding require accommodations in the workplace, and *those are your rights.* Use them.

Finally, embrace that you may feel grief. Grief over the ego deaths of no longer being the go-getter who could do it all, the #girlbossing "yes" girl, available for everything, always ready to jump in and lend a hand, and then suddenly not having that same time or energy anymore.

At the same time, however, that ego death is rebirth. You're ready. So, instead of just stewing in the grief, look to this as a point in your life where you can breathe and reflect on how, for the moment, you've done enough. That you've worked hard and earned your stripes and now are going to shift gears to a new direction.

This rebirth can be so freeing. Before I had kids, I used to proofread emails three times before sending, obsessed with making sure I made zero mistakes. Now, I just send them—and they're still good. I'm still excellent at my job *and* I'm happier. Motherhood unlocked skills and qualities I didn't have pre-baby, and I'm actually better at my work in many ways. But one thing I no longer do is ignore the natural pace of my body, and it is vital to embrace "good enough."

So, finding peace in "good enough" is important. These setbacks will be temporary. And when you do reemerge into your workplace, the strengths and skills that motherhood will have brought you will do so much to supercharge your career to the next level.

Motherhood Is Your Superpower

So why is starting a family actually so good for your career?

The way I see it, motherhood acts as the ultimate filter. It offers a chance to sift through your day-to-day life and see what truly matters.

Before becoming a mother, I did *so* much. I worked hard, I took on extra projects, I was involved in a whole bunch of volunteer activities. But once I had babies, I homed in on what truly resonated with me. Everything shifted focus toward my sons and the family.

In a sense, I had no choice *but* to refocus. When you have kids, time becomes precious; if you're going to devote a big chunk of your day to being away from your family, you want to spend it on work that truly aligns with your values. If the work doesn't feel meaningful, it's a tough bargain you're not likely to want to stick with.

So, in that sense, motherhood serves as a clarifier—it crystallizes your priorities. For me, having a baby meant shedding peripheral distractions, allowing my passion for women's rights to flourish, and acting as the catalyst that advanced my career and the impetus for creating my own niche.

But motherhood also instills a newfound assertiveness. Instead of getting sucked into unprofitable work projects or aimless volunteering, I felt empowered to say "no, that's not worth leaving my baby for" and retrain my efforts on focused, profitable work. More than that, though, I found that motherhood was an act of advocacy from the get-go. Being responsible for a small, helpless creature that we love with all our being *demands* that we speak up for them. Our fierce mother hearts won't have it any other way. Even if we're not naturally assertive, motherhood will get us flexing that muscle and strengthening it over time. And while advocacy is a skill anyone can learn, at any time, it demands a lot of stamina. Motherhood provides that stamina because you're doing it for your child—but the skill will translate to all parts of your life and work.

And then there's *mom guilt*. The nagging sense that we're failing our children by going to work, and failing our employers by going home to our kids.

People often say, "Just ignore mom guilt; it's internalized patriarchy." But my take is a bit different. I think ignoring guilt only feeds the spiral. Instead, I choose to see mom guilt as a compass. It tells us something our bodies are trying to communicate, and I refuse to ignore my instincts. It can signal adjustments needed in our careers, an urgency to shift priorities.

So, instead of brushing it off or burying it, I take that mom guilt seriously. Am I holding myself to an unrealistic standard? What would I advise a friend in the same situation? Take a breath—what's important right now? Your body, your baby, your family—they matter most. They are your North Stars, your unshakable commitments.

Your career, on the other hand, is malleable. It's like playdough; you can mold it. Work should be enjoyable, an expression of our humanity. A career is a lifelong project, not a race to do everything now.

With that in mind, motherhood is an opportunity to learn how to look at your career and say, "Not right now." To learn to trust that things will get done, just differently. When I became a mom, I didn't become less productive; I just stopped wasting time on nonsense. Work became more focused. My passions emerged.

So, let go of the assumption that motherhood will ruin your career, or that your career will ruin motherhood—it'll actually illuminate your desired path. The most essential thing you'll learn in this book is how to integrate the two, instead of fitting work in the margins of motherhood or fitting motherhood in the margins of work. And it's precisely this integration that will propel you to become the best version of yourself, and that's the version your child or children need.

We won't fade away into a mom version of ourselves; we expand. It's something to celebrate. This journey is about being fully alive, acknowledging the challenges without dwelling in fear. Embrace your motherhood identity, and be curious about how it'll shape your career and workplace: You will go places you could not even have imagined before motherhood, and it will be *because* of motherhood, not despite it.

Motherhood will make you better at your job. It made me more understanding and gave me a larger capacity to hold big problems and big causes. I became a master organizer and could put things in perspective. I was able to work under pressure or tired and became the opposite of frazzled (the stereotype)—I became unfazed and unshakable. Oh, you want me to negotiate a deal with a Fortune 500 company? That's nothing compared to getting a toddler to eat broccoli. Motherhood made me supercharged. It's a software upgrade. And that's a part that is really underappreciated in our culture. We think motherhood will take away. That the baby will make you unstable and hormonal and undedicated, unmotivated, and not ambitious anymore. And that you're just going to attend your mommy and me class and then you're just going to go over here and do your real work things. And it's just not the truth. We don't look at what we gain. I look at mothers and I am like, oh my goodness, just look at what they do on top of being a mother, and often precisely because they are a mother. It's incredible. The work they do comes from this place of deep love for all humanity. That is the best place to work from. It's not motivated by greed; it's not motivated by domination and crushing and grinding. They want to take care of the children, all the children. I mean, how beautiful is that?

The Employment Relationship
and Cultivating Neutrality

When one of my clients, Sarah, announced her pregnancy at work, her manager, Lina, did not respond to it very well.

Lina took about half a second to pause and soak in the news. "Well, your performance will probably get worse because of your hormones," she declared. "And you'll have to work harder now to make up for the time you'll be gone."

This was not the reception Sarah was anticipating. Nauseous, bloated, and exhausted, all she could think through her first-trimester haze was, *You couldn't even give me a congratulations?*

Unfortunately, while her symptoms got a little better, Lina's attitude didn't. When Sarah hit around eighteen weeks pregnant, Lina asked her, "Are you even pregnant? You don't look pregnant. Your boobs haven't grown." When Sarah asked for maternity leave, Lina responded, "Why are you taking time off? Don't you need money? You don't even have a place of your own." When Sarah asked for the promotion she was promised before she was pregnant, Lina told her, "Well, I'm not going to give it to you now that you're pregnant. You're lucky to even have a job."

Worse, Lina wasn't just rude—she was wildly inappropriate. When Sarah developed gestational diabetes, making her pregnancy high-risk, Lina brushed her off with, "Diabetes isn't that bad. It's not like the fetus will be deformed." And in the weeks leading up to her due date, Lina asked Sarah almost daily, "How is your vagina? How many centimeters are you dilated?"

Understandably, Sarah quickly reached her wit's end with Lina and tried to deal with her as little as possible. But since Lina was her supervisor, Sarah had no choice but to confront her when it came to the issue of legally mandated leave, which in the State of California lasts several months after the baby arrives.

This time, Sarah wasn't going to be blindsided. She took a deep breath, steeled herself, and came into Lina's office prepared, explaining that she would need time to recover from birth, establish a breastfeeding relationship, and bond with the baby.

Lina's response? "I don't care about your stupid baby."

Not all managers are as toxic (or law-breaking!) as Lina. In contrast to Sarah's experience, I worked with a woman named Audrey. When she announced her pregnancy, her boss cried tears of joy and instantly called the office contractor—*to design a nursery*. She proposed hiring a nanny for Audrey and even put her on the company payroll. What a dream!

Yet so many women, when announcing their pregnancies at work, are shocked to find that their boss's first reaction isn't to jump up and down with excitement, or even say "congratulations."

Now, make no mistake: Having a baby *is* wonderful. It is a beautiful, exciting, jump-up-and-down-for-joy moment in your life that deserves to bring you every happiness. If I could reach through this book and give you a big celebratory hug, I would. So please know that I, Daphne, am absolutely thrilled for you—and here for you.

That said, this kind of excitement—a warm, delighted, compassionate response to your pregnancy announcement—is just not likely to happen at work.

Again, that's not because motherhood isn't incredible and worth celebrating. It's because capitalism and motherhood are fundamentally at odds. And while, over the long term, motherhood is a wonderful and energizing thing for your *career*, over the short term, the effects on your *job* can cause some turbulence.

In addition, our managers are humans who experience all the complex human emotions we all do. Audrey's manager was so happy because none of her own children wanted to have kids, and she was so eager for a grandmother experience that she shifted all those hopes and dreams to Audrey. On the other hand, in the course of depositions, we learned that Sarah's boss had been a teenage mom who was forced by her parents to give her child up for adoption. Suddenly, her rage and rudeness toward the mother employees made more sense: She couldn't care about Sarah's baby because she wasn't even allowed to care about her own baby.

Your manager may have experienced fertility problems or feel the grief of missing her kids or be completely detached from the parenting experience and adhere to the bootstrappy "why is it *my* problem that you decided to have kids?"

Managers come in all forms, and their personal experience and beliefs will shape their reaction to your pregnancy announcement.

That might all sound scary and dramatic, but I promise you, it's not. It's simply reality, and coming to terms with this reality will do wonders for your mental and emotional health as you navigate becoming a working mother. When you can cultivate a healthy sense of *detachment* from your job, when you're able to emotionally divest from your work relationships to an appropriate level, you can set yourself up for success. You stop taking anything personally. You can exercise the rights you have, get the support you need, and not doom yourself to disappointment that your job isn't fulfilling something that jobs were never meant to fulfill.

So, let's start with the basics. Your work team is not your family. Yes, you may get along great with coworkers and supervisors, you may enjoy their company and have lots in common with them as people, but ultimately, your employer makes money by providing a service or creating certain goods. You get paid to be a part of providing that service or creating those goods. Your boss therefore needs you to be present to contribute to operations and production. When you have a baby, you need to temporarily stop doing that, and this is in essence a micro-rebellion against the tenets of capitalism—which demands an incessant, relentless pursuit of constant growth and production. Some bosses will tolerate this better than others.

So it's important to accept that having a baby *will* have an impact on your job and work relationships, even if just for a moment. Hoping that everyone will embrace your announcement with joy is not realistic and will probably only leave you feeling disappointed.

Next, you need to actively adopt a *neutral* stance toward your work relationships, so that the team's reaction to your family expansion cannot shake you as much. Some bosses will be kind and tell you they're happy for you. And they very well may be! They may feel genuinely excited that you are growing your family.

Other bosses may receive the news as a personal betrayal, even feeling victimized and projecting their frustrations on you. They will say things like (and these are actual things said to my clients), "It's so unfair you get to take a vacation," or "We gave you a job and this is how you repay us?" or even "Aren't you just a horny little bunny?" (that one was said to a client announcing her second baby!).

What is most likely is that your boss will feel conflicted. On the one hand, as a human, they may feel genuinely thrilled for you. But as a boss, they may be worried about how your pregnancy will influence business operations.

No matter what, though, if you can remain *neutral* in your own mind, and realistic in your expectations, you can plan ahead and be prepared. Remind yourself that the workplace is not where we should go looking for compassion and understanding about our motherhood experience—*and that's just fine.* It isn't good or bad; it just *is.*

Why does all this matter? Beyond your own emotional and mental health, this attitude and understanding is what will make you an effective self-advocate. It's only when you've come to terms with the reality of what motherhood means to workplaces, and cultivated the emotional detachment not to expect a warm reception where you're simply not going to find one, that you can talk to your employer so that they'll *really* listen.

Because in business, money talks. Which means you have to learn how to speak the language of money to get you what you need at work. We can't expect our employers to care about our baby—fine. That's not part of that relationship, and we're okay with that! But we *can* insist that our employers give us what is legally owed to us—because otherwise, well . . . it might cost them a lot of money.

When you know your rights, know that your employer might suffer financial consequences for violating them, and when you aren't emotionally enmeshed in your job, it will be *so* much easier for you to command your employer's respect.

Is there still risk? Yes, but your job is always at risk. Just ask the thousands of laid-off tech and federal workers. And if you lose your job because you stood up for your rights, then you will at least have legal options to pursue.

Remember Sarah, with the horrible manager? That's exactly what she was able to do. At first, she spoke up internally and bravely reported the discrimination to an HR rep, only to be told, "I'm not going to waste time on this."

Meanwhile, another of Lina's direct reports, Chelsea, became pregnant. Lina immediately demoted Chelsea, lowered her pay, and eventually permanently replaced her with a male employee, reassigning Chelsea from management to admin. "This is what you get," Lina told the company's owner, "for hiring women."

None of this was legal. And Sarah and Chelsea knew it. They were no longer willing to be polite and quiet when their employer wasn't following the law. In response to their managers speaking in the language of discrimination, Sarah and Chelsea spoke in the language of money—and they came to me. The two of them ultimately walked away with $1 million to compensate for workplace anxiety and depression (what we call emotional distress)—they were *not* fired.

To be clear, I will not teach you how to sue your employer, but how to *collaborate* with your employer. With the right employer (not Sarah's), you can present your asks in a way that actually *benefits* the employer. After all, you're helping them stay compliant. Companies pay attorneys and HR programs a lot of money to avoid risk, and if you're the number 1 risk manager looking out for the company's interest, you'll see that they can actually really appreciate that. I don't want you to position yourself in conflict toward your employer. In fact, staying aligned and united will be better for everyone, including your baby.

One way of doing this is to speak in the "royal we" instead of making individual requests.

> I've done some research and I learned there's this new law. Have you heard of it? We'll want to make sure we stay compliant with new regulations. This law is relevant to me, so I'm pretty deep in this research. Happy to discuss it more to make sure we know what we need to know and don't put the company at risk.

When the mothers I work with approach issues this way, often their employers will actually *thank* them. Yes, thank them, for helping them stay compliant and prevent financial risk!

The Success Audit

There's one last tactic that I think makes the collision of motherhood and work so exciting and empowering. Since I started advising mothers, I've counseled them that the leave planning process can be a great time to do a "success audit": to look back at your career and take stock of all the amazing achievements you've racked up.

Over the years, I received stories of moms who'd done exactly that same thing—and boosted their careers like they never had before.

One of my clients, Katie, shared her experience that particularly stuck with me. "I did it!" she wrote. "I prepared a full document when I asked for a raise. It included an executive summary outlining my objectives and my boss's objectives, a brief overview of my current job and its growth, and my compensation request. Then, I provided exhibits for each area, detailing my role, my impact on the team/company, management responsibilities, and specific compensation data like title, location, inflation, and cost of living comparisons. I closed with 'I'm ready to continue investing in you; I hope you'll continue to invest in me.'"

I was so proud that she implemented my guidance so well. When her employer began bringing people back to the office, she advocated to work remotely two days a week, because she was pumping—and not only did she get that request granted, but it became company policy. She knew what she needed, but realized it might cause friction if it was just her being given this schedule, so she presented it to her employer as an opportunity to show appreciation and support for moms. It was something they couldn't argue with. And now all the moms at her workplace get to reap the benefits of her advocacy.

Another client, Lyla, shared all the things *she* had accomplished in her career since having kids: "As you recommended, I keep a screenshot of my successes and compliments when they are little, so one day they can see what was possible for a mom to achieve. It also allows me to create my own book of exhibits for when I feel down or like I'm 'failing' everyone. My book of exhibits reminds me that I have done so much, I am so valued, and that I can trust my own chartered path."

Katie and Lyla are just a few of the moms I've supported for whom motherhood was an incredible leap forward in their careers, and their overall sense of self. Through their success audit, catalyzed by their immi-nent leave, they learned how to frame their requests in a way that ben-efits their employer—whether from a PR perspective, retention, or to help your employer stay compliant—and got what they wanted. Having babies revealed to them the inner strengths, passions, and priorities that ultimately unlocked a better, more rewarding life, not just at work, but all around.

I know stories of triumph aren't what you picture when you think of "motherhood and the workplace." More likely, the collision of these two realms gets you racked with a combination of heavier emotions: anxi-ety, guilt, grief, fear. You know—well, "know"—how challenging it is for women to "have it all," and you're terrified that starting a family is going to torpedo your career—or that having a job is going to kneecap your ability to parent.

I'd like to gently challenge that and invite you to do a success audit of your own. This can take any form that you like: a journal entry, a list, a voice memo dictated to yourself on a walk. But as you brainstorm, here are some things to consider:

- What do I do that nobody else can (or nobody else can do *as well*)?
- How does my work save my colleagues and company time and/or money?
- How has my work provided intangible benefits to my employer—promotion, publicity, networking, anything like that?
- What specific praise have I gotten for my work? (Bonus points if you can shore up the emails or other written evidence as testimonials.)
- How will my experience of motherhood open doors to an expanded market that my employer hasn't tapped into yet? How can I position myself to be the bridge to this new market?
- What are some visions, strategies, or improved processes I see for the organization that only I can lead? How will these benefit the organization?

- If I'd hire a top-notch PR team to articulate my accomplishments, how would they write and speak about me?

You Are Divine

We've discussed all the amazing things motherhood will do to transform you and your career, detoxing from our "yes girl" mentality, the reality of the employment relationship, and now I want to end this chapter on something a bit woo-woo.

As a mother, you are Divine.

You are a life creator, a regenerative force.

And motherhood is a creative act and *adventure*, the greatest one yet.

Yes, it's going to be hard. But you're going to love it. Not all the time, of course, but you'll surprise yourself with how strong you are. And you're going to love *yourself* for doing it and putting in the hard work. You'll see in dimensions you can't even imagine yet. In that way, having a baby opens up everything. It's like a cosmic catalyst, a Divine interloper in the form of a baby here to shake things up, and you are going to embrace it, roll with it, and *rock* with it—yeah, baby!

If you are afraid you're unprepared, unworthy—don't be. Babies come with an instinctual handbook; the guidelines are etched in your bones. And the joy they bring is unmatched by anything else.

Take it from me: I've been onstage accepting awards for my work. I've won massive victories for my clients in court. I've outperformed revenue goals quarter after quarter.

But ultimately, those successes are temporary, fleeting things. My career matters, but it's not the central thing I shape the rest of my life around. I trust it's sturdy enough to handle whatever comes. I've laid the foundation, put in the grunt work.

My kids, though? They're here with me now, and they'll be with me for life. They're the real deal, the greatest love story I'll ever experience.

So remember that as a mother, as a mother living and working *today*, you are powerful. We have agency. Moms today can run Etsy shops from their garages, start online businesses in between nursing, work flexible hours so they can cuddle their kids to sleep, and still achieve their professional goals.

We are the first liberated mothers in our lineage to have this opportunity to say: *I decide.*

I'm not just going to be a mom. I'm not just going to be a wife ironing your shirts. I have my own vision and dreams and ambitions, and I will bring *all* of them into existence however they fit my needs. Just give me a solid breast pump and some strong coffee, and watch me weave my own purpose into existence. Not by fitting motherhood into the margins of work, or by fitting work into the margins of motherhood, but by weaving it all together into one beautiful, colorful tapestry of love and creation and purpose and passion. The mother—where all human life comes from—has the raw power and pure potentiality to create whatever the F she wants into existence. Just wait and see. You'll do it too. I promise.

2

Maternity Leave

Laws, Policies, and Your (Birth) Rights in the Workplace

As a mother, you're going to get a lot of . . . well, *questionable* advice. Don't lift your arms above your head or you'll hurt the baby!

Don't go swimming or you'll hurt the baby!

You shouldn't be drinking that coffee—don't you know caffeine will hurt the baby?!

DON'T TOUCH THE CAT! DON'T EAT THAT SANDWICH! DON'T DO YOGA!

All this advice can be flummoxing and overwhelming, even if it's well intentioned, and it can be even harder to know what parts to follow. So let me keep it simple here: When it comes to maternity leave, the best advice I can give is, "Don't *ask* HR. *Tell* them."

Because the worst—and most common—advice when it comes to the workplace is, "Just ask HR."

Caroline was one of many women who did just that. At twenty weeks pregnant, she was thrilled when she came back from a successful anatomy scan showing a healthy baby. She'd told her boss of her pregnancy early on, during her first trimester, but with the twenty-week scan under her belt, she dutifully emailed her HR department to get the ball rolling on some more logistics.

> Hi Donna,
>
> As you know, I'm expecting a baby in the fall and I'm working to prepare for my absence. Could you tell me what the company's maternity leave policy is? Thank you.

A few hours later, Donna's reply came back:

> Hi Caroline,
>
> Our company does not have a maternity leave policy. Please let me
> know if you have any further questions.

Caroline was in shock. She almost burst into tears at her desk—how could this be possible? She knew maternity leave in the United States didn't stack up well compared to other countries, but she'd figured surely she could take *some* time, even if it was unpaid. Now she felt paralyzed, completely unsure what to do next.

Tina was also pregnant, about twelve weeks along with her second baby. She'd been working freelance when she had her daughter two years ago, so this would be her first time navigating pregnancy and leave in a corporate environment. When Tina sent a similar email to *her* HR rep—hey, what's our parental leave policy?—the response she got was:

> Hey Tina,
>
> Thanks for asking. Our company offers four weeks of paid parental
> leave. The necessary paperwork is attached.

Tina wasn't thrilled . . . but four weeks was better than nothing, she supposed. Honestly, knowing what she did as a second-time mom, she'd happily take eight or twelve weeks off—even unpaid—just to give herself time to recover, bond, and get back into the swing of life with a new baby. Her husband's salary would be more than enough to keep them going that long. But she couldn't risk losing her job *entirely.* So, she figured if all her job offered was four weeks . . . then four weeks it was.

Again, Caroline and Tina were just doing what a lot of parents-to-be do. They knew they were pregnant, they wanted to be proactive, and so they followed the advice that "everyone knows" is the next step. Say it with me now: "Just ask HR!"

But that advice nearly shortchanged them out of the leave they were *legally entitled to.* Why?

Because you do not ask your HR what kind of maternity leave you get. You *tell* them what leave you're legally entitled to. (Or, if you want to be gentler, you ask them to confirm your understanding of your leave rights is correct. More on this later.)

But to do *that*, you need to know your rights. You need to know what "maternity leave" actually means. You need to know an alphabet soup's worth of acronyms from FMLA to STD to PTO and understand which ones apply to you—then insist on them.

Fortunately, Caroline was one of the many moms who found their way to my Instagram comments, and ended up joining my program—where, I'm happy to say, I was able to share the advice that would remedy her situation.

"I got six months total off!" Caroline later shared. "My HR helped me, but didn't tell me everything—they just had no idea this was even possible. I learned about my rights from you and then educated my HR, and they ended up amending the handbook. They simply didn't know there were even state rights they had to follow. They assumed they were exempt as a small employer. In fact, they were actually very *grateful* that I highlighted this to them because they didn't want to get in trouble."

Tina was a mom in a similar situation. She discovered that while her employer would give her only four weeks *paid* off, she was eligible to take an additional eight weeks *un*paid under the Family and Medical Leave Act and still have her job waiting for her when she came back. As a result, she spent a full twelve weeks out from work and was able to heal and spend time with her baby instead of hustling back to the office just a month postpartum.

Caroline and Tina are both success stories I'm proud of, but both could have saved themselves a lot of time (and stress!) if they'd been prepared from the get-go.

Every mother needs to know what "maternity leave" actually is (spoiler: It's a bunch of things) and the options that *you*, personally, are entitled to, based on your current employer, state of residence, and family situation.

That's what this chapter's for. We'll cover all the laws, policies, and optional benefits that you'll draw upon to put together your maternity leave, including all the confusing places they overlap, intersect, and (appear to) contradict. You'll know what's required by the law, what's provided by your employer, and what all those zillions of acronyms mean. Armed with this information, you'll know how to put together a maternity leave plan that maximizes your time off *and* the money you're paid, all with as much job protection as you're legally entitled to. (Then, in the next chapter, we'll cover how to *actually* set all this up with HR.)

I want to acknowledge up front—this is a lot of information to cover, and it can *feel* like a lot to absorb too. That's okay. Take your time. Remember that not all laws will apply to you and your situation, and feel free to skip around based on what you know about your job and state of residence. Also, do not at all feel obligated to process all this info at once. Skim it, then come back to read more closely, maybe take some notes (or take a nap), and then revisit again. You've got this.

There's No Such Thing as "Maternity Leave"

If reading that headline made you panic, hold up!

When I say there's no such thing as maternity leave, all I mean is that "maternity leave," as a concept, doesn't have a consistent, let alone legally mandated, definition.

I saw an article trending online recently stating that 96 percent of all US corporations "offer maternity leave," and 93 percent offer paternity leave, up from half of the companies about a decade ago. The comment section was berserk: "What are you talking about?" "Not my employer!" "Huh!!!? Sources?"

I understood the confusion. After all, *any* time off after birth can be classified as maternity leave or paternity leave, whether that is a leave of absence based on the law, PTO, or a company policy leave.

So the question that was asked in this survey, to employers, was basically, "Do you give any time off after birth?" Of course, companies tend to offer some time off. The questions we all have is: *How much time, and is it paid, and how do I get paid?*

Speaking about "maternity leave" does nothing to answer these questions, because "maternity leave" actually means . . . nothing at all. At least legally. It is a colloquial term used in the workplace to describe the period of absence after birth.

When we talk about "maternity leave" in a legal conversation, what we're *actually* talking about is a network of overlapping state and federal programs, legally protected rights, employer policies, and benefits and insurance claims. There are company perks (like paid time off and short-term disability policies), there are federal laws (like FMLA), and there are state-sponsored paid-leave programs (in places such as California, Washington, Massachusetts, and New York, among others).

Even apart from legal definitions and specific policies, there isn't even one single *objective* for "maternity leave." "Maternity leave" can refer to simply the period of time you're not at work after having a baby, it can refer to your right to job protection (i.e., to not get fired for being away from your job post-childbirth), and/or it can refer to the money you receive while not actively working at your job. (And to make things more complicated, that money can come from multiple places: your employer, as a perk; an employer-sponsored insurance policy; or a state program funded by paycheck deductions, to name the big ones.) And because it can refer to any of these things, it kind of refers to none of those things specifically.

Because "maternity leave" doesn't refer to one single *thing*, what can end up happening is that you as the mother and the people responsible for administering any and all of these aspects of leave end up talking past each other. Sometimes, this is because the person you're asking (be they an HR rep, a state government employee, an attorney, or a benefits administrator) simply doesn't know what you're entitled to—maybe because they're genuinely ignorant of how things work overall, or maybe because they specialize in another area of "maternity leave" and know only part of the picture.

Many parents go to the wrong place with their questions. For example, they may spend hours on the phone with their state's disability benefits provider, asking them questions about their company's paid leave policies.

In that situation, it's sort of like arriving at the airport and asking the TSA agent if your carry-on bag will fit in the overhead compartment, or how to log onto the Wi-Fi on the plane. Even if they want to help you, that's just not their job! They don't have the individual airlines' policies memorized because why would they?

The reverse happens too. For example, many parents ask their employers to help them with their "paid leave," when the payment comes from an external source that is unrelated to the employer, like the government. This would be like asking the administrator at your kids' daycare how to sign up for the WIC program. They may have some understanding, but these benefits come from the government, so the school would not be the best source to advise you on this process.

Then, if they are remote workers, they may ask their employer about benefits that do not exist in the employer's state. This would be like asking a coffee shop in Arizona why they aren't selling you pot. ("Because this isn't California, ma'am.")

Managers tend to be so confused about all this themselves, so why would we expect them to be the best source of information? They are busy doing *their* jobs, and we also expect them to be high-level benefits experts and employment law ninjas? It's just not a reasonable expectation.

Other times, however, the miscommunication is more intentional. Keep in mind, HR's job is basically to 1. ensure legal compliance and 2. administer company policies (in other words, 1. cover the company's butt and 2. make sure you get what you're entitled to . . . but no more). And since "maternity leave" isn't a legally defined term, *technically*, a company can respond just like Caroline's did: "Our maternity leave policy? We have none." Or they can respond like Tina's did: "We offer X weeks of paid leave."

Put another way, when you ask your HR for "the maternity leave policy," you're asking, at best, for an internal company policy—a policy that your employer is under no legal obligation to have in place (like Caroline's company) or that might provide less paid leave than you'd be entitled to take *unpaid* (like Tina's company). Even if they *do* know your rights, they might be specifically expected to avoid disclosing them to you (because that saves the company money). Lastly, they may be well-intentioned and genuinely interested in helping you maximize your options, but they simply may not know or do not want to inadvertently misrepresent something serious like the law, so they end up telling you nothing or deferring you somewhere else, in which case you telling them instead of asking them actually makes their job easier and less stressful.

The upshot of this jumbled-up system and lack of clarity of terms means that too many women end up either returning to work while still in physical pain, not taking full advantage of state-provided benefits they may be eligible for, or straight-up quitting their jobs—simply because they are not asking the right question, and they're not asking it to the right person.

I am fully convinced that this confusion is one of the primary reasons why women are returning to work too soon. They just don't know what they don't know.

The good news is that when you know your goals, and you know your rights, *you* get to define what "maternity leave" ultimately means. No, you can't wave a wand and change the law (or your company policy) to grant you eighteen months off at full salary, but you *can* drill down on your own priorities, risk tolerance, and financial situation to get a clear picture of what you'll need in order to recover from childbirth, bond with your baby, and return to work at the right time. With that in mind, you'll be able to marshal the laws and policies that apply to you, adjust your plan where necessary, and get as close as possible to what you need.

But let's be super clear: **You are the best advocate for your baby**, and your employer is not going to be the place where you will receive a fully integrated picture of all your "maternity leave" options and benefits, mainly because a lot of this may just not be in their field of awareness or control, and it's also just not reasonable to expect of them. In the end, making sure you have a comprehensive plan to prepare for your bundle of joy's arrival is your job. You cannot outsource the task of your baby's well-being, and certainly shouldn't outsource it to the people who are most incentivized to get you back to work as soon as possible.

So, with all this in mind, let's break down what "maternity leave" actually is. I'll start with an at-a-glance overview of what those different policies and laws do and do not do, and then delve in deeper to how each of them works.

Maternity Leave Programs at a Glance

Here's how I do maternity leave planning with clients. First, we figure out how much time off she will be entitled to. These are her *leave of absence rights*, i.e., the amount of time off she will be able to take off work without losing her job. This will either be through FMLA, or state regulations, sometimes both.

We then draw that timeline out on a piece of paper. (I will quite literally draw a line and write the leave law on it, with the specific dates.)

It's only after we understand the time off rights that we review the financial side. We'll go over her benefits, and I will add them to the leave timeline diagram as new lines underneath: each benefit a different color, with the source of the benefit written above it for reference.

What you end up with is usually a patchwork of colors and gaps. That is normal. And that is your "maternity leave." It's different for everybody, which is why it's so hard to talk about in generalized statements.

To start, here are the potential sources for job-protected time off programs:

1. Federal law
   - FMLA
   - PWFA leave of absence accommodations

2. State law
   - State medical (or disability) leave
   - State bonding (or family) leave

Accessing these rights will depend on different eligibility factors, including where you live, your medical restrictions, and how long you've worked for your employer. (Note that these laws may or may not be included in your company handbook. It doesn't change your eligibility for them.)

Once you understand your eligibility generally, you can review the length of time you are eligible to take off. Again, please know that this can vary depending on your postpartum restrictions and other location-specific factors.

Now, once you understand which laws apply to you and how long your leave of absence can be, you can proceed and review whether you can be paid during this block of time off.

This is where a lot of people run into trouble: Most people do this in reverse (look up benefits first, then look at job protection), and that can really jeopardize your job. Doing so can lead people to assume their jobs are protected during the entire benefits period, which is not true. These are separate systems.

Here are the potential sources for financial benefit programs:

1. Federal law
   • FEPLA

2. State law
   • State disability benefits
   • State family benefits

3. Private benefits
   • Short-term disability insurance
   • Paid parental leave

Time-off rights and financial programs will overlap, but there is rarely one policy or program that does both (i.e., grant protected time off and also money). You will most likely be using a combination of these programs (often two or more) at the same time.

The Good News:
Maternity Leave Mythbusting

While the United States has a *loooooong* way to go when it comes to maternity leave, the picture is *not* as doom and gloom as you might have heard. Here are some quick myths to shatter about the state of maternity leave in America.

MYTH: American moms just don't get any maternity leave.

TRUTH: American moms get medical/disability leave and/or family/ bonding leave, subject to eligibility. Maternity leave is not a right, but other leave rights exist!

MYTH: American moms don't have paid leave rights.

TRUTH: 60 percent of American moms don't have paid leave rights . . . but 40 percent *do* (not counting employer or private insurance benefits!).

MYTH: America is the only industrialized country without federal paid leave.

TRUTH: America *does* have a federal paid leave program, but it's only available to federal employees (including military parents).

MYTH: American moms have to go back to work at six weeks postpartum (while dogs get eight weeks before their puppies can be taken away!).

TRUTH: There is no six-week limit on leave anywhere in America. Women go back because their doctors are declaring them "no longer disabled," but they are not *legally required to*. They just have to switch from disability leave to bonding leave to continue their leave!

MYTH: The maximum leave time for any mom in America is twelve weeks (under the Family and Medical Leave Act).

TRUTH: The maximum leave time a mom can get in America—if she lives in California—is seven months (of which six months are paid), and up to ONE YEAR AND EIGHT WEEKS of paid leave if the employer accepts all disability extensions.

MYTH: There are no other leave options when you don't qualify for FMLA. America sucks for parents.

TRUTH: There *are* other leave options when you don't qualify for FMLA. (But . . . America does kinda suck for parents.)

MYTH: It's entirely up to your company whether you get any paid leave or not.

TRUTH: Access to paid leave depends on your state. An employer is allowed to provide paid leave benefits, but those are a perk, not a right. If your state is one that offers paid leave, and you're eligible for it, your employer cannot deny you that leave.

Exercise:
Designing Your "Maternity Leave"

When taking time away from your job to have a baby, there are a few main factors you'll want to consider.

1. How long do I think I'll need/want to be away from work? (If you could choose yourself. This may not be what you will be entitled to, but it's a helpful benchmark.)
2. How long can I cover my expenses while I'm not working as usual? (We'll need to do some good old spreadsheet action here.)
3. Am I anticipating a long-term career with this employer? (If so, taking a more conservative approach when you make your requests can result in less impact on your professional advancement.)

Take some time to jot down ideas on these three questions. A few more details to consider:

The standard recovery time is considered to be six weeks for a vaginal birth and eight weeks for a C-section. However, that's the bare minimum for physical healing, and my informal observation is that most women do *not* feel like their usual selves at that stage. Still, it's useful to know, as this is the medical default.

Does your medical team foresee any complications leading up to or after birth (e.g., a prepartum hospital stay, a planned C-section)? If you're not pregnant yet, think about any ongoing or chronic health issues you manage and how those might play into your recovery. (This includes mental health conditions like anxiety or depression, which can be exacerbated postpartum and may result in the need for leave extensions.)

What are your average monthly expenses currently? Do you have savings you can spend down while not drawing a paycheck? What about other sources of income? If you have a partner, how much could their paycheck cover? Can you put a mat leave fund on your Babylist?

How big is your employer? Do you work on-site or remotely? Is your employer based in the same state as you are? Are you a member of a union? (If so, while you will have the same legal protections as everyone else, you may have access to a different benefits system, as well as additional protections. These will be laid out in the collective bargaining agreement.)

What is your (tentative) plan for childcare when you go back to work? Knowing you'll have a stay-at-home spouse or free childcare from family can make it easier and more flexible to get back to work, whereas finding (and paying for) daycare or a nanny will take time and money (and keep in mind that the younger the child, the more expensive the care typically will be).

Don't worry just yet about what you're actually entitled to (we'll get to that later!), but think in terms of "practical best-case scenario." By the end of the exercise, you should have more of a bead on what your ideal-yet-realistic maternity leave looks like.

With that sketched out, it's time to learn the laws and policies that you'll use to help make this happen.

Are You a 1099 Employee?

Trick question! There is no such thing.

Many people mistakenly think they're employees when they're really not. If your job pays you with a tax form 1099 at the end of the year instead of a W-2, you are not, in fact, an "employee" at all: You're an independent contractor, which means, in the eyes of the law, you are your own boss . . . and your own HR, payroll tax admin, and benefits coordinator. No paid maternity leave is coming from Uncle Sam or your "employer"—because, well, you're the employer. Be cautious of misclassification. If the person you are working with is giving you specific instructions, directives, and schedules, you are not a contractor; you are an employee. A contractor is a *freelancer*, and the work is usually project-based or on a specific retainer. It is a business-to-business relationship, which means you don't have a "boss"; you have a client. This client is allowed to give feedback about your work, but is not allowed to assert any control over your working conditions.

This kind of misclassification—when you're expected to work as an employee but paid as a contractor—is a big deal for a host of reasons, among them the lack of job protection and the unfair burden of employer-side taxes. If you suspect misclassification, you can report it, but it will take some time to sort out. In the meantime, you can explore state-specific family leave programs (some states offer paid family leave to freelancers, but you may need to opt into it in advance) and save up to self-fund your time away from work.

Leave of Absence Protections: Federal

The good news: Federal law applies to all US citizens and employers, regardless of which state you live in or work in.

The less good news: Getting your dream mat leave depends on winning the zip code and employer lottery. Most federal laws around job protection and pregnancy discrimination don't kick in unless your employer is larger than a certain size. (This is, in theory, to reduce the burden on smaller businesses who couldn't sustain operations if they had to allow employees unpaid leave. But it's also a huge bummer.)

Regardless, it's important to be familiar with these laws because they're as all-American as it gets (and because you'll probably see them popping up a lot throughout your pregnancy and motherhood, even if they don't apply to your employer).

Moreover, some of these laws actually cover the period *after* your leave ends, which is important to know so that you can plan accordingly (for example, knowing that you *must* be provided pumping time at work might mean you're willing and able to return to work before you plan to wean). So, while these don't all strictly apply to the time you're away from your job after childbirth, they're all relevant to piecing together the full picture of your leave plan.

FAMILY AND MEDICAL LEAVE ACT (FMLA)

Company Size: 50+ employees

If you're dreaming of bonding time with your newest child, the Family and Medical Leave Act (FMLA) has your back. Whether you're a mom, dad, adoptive parent, or foster parent, if you're eligible under this legislation, you're entitled to twelve weeks of job-protected bonding leave. Your employer can't fire you for taking this leave or requesting this leave—that would be considered leave interference and leave retaliation.

If you are eligible, it is an absolute right. This means they have to grant it, even if it's an inconvenience to them. They cannot try to negotiate with you, haggle down the time, or convince you to take it during the slow quarter. They cannot try to get you to come back sooner because they really need you. The right is absolute—when you are eligible, all you have to do is give timely notice of when you want to take it. They just have to figure out how to make it work.

One of my clients, Esmeralda, called her employer halfway through her leave to confirm her return date. They responded and said, "Best we can do is two days per week, part-time." Employers are not allowed to negotiate lawful leaves, as long as you are eligible and have time left in your leave bank.

Passed in 1993, the FMLA is the closest thing we have to a national leave program. It doesn't provide paid time off, but it *does* protect your job: If you are recovering from birth or bonding with a baby, the law states you can take time off work. Specifically, you can take up to twelve weeks of unpaid leave in a year, and your job (or an equivalent one) will be waiting for you when you get back.

Of course, there is a catch: Even though this is a federal law, and covers all fifty states and DC, there are significant eligibility obstacles.

Do You Qualify for FMLA Leave?

Answer these questions:

Do you work for a company with fifty or more employees within seventy-five miles of your jobsite?

Have you worked for this company for at least one year as of the start date of your leave?

Have you worked for more than 1,250 hours (about 24 hours/week) as of the start date of your leave?

If you answered yes to all three, you are eligible for FMLA leave. Congratulations!

If you are not eligible, you can request time off under another law, called the Pregnant Workers Fairness Act (PWFA). We will cover this law next.

When it comes to having a baby, there are four main reasons that qualify you to claim your right to FMLA leave.

1. For Pregnancy

Before your baby is even born, you can use FMLA if you are incapacitated due to pregnancy (for example, if you have hyperemesis or preeclampsia and physically cannot work). However, any leave you take *during* pregnancy will count against your twelve total weeks—so one week before baby means one less week *after* baby. Yes, this is totally unfair. But it is unfortunately a part of the law. Most women will try to work through their pregnancy for this exact reason. (You can also try a PWFA accommodation if you want to save your full leave bank.)

If you do need the time off, you will tell your doctor first. Your doctor will then write a note for you to provide to your employer, and the time will be deducted from your overall FMLA leave bank.

2. For Prenatal Appointments

You can also use FMLA to cover time away from work to attend prenatal appointments. To be sure, you don't *have* to—if your employer does not track time off for medical visits, for example, it's better *not* to request FMLA for those visits because that will deduct from your FMLA time *after* giving birth. (Again, total bullshit. But it is the law.)

However, many employers do count your doctors' visits against your attendance record. In this case, if you don't assert your FMLA needs, you can risk exceeding the attendance policy limit and losing your job. If that's likely to happen at your workplace, you have to be very clear when taking your time off to document that you are attending prenatal visits and that you are seeking FMLA protected time off. (You can also request PWFA accommodations for prenatal care, and this will also protect your leave bank.)

Do not assume your employer will know that you can request leave rights for prenatal care. One of my clients, Julia, actually worked for a medical office and asked for time off for prenatal visits. Her employer started tracking her time under the company attendance policy. After a few weeks, they emailed her, telling her she's on "attendance probation." Julia explained she needed the time off for medical care, to ensure the safety of her pregnancy. Her manager told her that her attendance needed to improve. She then texted her manager, "I feel like I am being discriminated against for these prenatal appointments. I am high risk and under a lot of stress. This is not just me, you're affecting my baby as well." A few days later, she found her job posted on Indeed. The company then sent Julia a furlough note, using the pandemic as a disguise to cover up an illegal termination. Both the tracking of protected time off under the attendance policy, and the termination in response to her complaint, are against the law.

3. For Birth Recovery

Since childbirth is a major physical event, you can take FMLA to recover. After you have the baby, you will be considered disabled for about six weeks after vaginal birth, or eight weeks after a C-section, and you will be able to take that amount of time off from work as job-protected leave.

Now, if you're even halfway decent at math, you probably noticed that six and eight are both less than twelve. In order to take all twelve weeks of your FMLA at once, right after giving birth, you will need to provide another "qualifying reason" for the additional leave—in this case, the reason is bonding. So, if you plan on taking the entire twelve weeks following your child's birth for recovery *and* bonding, you can bypass the need to provide medical documentation by simply requesting your full FMLA leave rights for bonding leave.

4. For Parental Bonding

All parents—birthing and non-birthing and adoptive—can use FMLA for bonding with a new baby. All you need is a baby under the age of one. Unlike taking leave for medical reasons, you don't have to submit your medical notes if you use your FMLA leave for parental bonding. Again, if you work straight through your pregnancy, and you want to take all twelve weeks of your FMLA leave at once, you may want to request it for parental bonding because then you can avoid all the hassle.

The exception to this is when your disability period may exceed twelve weeks, for example, due to a traumatic birth, postpartum complications, or mental health conditions such as postpartum anxiety or depression. If this is you, and you have your medical team's cooperation, then staying on disability status will put you in the best position to try to extend your leave or seek additional postpartum accommodations (such as telework) on the basis of medical reasons. It is not possible to seek additional accommodations if you want more time for bonding. Bonding time is always capped at a specific max. Only disability/medical leave can be extended if there is medical justification.

Timing also matters with taking FMLA leave. You are entitled to twelve weeks of FMLA in one year,* and bonding leave rights expire when your baby turns one.

---

* Your employer can define what it considers an "FMLA year." This might be a calendar year, or it may be based on your workplace anniversary date, or the start date of your leave—this is called a "rolling" twelve-month period, measured backward from the date you start your leave—but might not.

Intermittent Leave

Did you know you can generally use the medical leave portion of your FMLA leave intermittently? If those smaller blocks of leave are supported by medical certification, your employer would not be able to object. Intermittent leave is a right if it is used for medical purposes.

However if you want to take your bonding leave in smaller blocks, your employer has to agree. If your employer does not agree, your bonding leave has to be taken in one block. Note that you can still decide when to start your bonding leave, it just needs to be completed before your baby turns one, and you do not have to take all your bonding leave immediately after childbirth.

All this means you can take your medical leave first, go back to work, then go on bonding leave for the remainder of your leave. In other words, even if your employer does not agree to you using intermittent bonding leave, you can delay or save a continuous block of bonding leave. (Please know your state may have more generous rules, too.) Again, you don't need any employer approval for intermittent medical leave (for example, if you return to work, but symptoms reemerge and you have to go back on medical leave, or if you need to use more time for postnatal appointments).

Another example of intermittent leave is to request a part-time schedule to ease back into work.

It's important to know what else the FMLA requires of your employer. They must continue your health insurance coverage, they must allow you access to any benefits you accrued prior to taking leave, and they must give you your old job (or a nearly identical one) when you return. (This all comes from 29 U.S.C.A. § 2614, if you want to get technical with your citations.) An exception to this is when the job disappears for reasons unrelated to the leave, like a department-wide layoff. However, an employer may not replace you and then just decide that it's easier to stick with the current team. Put simply, your employer can't toss you aside because you left to have a baby. Even if you were replaced, you have to be returned to work. It's your right to return to work with your head held high and your position secure.

Do I Get More Leave with Twins or Multiples?

There is no "double" leave for twins or multiples. However, you are more likely to receive accommodations (see below) as your needs and limitations are likely multiplied too.

THE AMERICANS WITH DISABILITIES ACT (ADA) AND THE PREGNANT WORKERS FAIRNESS ACT

Company Size: 15 employees

For all the shortfalls our country's social safety net has compared to other developed nations, we do have one crown jewel to be proud of: the Americans with Disabilities Act. This landmark legislation, passed in 1990, protects people with disabilities (including disabilities related to pregnancy and postpartum) from discrimination and mandates a baseline level of accessibility for things like building codes and public services. It's the reason you'll see curb cuts on public sidewalks, accessible stalls in bathrooms, and Braille lettering on signage. It was the first comprehensive disability civil rights law of its kind in the world, and many countries *still* do not have comparable protections and accessibility requirements (one walk through a European city with tons of stairs and narrow sidewalks, and you'll see what I mean).

So, if you're dealing with a high-risk pregnancy and the associated medical complications, the ADA gives you the power to request accommodations at work, from a flexible schedule to extra breaks to extended leave. Your employer must grant your accommodation requests to keep you working at your job if those requests are reasonable and won't sink the ship.

The Pregnant Workers Fairness Act is like the ADA's little sister. Passed in 2022, it officially took effect in June 2023 to protect pregnant workers who might otherwise have fallen through the cracks of existing laws. Basically, the PWFA goes a step further than the ADA by specifically requiring employers to provide reasonable accommodations for workers who are pregnant, recovering from childbirth, or dealing with related medical conditions, regardless of whether those pregnancy-related symptoms would otherwise be considered a "disability" per se. In other words, it lowers the bar for requiring accommodations from "high-risk pregnancies only" to "any pregnancy-related symptoms."

Despite the specific name, the PWFA also covers the postpartum period, and it can also be used as a leave of absence law. However, the PWFA is not a straightforward leave of absence law and does not provide an absolute leave right protection like the FMLA. Instead, the leave rights under the PWFA are negotiable and a type of accommodation that can be requested among a list of other accommodations (such as telework, flexibility, etc.). However, many of the mamas in my membership have used PWFA for anything from prenatal appointments and fertility treatments to extended mat leaves and even mat leaves when the mother was not eligible for FMLA.

(We'll cover requesting these accommodations in the next chapter. For now, just know that the ADA and PWFA have your back!)

FEDERAL EMPLOYEES ONLY (FEPLA)

Do you work for the federal government? Congratulations—you may be one of the rare US workers who gets federally provided paid leave, under something called the Federal Employee Paid Leave Act (FEPLA).

FEPLA, though winning at being the most fun acronym to pronounce, loses at visibility. It's not a well-known law and is severely underused.

While FMLA provides job protection during time off (but no pay), FEPLA covers the wage portion of your leave and runs concurrently during an FMLA leave. A federal employee can only receive FEPLA pay if they are eligible for FMLA. The agency that employs you should have a process in place for providing FEPLA pay, and usually a form will be available on the public website or an internal portal. The only federal employees exempted from FEPLA are postal workers. (Sorry, USPS—we love you, and it's total bullshit!) Military employees have a separate system of paid leave, known as Primary Caregiver Leave (PCL), which can be requested by eligible service members who are designated as the primary caregiver for a new baby.

When I advocate for federal paid leave, I always remind lawmakers that a federal paid leave policy already exists. We just have to expand FEPLA to apply to everybody.

Leave of Absence Protections: State

If there's one thing I find myself telling expectant parents over and over again, it's "that depends on your state."

For better or worse (and I'd argue "for worse" because it makes my job infinitely harder), in this beautiful, expansive, diverse country of ours, no two states seem to want to do things the same way, and that's especially the case when it comes to parental leave.

I'm not going to be able to detail every single state's options here: That'd quickly make this book a door stopper of a legal textbook, and it would also be constantly out of date given how often laws can and do change.

So what I will do is break down the different *categories* of state laws and programs that help provide job protection and/or paid leave after giving birth. That will give you a solid understanding of what kinds of options are on the table, generally speaking. From there, you can visit my website at themamattorney.com to download a free, updated resource guide tailored to your state that will help you learn exactly what's available to you.

What If I Work Remotely?

As if state-level laws weren't confusing enough on their own, more and more people now work from home for an employer based in a different state. The short answer is that, typically, the state where you physically perform your work (meaning your home state) is the state whose employment laws, including maternity leave laws and benefits programs, will apply to you . . . which can really suck if your employer is in a state with paid leave but *you* work remotely from a state that offers zilch. I tend to advise parents in states like California or New Jersey to wait to move to cheaper states until they are through the baby stages with their kids, because they usually spent years paying into benefits systems that they will finally get to benefit from.

However, your employer *may* have a policy to extend its own state-level benefits to all employees regardless of location, so it's worth asking. The best employers will look at the most generous state where they have employees and apply these policies nationally. (I'd argue that this is in fact economically wise, because keeping track of all the different states is *expensive*. Risking noncompliance is expensive, too, so might as well just harmonize these policies and make it fair for everyone working in your company.)

STATE MEDICAL AND FAMILY LEAVE LAWS

Some states have laws that offer job-protected leave that goes beyond the federal FMLA, either by offering additional leave, covering more employees, or removing FMLA eligibility barriers. This means you might have legally protected leave even if your job doesn't qualify you for federal-level protections.

For example, Massachusetts has something called the Massachusetts Parental Leave Act that applies to employers with *six* or more employees (as compared to the FMLA's fifty or more employees) and grants up to eight weeks of job-protected leave. Minnesota does even better with the Minnesota Parental Leave Act, which applies to employers with *one* or more employees. California has the Pregnancy Disability Leave Law, which gives up to four months of medical leave for pregnancy or birth recovery, and also the California Family Rights Act, which provides an additional twelve weeks of bonding leave. Both laws apply to employers with five or more employees.

There are two categories of laws that will cover time after birth: medical leaves and family leaves. Your state may have one or both. Only birthing moms can use both medical and family leave options. All parents can use family leaves. So you'll want to make sure you know your rights under both categories of leave laws (this is something I cover in my program).

A mistake many moms in these states make is to confuse the family leave for their medical leave, resulting in taking only family leave. They often assume the same principle applies as with FMLA, meaning that you get to the same max whether for medical or bonding. This is not true in states with additional protections. In these states, birthing mothers tend to net out many more weeks or even months beyond the federal twelve-week limit. Technically speaking, family leave is not for pregnancy or recovery from childbirth, only for bonding with that new family member (i.e., your baby). This kind of leave protects your job (meaning you can't be fired for taking it).

Another mistake mothers make is to confuse the leave laws with the benefits programs and conflate these terms when asking for their rights or their benefits. It's essential that you use the proper acronyms in your communications.

For example, New Jersey has a law called New Jersey Family Leave Act that protects your job for twelve weeks of unpaid bonding leave (on top of your twelve FMLA weeks too!) but does not, in itself, pay for that leave, and you'd have to use the New Jersey Family Leave Insurance program for payments. What many parents do is ask their employers for the Family Leave Insurance instead of the actual leave law.

In California, many parents ask their employers for "PFL" (Paid Family Leave), but this is the name of the financial benefits program. The leave law is called CFRA and is four weeks longer than the benefits program. Parents end up losing four weeks of leave due to this mistake.

Mothers also get justifiably confused when there are laws like "California Pregnancy Disability Leave" and assume these are protections only during pregnancy, but these laws cover the postpartum period too.

I know it's hard, but fully diving into the alphabet soup is the only way to maximize all your protections. And if you find yourself cross-eyed, come join me in my program where I spell this out per state, including all the updated templates to send to your employer.

STATE BENEFITS PROGRAMS

Jackpot! The gold standard for state-level parental leave are paid family and disability benefits programs. These programs typically allow you to be paid with partial wage replacement so you can heal and/or bond with your baby.

Typically, you pay into these programs through small payroll deductions, and when you need to be paid, you must apply for benefits from the appropriate department of your state government. The amount you get paid varies from state to state, but it's usually set as a percentage of your regular wages, with some kind of maximum cap (weekly, monthly, and/or total) plus a time limit.

There are two types of state benefits programs: (a) state disability benefits, which are accessible to birthing parents only and are used for pregnancy or postpartum recovery, and can include mental health conditions; and (b) state bonding benefits. States often call these "paid family leave" programs, but this is a bit of a confusing name, as these are not job-protected leave rights, but financial benefits funds. (To prevent confusion, I call these "bonding benefits" to differentiate from the actual family leave laws. They are accessible to all parents.)

STATE DISABILITY BENEFITS

In a few states, you might be eligible for disability benefits after giving birth. These programs provide partial wage replacement when you are unable to work due to a physical or mental condition. For these benefits, you usually must have paid into the fund for quite a while to be eligible. This is actually the first thing you want to review when you are pregnant. You will see these deductions on your paystub. It will look like a couple of dollars taken out of your pay every month.

Once you're eligible and have paid into the program, you will give birth and then apply for benefits, often with documentation from your medical provider. You'll then receive regular payments that replace a portion of your income while you recover. Once you're physically ready to return to work, the payments usually stop.

Note that these benefits systems are not where your leave rights come from, just where your money comes from. A lot of parents make the mistake of applying for benefits and assume that this action alone protects their job and time off. Your leave rights need to be ironed out and confirmed by your employer. The state is not involved in protecting your job, only in getting you paid. I have seen so many mothers lose their jobs by assuming these benefit programs protect their jobs. Often the disability benefit systems will have a longer window than the leave laws, and the mothers often assumed the leave laws track the disability benefits systems. They do not. In fact, benefits systems and leave laws are rarely aligned. This mismatch is frustrating, and it's here that so many jobs are lost. In fact, the most common call I receive is precisely this scenario: A mother goes on leave and just keeps sending in medical forms to the state without alerting the employer that they need more time than what the leave law allows. They'd then suddenly get a termination letter for "job abandonment" in the mail. This is not a wrongful termination. When we hit the max on our leave protections, we need to return to work or negotiate an extension with our employers. I'd always ask these mothers if they got approval from their employers on their leave plans, and the moms would tell me they assumed the state (or their doc) would communicate with the employers. They don't. Securing your leave plan, and getting your employer's understanding and signoff on your leave plan, is your job. And it's a job so important that it can cost your actual job.

STATE BONDING (OR FAMILY) BENEFITS

An example of a state bonding benefit is the New York State Paid Family Leave program and the California Paid Family Leave program.

State bonding (or family) benefits provide payment during family or bonding leaves. They are only accessible to you if you are actually employed. These benefits are also accessible to non-birthing parents and are intended to cover the bonding (not disability) portion of your leave. Unlike disability benefits, family benefits tend to be taxed as they are wage replacement benefits.

State Paid Sick Leave Laws

In some states, paid sick leave laws can be leveraged for maternity leave. (Because, yes, not all states require paid sick days. Insanity.) If your state mandates that your employer allow you to accrue sick time, you may be able to use that sick time to recover after the birth of a child.

Employer Perks

I like to say that employer paid leave policies are like foosball tables in the break room: It's great if your employer provides them, but they're not guaranteed, and they can always be taken away—with no legal repercussions. They are a perk.

Complicating matters is the fact that you'll almost certainly be claiming both employer-provided policies *and* legally mandated rights (both federal and state), meaning you'll be dealing with tons of similar (or contradictory) definitions, overlapping time frames, and endless requests for documentation.

We'll cover talking with HR and claiming what's yours in depth in the next chapter. For now, here's a rundown of the *types* of pregnancy- and parenthood-related benefits your employer might have on offer.

PAID PARENTAL LEAVE POLICY

Paid parental leave is basically a form of paid time off. In that sense, it's a benefit just like paid vacation time, except that it can be tapped into only under a specific circumstance (namely, when you have a new child in your life).

The setup of employer-provided paid parental leave can vary a whole lot. Some employers might offer a set number of weeks (or months) of paid leave to all parents, while others might provide a certain amount of paid time off that you can use for parental leave, but only *after* you've burned through your regular vacation or sick days, while others may offer different lengths of leave for birthing versus non-birthing parents.

Eligibility can also vary a lot—because, again, it's up to the company. Typically, you'll need to have been with the company for a certain amount of time before you're eligible for parental leave benefits. There may also be different eligibility rules for full-time versus part-time employees, or for salaried versus hourly workers.

Now, before you say, "Great, so I don't need FMLA leave because I have paid parental leave through my company!" wait just a second. It's important to understand that paid parental leave isn't a *replacement* for FMLA leave, but a *complement* to it. Paid parental leave just means that your company has agreed to issue you a paycheck for a certain number of weeks while you're out caring for your new baby. FMLA leave ensures that your job is not at risk if you're on leave from work due to covered reasons (such as the birth of a child) for up to twelve weeks. In other words, if your company offers paid parental leave, it could run concurrently with FMLA leave, and you should request and use both.

This means it's also possible to have paid parental leave through your job and *not* be eligible for FMLA-protected leave. I know, it's confusing. But because companies are only subject to the FMLA if they have more than fifty employees, many small businesses will not have to offer job-protected leave to their employees because they're simply too small. However, that doesn't stop those businesses from being able to offer paid parental leave as a perk *if they choose to do so*—and some do! But, assuming you're eligible for FMLA leave and your company offers paid leave, ensure you're requesting both: FMLA leave to make sure your job is still there for you after twelve weeks, and paid parental leave to use the benefits that your employer has agreed you are entitled to.

What if my employer offers paid leave and I also live in a paid leave state?

If your employer offers a paid leave policy and you work in a paid leave state, do not forfeit your state benefits. Many parents will just decide to request the paid leave policy because it's easier, and because they don't want to deal with the hassle of all the forms. However, doing so is giving the government free money. You have already paid for these benefits. In addition, unlike state benefits, employer paid leave policies can be revoked and sometimes even clawed back. They are also taxed fully, while disability benefits are usually untaxed. Plus there is a process for benefits, while there are no legal entitlements to paid leave policies.

Ask your employer about the integration policy. It's also possible that they were unaware. Many generous employers just want to do the right thing, and as we've covered, most people don't know that American maternity leave is a lot more complicated than "America doesn't have paid maternity leave." Most employers are operating under the assumption that paid leave is their responsibility, because that is the public myth. It's very likely that your employer may not know that they operate in a paid leave state. It will be a happy surprise to them when you educate them that they don't need to pay you, because they've already paid you through payroll deductions. They would essentially be paying twice and also giving free money to the government (as would you). Instead, ask them to supplement the difference. State benefits are rarely at 100 percent, and employers can "top off" your benefits to offset the differential. That way you will accrue zero financial losses, and you may actually net more as you may be taxed less than on traditional wages.

SHORT-TERM DISABILITY INSURANCE

Short-term disability insurance (or STD insurance—unfortunately—for short) is another employer-provided perk that can help you maintain some level of income while you're out of work due to a disability . . . like having recently given birth. This is a private policy that your employer offers, but which *you* are responsible for paying for (in part or in whole), similar to other benefits like a healthcare plan or a 401(k) plan. If you subscribe to the policy (and it *is* something you have to actively opt into—more on that in a sec), then, should you become disabled and unable to work, the policy will pay out a certain percentage of your salary over a set period of time as defined in your coverage.

To be clear, these are independent, privatized programs that have to be distinguished from the state disability benefits that are paid and administered through your payroll system.

For the latter, you do not take any action. These payments will happen automatically because your state government mandates it. However, for the insurance programs, you are dealing with a private provider akin to a healthcare insurance provider. This means: Prepare to be extremely frustrated.

If you are seeking STD insurance, make sure you're enrolled as soon as possible because you will almost certainly be required to have paid into the program for a set period before claiming benefits.

The first thing you'll want to determine is: *Do we even have STD coverage here, and am I opted in if so?* If your employer does offer it, and you're *not* signed up, then get signed up ASAP. Like, put this book down and go do it now. Here's why: Insurance is always a game of odds, right? The insurer is betting the Thing *won't* happen because that way they don't have to pay out. The more likely they think the Thing is to happen, the more they'll charge you in premiums, as a way to hedge their bets. But if the Thing is all but *certain* to happen . . . they will deny you coverage entirely.

In other words, if you're already pregnant, it may be too late. You're *very very* likely to want that disability payout . . . which makes you a "bad" bet for the insurance company as they would get a negative ROI (I know . . . barf). Therefore, most STD policies require at *least* ten months of premiums paid before childbirth will be covered as a disability.

When you apply for STD coverage, you'll be applying with the insurer, not with your employer or with the state. The application process can be quite uncomfortable because they can often send you super-long questionnaires to fill out to verify your medical history and details of your personal life (like whether or not you skydive—seriously). As these processes take place between you and the insurer, instead of you and the employer, employment laws don't really apply here; consumer laws do. This means these investigations will be more invasive and private than what you would expect (and what would be allowed) in a workplace setting. Due to the invasive nature of these systems, many mothers conclude it is not worth it. This is a decision only you can make—just remember that you are outside of your employment protections. You are in a relationship with the insurer, and the insurer is a business, and businesses don't make money by just handing out payments. There are certainly protections here, too, like bad faith insurance denials, but the remedy for these issues would fall under consumer protection law, not employment law.

Once you have a policy, you'll pay a monthly premium, directly from your paycheck. Just like with healthcare, there can be both an employer contribution and an employee contribution. Some employers contribute $0 to your premium payments, and consider the ability to apply for coverage in itself a perk (which, actually, it is, since single-person STD policies are very difficult to get), and some will chip in more.

As a recap, short-term disability covers your paycheck for a certain percentage for a certain amount of time. To be clear: **These providers do not give you any leave rights, nor do they protect your job.** Many mothers make the mistake of relying on these companies (which are third-party vendors) to fully administer their leaves, when they don't actually have the authority to do so, because your employment rights are with your employer.

Often, you have to show that you can't do your job duties through documentation from a medical provider. These companies tend to be over-zealous when it comes to interfering in the doctor-patient relationship, substituting their opinion for that of your doctor.

Again, these companies only have the authority to decide whether you should get paid. They don't have the authority to decide whether you should get accommodated, get that leave extension, or are disabled for purposes of your leave rights.

What makes this complex is that they are allowed to make a determination regarding your disability when it comes to your benefits. *And*, this decision may differ from your provider's, or from your employer's. So you may end up with the time off, but not the money. Ugh . . . I know.

Remember that companies tend to refer to these benefits as "salary continuation," which is exactly what they are.

Currently, five states mandate this coverage, including California, Hawaii, New Jersey, New York, and Rhode Island.

In other states, coverage may be voluntary and you'd need to opt in. Sometimes, employers provide the full cost of premiums, a portion, or, if it's voluntary, you may need to pay for the full premiums.

When filing for these benefits, they will ask for some sort of medical letter. Just like healthcare insurance companies, these companies are incentivized to ignore your claims. And just like with healthcare insurance companies, you have to be persistent, a.k.a. *annoying*. Keep sending in these letters and notes. These providers often reject mental health claims, and you'll need to show a ton of documentation and may still face denials. I could write a book about my frustration with insurance companies, but I'll leave you with this: I've seen mothers put these companies in their place and get payouts, so it's possible, but if the hassle and invasion of privacy isn't worth it, I respect that choice just as much. Sometimes we have to just protect our peace and stop wasting all of our time and getting depleted in the back-and-forth with exploitative systems. I fully believe that's part of our revolution too. Sometimes these payouts can be very low, so be clear on what type of money you're talking about, because it may all be worth less than the value of your time.

OTHER PERKS

Technically speaking, companies can offer almost anything (so long as it's legal) as a reward for all your hard work. Most don't, but some do. These perks are the things that fall into a kind of grab-bag category of stuff that's nice to have but far from common—which is why, if your employer offers them, you should totally take them up on it.

Also, I don't share these here just to give you major FOMO: Perks like these can be a great thing to suggest to your employer because they're innovative and a great way to help a company tout itself as "family-friendly." So, if your employer is building out their parental leave offerings from scratch, for example, or has solicited feedback on what else it can offer employees for "wellness," or if you just think they'll be receptive to these ideas—try suggesting one of these. I've included some talking points on what makes them such a good benefit . . . to your employer.

Portable pumps

Benefit for you: For traveling professionals or those with demanding jobs (like healthcare or education), portable pumps like Willow let you pump discreetly during meetings, commutes, or even (take it from me) while cross-examining witnesses in court—no lactation room required.

Benefit to your employer: While insurance rarely covers these, they're a smart investment. Employees maintain productivity (I've pumped while driving to hearings or mediating cases) and avoid lengthy pump-break disruptions.

Breastmilk shipping

Benefit for you: Travel a lot for work and planning to breastfeed? A service like Milk Stork will transport your pumped milk from wherever you are in the field back home to your baby, so you don't have to pump and dump and your baby can still get their food from you.

Benefit to your employer: Your star salesperson is a lactating mom? This will be a huge help and a load off her mind so that she can keep up her numbers while traveling, *and* feel like a valued member of your team.

Fertility programs

Benefit for you: With the cost of a single IVF cycle going as high as $20,000, conceiving through fertility issues can be both emotionally and financially draining. Having your employer share (or cover) the cost can make the decision to pursue IVF easier—and the sooner you start, the sooner you're likely to see success.

Benefit to your employer: Imagine your company offers a benefit that is an instant sell for 16 percent of top talent. Well, around one in six people worldwide will be diagnosed with fertility issues, and that includes the best people in the workforce. Giving this as a benefit not only shows you care about employees and their families, but also sets you apart from your peer companies as *the* place to work.

Adoption assistance

Benefits to you: Preparing to adopt can be like a second job in itself, except you're paying to do it instead of the other way around, and it can be *quite* costly—as much as $40,000.

Benefits to your employer: Helping employees defray the cost of adoption is a meaningful act of showing your family values—for *all* kinds of families. It sends a message to adoptive couples (both same-sex and opposite-sex) that you recognize them as valid and valuable as much as any family.

Smart bassinets

Benefits for you: Bassinets like the Snoo (which automatically rocks and plays white noise for your infant) can be a godsend for getting just a few more hours of peaceful sleep in those first six months . . . but they're not cheap.

Benefits for your employer: Beyond the fact that there is nothing, *nothing*, more precious to an exhausted new parent than the gift of sleep, a tired employee isn't at their best.

On-site childcare

Benefits for you: Childcare—finding it, paying for it, and the daily pickups and drop-offs—inevitably ends up taking much more of your mental real estate than you'd like as a working parent. Being able to co-commute along with your child to the same "worksite" gives you more time together and less stress about coordinating schedules.

Benefits for your employer: Absenteeism because of childcare gaps is no good—for anyone. Making childcare a "no-brainer" by offering it at your company location helps your employees get to work smoothly and routinely.

You can come up with your own ideas, but the trick is to present it to your employer as a benefit to them—whether through increased productivity, talent retention, or goodwill. Remind them that you now have a family to support, you are paying for childcare so you can work there, and you would like to keep investing in them and are simply requesting reciprocity. If there are other parents, requesting these benefits collectively will give you an even better shot at getting them approved.

WHAT ABOUT DADS AND NON-BIRTHING PARENTS?

Hey, dudes, dads-to-be, and all partners of pregnant people. I've got great news for you: America is actually a leader in paternity leave. U-S-A! U-S-A! Other than a few outliers (looking at you, Swedish latte papas), the average length of paternity leave on a global scale is two weeks (per the International Labor Organization). In America, dads and non-birthing mamas can take twelve weeks of bonding leave under FMLA. Plus, depending on your state, you may also be legally entitled to paid leave and additional benefits.

But, just like your partner, you will get these rights only if you ask for them, and you need to be proactive. Really, everything I say about timing, communication, expectation- and boundary-setting throughout this book goes for you too. Don't be the guy texting your boss on the L&D floor, *Hey, need 2 take PTO for a few weeks, wife in labor.*

Instead, keep on top of the process together. Here's what I recommend.

Review the rules ASAP. Right after your partner pees on the stick (okay, maybe not *right* after), the two of you should sit down together and review your leave benefits and rights from both your employers and your applicable state laws. I often see parents spend hours reading Amazon reviews on baby items like the Snoo but very little time doing in-depth research to prepare for their family leave plan together. These leave preparations are as important as the medical and logistical preparations, as they are intertwined. Build regular time into your calendars to prepare your joint leave plan.

Build a joint leave plan. Once you know what your rights are, as well as any policies that supplement those rights, you can build a leave plan *together*, for both of you. It's kind of like a game of *Tetris*: You can each fill up different chunks of time at different stages postpartum, but it doesn't always have to be "both parents on leave at the same time." What I recommend parents do is take a little bit of time together in the beginning for bonding, cherishing the new family, and doing all the nourishing and nurturing back to health that's necessary after childbirth. At that point, Dad could go back to work (i.e., not exhausting all of his leave yet) while Mom is still on leave, ideally with other support (because even a four-week-old infant is a lot to handle alone). Then, when Mom goes back to work, Dad stays home with the baby for her first few weeks: the perfect time for Dad to get comfortable solo parenting (when baby's less of a blob and hopefully past the cluster-feeding stage) and Mom to have the peace of mind knowing her baby's at home with a parent. The key to this format of *Tetris*-leave plan is to review your intermittent-leave rights. Remember: FMLA can be used intermittently for medical leave (birth recovery), and for bonding (but only if the employer agrees). Few employers will promote these rights in handbooks because it tends to be more challenging to accommodate.

It is helpful to draw out your leave calendar. I do this with clients, and I actually still do these by hand and with a calculator, but tech tools can support you here too. Many employers use fancy software with different color codes for different leave laws, but these plans will be incomplete because they may not include all the financial benefit sources and will also not include the entire family's plan. Create a large timeline for both parents with all the applicable leave laws and financial benefits so that you can visualize who will be home at what time, and where the money will come from.

For an example leave calendar you can download, visit themamattorney. com.

It's okay to feel nervous. Dads feel nervous, even terrified, about a lot of this whole parenthood thing, a lot of the time—but they rarely talk about it. Those fears aren't unjustified, either—some research has shown that taking paternity leave can in fact have professional consequences down the road—but at the same time, it's essential to embrace the reality. This is what it means to be a provider (or, in this case, co-provider with your partner) and to be supportive of your family. (Plus, moms are *also* scared about the professional implications of having a kid and taking leave, but *we* don't have a choice when it comes to taking time away from work.) At the same time, you *don't* have to be some stoic rock of a person who never wavers or has doubts or anxieties. No one is expecting you to have all the answers, just to ask the right questions—so ask, and keep asking until everything is super clear.

Create a fantasy map. Dads often ask me what else they can do. After all, it can feel like you're having a more passive experience than your baby mama because it's not happening in your body. Your baby mama will be going to a lot of appointments and sending a lot more workplace emails than you, asking for different forms of benefits and accommodations. This is an anxiety-producing process, and you can help her by keeping her "file" complete and organized. You can even read this book, prewrite emails, and strategize her employer's next move. You can make a spreadsheet! Think of it as a fantasy football game, anticipating risk and planning accordingly. Just like "What will we do when this player is benched?" anticipate "What will I do if my wife develops PPD symptoms?" If you have the emails ready, the policies in your back pocket, and a mental health specialist's number at the ready, your baby mama will feel so protected and held by you, which will reduce her symptoms significantly.

And if no one has told you yet, thank you. You will never regret this, and your child is so lucky to land in your hands.

3

Help Them Help You

Collaborating with HR Effectively

I want to be clear: Despite the many HR professionals I've cross-examined on the stand (and despite the subtitle of this book!), I am not anti-HR by any means.

In fact, you'd be surprised how many HR professionals I end up helping navigate their *own* parental leave, or even their own cases.

Leyla, an HR professional, knew the ins and outs of maternity rights like the back of her hand. So, when she got pregnant, she had everything in place for her own maternity leave: She was quick with the documentation, proactive with the communication, and incredibly on the ball with her employer.

However, when her husband approached *his* company's HR manager to request FMLA paperwork, they repeatedly handed him their standard parental leave policy instead—a policy that would give him four weeks of paid leave to spend at home with his wife and new baby.

But while the four weeks of paid leave offered by the company was a nice benefit, it was *not* what he was asking for! He wanted his legally protected twelve weeks of FMLA leave, and he needed the proper paperwork to do so.

It was ultimately Leyla who had to encourage her husband to advocate for his rights (using some tips and tricks from my program) until the company finally provided the necessary documents.

"I wish more HR managers had the same mindset that I do," Leyla confessed after the fact. "Thank you for spreading the word to help those that are not familiar with these laws."

In today's workplace, HR is in charge of a *lot*—everything from regulatory and legal compliance to planning the company picnic—and they're going to be a key player in your motherhood-at-work journey. This chapter will teach you how to deal with them and get what you need for you and your family—and no, it's not going to be a free-for-all HR-bashing fest.

Make no mistake, though: HR works for the company, not you. The company pays them, so no matter how friendly and well-intentioned they are as people, HR professionals have a tough time doing their job well because it would mean going against the people who pay them. In fact, if they go against the company's interests too much, they can get fired.

That said, I applaud those HR professionals like Leyla, who genuinely want to help, or the countless others I've met with the courage to confront management over misconduct or legal compliance issues. I know that they're out there, and I'm grateful that they exist.

The others, though? The ones who are not so brave and just have a blind loyalty to the executives? They often end up in my deposition chair.

And since I don't know where you work or what kind of HR folks you're dealing with, I'm going to give you the whole playbook.

Knowing is half the battle—but it's only half. Now that you know what you're legally entitled to, it's time to investigate what your company has to offer, and that means interacting with HR. You'll go into these meetings educated and empowered, because when they know that you know your rights, they are a lot more likely to respect you and your needs.

What HR Is and What HR Isn't

I've cross-examined a lot of HR managers, but there's one in particular I'll never forget.

This woman was perfectly personable and easy to talk to. While being cross-examined, she wasn't frowning at us like we were the devil incarnate or sneering down at us with superiority. She actually seemed eager to help and answer our questions, even though, technically, as the lawyers for an aggrieved former employee, we worked for the "other side."

Before getting into the nitty-gritty, we wanted to get some basics on the record. We started simple: "How many subordinates do you have?"

She looked at us for a moment. "What's a subordinate?"

It didn't get better from there. In fact, it got worse. At one point, we asked if a safety issue had been reported to OSHA and her reply was, "What's OSHA?" As friendly and willing as she was, this HR woman showed a complete lack of basic understanding.

This might be an extreme example, but it illustrates the problems with our current HR system. I don't blame this woman for the gaps in her knowledge—if anything, I blame the whole setup she's working in.

Although the term "human resources" might sound a little creepy when you really think about it (are these the people in charge of turning us all into living batteries à la *The Matrix*?), the modern HR department actually has its roots in administrative work: In the early twentieth century, individual companies suddenly found themselves managing much larger numbers of workers (because of the Industrial Revolution) and needed to set up a dedicated department for things like payroll, hiring, and record-keeping. By around the 1930s—after a world war and during a burgeoning depression—this evolved into a more holistic responsibility of taking care of workers' welfare (as well as interacting with growing labor unions), and "personnel management" became the norm. In the 1940s, wartime wage freezes saw companies offering health insurance as a non-cash incentive to employees—yet another program that needed someone to administer it—and then the 1960s and 1970s brought the civil rights movement and labor law reforms that outlawed certain types of discrimination (and needed someone in charge of keeping the company compliant). Throw in the 1990s-era Americans with Disabilities Act, a renewed focus on equity, and tons of back-and-forth over remote work, and you have the huge purview of today's HR department.

With that kind of pileup of responsibilities over the past century or so of modern work, it's no wonder that HR is expected to cover so much. They are essentially in charge of the entire universe of personnel issues, everything from investigations to tax forms to organizing the holiday party to administering your leave. The job also requires a supernatural level of emotional caretaking, as well as the strange discomfort of being the one who is kind of like the team police, while also being an intrinsic part of the team, deserving of the protections of the rules themselves (but often with no one to enforce them for the HR staff). I had a close look into the job through my husband's professional path, and it looked exhausting.

The contradiction and tension of interests, the enormous smorgasbord of diverging tasks, and the cacophony of relentless staff complaints, juxtapositioned against unskilled managers—let's just say I was grateful to have my very stressful litigator job, mainly because it was simpler to represent one side of the issue. So, yes, HR is so many things. And because we have accepted HR as a sort of *waves at everything* kind of job, it's essential to understand what HR isn't.

This brings me back to my HR witness and her "what's OSHA?" level of expertise. It might seem astonishing that someone in her role didn't know about the Occupational Safety and Health Administration, but technically, there's no requirement that she *has* to: There are no real professional prerequisites for working in HR. You don't need to pass a qualifying exam like the bar or medical boards. True, some HR professionals have advanced degrees specifically in human resources, but many do not (especially at smaller companies, where the HR "team" might be one person who's gradually assumed more responsibilities over the years).

So, while HR folks do deal with employment law, they aren't lawyers themselves and often don't receive any legal training. By nature, they're generalists who have to handle a wide range of responsibilities, from benefits management to organizing company events, so they may not have deep expertise in *any* specific area. (Again, #NotAllHRPros: Many HR professionals *are* extremely competent and knowledgeable in employment law, but many are not and may not have even been trained or tested on the information.)

The upshot for you is that employment law is complex, and you cannot assume HR will know the ins and outs of this field.

And even if they do know, they might not tell you. In fact, they might be disincentivized to do so.

This brings me back to the other thing that HR isn't: Ultimately, they're not on your side. HR works for the company, not you. The company pays them, not you. They may be friendly and well-intentioned, but at the end of the day, maximizing *your maternity leave* means taking more money out of the company's pocket, and that's the opposite of what they're paid to do.

When you go to HR and ask them to help you, you are setting yourself up in an imbalanced dynamic, because HR has access to resources and experts (including the company's attorneys—who are paid to protect the company), and you don't. You'd be starting off with the wrong energetics, because you're asking the help of people who are paid to help the entity that tends to have opposing needs to you (i.e., maximizing your labor, presence, and production).

This makes it really, really hard to do this job well. And that's why I have so much empathy for those good-hearted HR professionals that I know are out there—and you should too.

Empathy, ultimately, is going to be your secret weapon.

Actually, it's not a weapon at all. It's more like a gift.

"Help Me Help You": The Golden Rule of Dealing with HR

With all that in mind, here's the one thing you need to deal with HR successfully.

Ready?

Repeat after me: "Help me help you."

That's it. That's the mindset you want to bring to every interaction with your HR department.

You know their job is thankless, endless, and difficult. You know they wear a ton of different hats and may not be trained for half the things in their job description. You know they are management, but not always treated as such. You know they have to do a ton of hand-holding. You know they are deployed for any tricky, contentious issue. You know they are expected to keep up with massively changing regulations. You know a lot of people, including their superiors, eye-roll when they are in the room.

One thing that has been consistent in my dealings with HR is that they are underappreciated and overworked. Often, they feel like they don't really "belong," which may be why they default to siding with management over employees, because they're incentivized to appear loyal.

So, when you go to talk to HR, know that in their mind they may be thinking, *Oh no, what now?* like a teacher who has too many kids in her class and no subs to give her a goddamn break.

You're not there to start a fight or cause trouble—you don't want that drama any more than they do. You simply want what you're entitled to.

So, by ensuring that they give you your full legal rights, don't violate any laws, and stay true to the promises of the company's policies, you're literally making their job easier. You truly are there to help them get everything to do with your pregnancy and leave wrapped up as quickly and smoothly as possible.

In practice, this means you need to do three things.

You'll be **prepared.** You'll get educated on the law (check, thanks to chapter 2) so that you know what you are and aren't entitled to and can cite the specific language necessary to invoke the magical force field of legal rights and protections. You'll also know the relevant parts of the handbook so that you can refer to specific policies accurately.

You'll be **persistent.** You're going to be an organization and project management queen, taking charge of setting meetings, following up in writing, asking clarifying questions, and managing deadlines. No matter how busy *they* are, you'll make sure things don't fall through the cracks.

You'll be **personable.** The whole time, you'll stay confident and comfortable in every interaction you have with HR—because, again, you're there to help them get the job done.

Again, this mindset is an exercise in empathy. As much as possible, lead with that. You understand how busy and frazzled an HR person can get, especially when dealing with (gulp) a pregnant employee—unless they're totally incompetent, they'll recognize that your being pregnant means they *really* need to cross their *t*'s and dot their *i*'s. What you're saying, by being prepared, persistent, and personable, is: "I know this is a lot to handle, and that the stakes are high, but you don't have to worry—I'm here to help keep you compliant."

What if you're nervous, or you've seen instances of retaliation? Frame your need in the form of a question. It's a lot less threatening to say, "I was looking into this new law, the PWFA—am I understanding correctly that this law applies to the company? Can we sit down and discuss this together?" than it is to say, "I'm entitled to PWFA rights. Here is my request: x, y, z."

Prepared:
The Almighty Employee Handbook

We've already covered the legal protections you have as a pregnant employee. Those are the law of the land and cannot be violated without risking a visit to court (or a stern letter from a lawyer like me).

Now it's time to learn what rules and regulations apply to you within the confines of your employer—the rules you'll find in your employee handbook.

You can think of the requirements in an employee handbook like the code of conduct at a place like Disney World. Organizations are allowed to have rules of engagement for participating in their activities and using their facilities. For example, it's legal to ride your bike down the street. Generally speaking, you have the right as a cyclist to share the road with cars. But at Disney World, there's (probably) a rule that says "no bikes." If you cruise down Main Street USA on your ten-speed, the cast members are allowed to ask you to leave. Disney World isn't saying you can't *ever* ride your bike; they're just saying that, within the confines of their theme park, it's not allowed.

To be clear, this doesn't mean employee handbooks can supersede the law. A handbook can't require something that violates the rights of a protected class. So Disney World can say "no bike riding allowed," but they *can't* say something broader like "no wheeled vehicles allowed," because that could arguably violate the rights of wheelchair users to enjoy their park (a right that's protected under the ADA). Similarly, an employer can require its employees to adhere to a "professional dress code," but they can't stipulate that this dress code prohibits, say, natural Black hairstyles, because that would constitute race-based discrimination.

Policies are not the law. They are not enforceable in court. These are just internal guidelines for specific organizations. Policies should reflect the law. Sometimes they don't. If they don't, the law always wins. What I see a lot is that an employee exhausts her leave per the policy, and then the employer tells her she's not allowed to take more time off. Often this employee is entitled to much more time off under the law, but the employer is not aware of the law, and incorrectly assumes the policies reflect the law, or simply doesn't research the correct rules.

So if you encounter this scenario, where the employer is dangling the policies, code of ethics, handbooks, and other self-serving documents above your head, be cautious. The employer may be trying to justify doing something shady by pointing at its own rules, as opposed to providing you with the protections you're entitled to under the law. Always ask the employer to provide you with the actual law instead of the company policy.

In an ideal world, your employee handbook would be thorough, clear, up-to-date, and easy to access. In practice . . . well, that's rarely the case. (Honestly, the next employee handbook I see that fits that description will be the first one.)

Handbooks are often outdated or incomplete, as they tend to be one of those "perpetual projects" that's never an emergency or high priority, especially in a small company or one where HR is stretched thin. Even if they're complete and relatively recently updated, there's no guarantee they reflect the latest changes in employment laws, because those change!

Handbooks can also be confusing. They'll mix together legal rights and company policies without clearly distinguishing between them, leaving you without a clear sense of what you're legally owed versus what's technically a perk. Moreover, they may not provide enough detail or guidance on how to actually exercise or maximize your rights as an employee, especially when it comes to issues like pregnancy, maternity leave, and childcare.

Keep in mind that handbooks are written by the employer, and while they can certainly include pertinent laws, the language is often intentionally designed to protect the employer.

With all that said, here are the main topics you can expect your company's handbook to cover:

- Mission statement and company philosophy
- Employment policies (e.g., attendance, dress code, conduct)
- Benefits (e.g., health insurance, paid time off, retirement plans)
- Workplace rules and regulations (e.g., use of company equipment, handling of secure information)
- Reporting procedures for issues or concerns
- Disciplinary actions

(Not all of these are going to be directly relevant to your pregnancy and maternity leave, but it's a good idea to be up to speed on all of them regardless.)

The handbook should also have a "last updated" date, either on the cover page or within individual sections. This is important to note because some legal requirements that *are* directly relevant to your work as a pregnant and postpartum employee (such as the PWFA and the PUMP Act) are less than five years old, and your handbook might present conflicting or outdated information.

When it comes to reading the handbook, there's more than likely going to be a lot of fluff and irrelevant nonsense in there, so don't think you have to go cover to cover: No one reads the whole handbook. Just read the part related to your situation and know where to find what you need (keeping in mind that pregnancy is often covered by disability, so make sure to read everything on disability). It's also helpful to make notes as you go so that you can follow up with HR on anything you don't understand.

As you read, here's what you'll want to do:

Look for outdated or irrelevant policies that may not actually be enforceable.

Remember, just because it's in the handbook doesn't mean the company can legally enforce it. Refer back to the federal and state-level protections you have and make sure none of the company's policies require something contradictory.

Examples you might see:

You're not allowed to discuss your wages with your coworkers. (This goes against federal law.)

You can only take seven days off per year. (This omits your important leave rights.)

Distinguish between company policies and legal rights/ protections.

The handbook often mixes these together, so it's important to understand which is which—and make sure you don't take *only* what's provided by your company. When in doubt, refer to the text of a law to make sure you know what you're legally entitled to.

Examples you might see:

"We offer four weeks of paid parental leave." → Great! But if you're a qualifying employee under FMLA, you are also entitled to an additional eight weeks of job-protected leave.

"Violating attendance policies can result in termination." → This ignores that policy has to be waived for legal rights, to include prenatal appointments, medical leave, bonding leave, pumping, etc., and that it may not lead to termination.

"Employment is at-will. Employees can be fired for any reason, including no reason." → This often leaves employees assuming they can be fired for being pregnant, or for being a woman, or for missing a meeting during a pump break. However, an at-will employment policy does not insulate an employer from following employment law, including protections based on pregnancy, disability, gender, race/ethnicity, religion, marital status, or military status. The full statement should read, "Employees can be fired for any reason, including no reason, but not for an illegal reason."

My former client Miriam, a preschool coordinator, asked for time off for birth. Her manager fired her, telling her, "You'll be out of the office for too long, so I'll need to replace you. I'm sorry, but you're at-will." This is against the law. Employers have to respect our rights whether or not we're at-will (in fact, nearly all employees in the United States are at-will).

Identify any vague, ambiguous, or incomplete language.
Any bit of wiggle room for the company in how something is defined is a potential opportunity for your rights to be violated. Not saying this will happen, but you'll want to know ASAP if there's something hinky in the language that could be leveraged against you.

Examples you might see:

"Employees are expected to dress neatly and professionally while working for [COMPANY]." → Okay, but what if I'm pregnant and I can only wear maternity leggings? Is that still "professional"? (I had a client who was disciplined for doing just that, because the big-box store where she worked—ironically a leading "mom store"—required khakis as a uniform.)

"At termination, any sick days, vacation days, PTO, and any other time-off benefits lapse." → This ignores that some states require companies to pay out sick time and/or vacation time at termination, and that some employees can receive disability benefits even after termination.

"Staff should arrive at least thirty minutes before any client meeting, and must be prepared for the meeting, or be subject to discipline." → What if the meeting starts when the office opens? Are the thirty minutes paid time? What does "prepared" mean?

"Parental leave cannot be extended beyond sixteen weeks." → This ignores that leave can be extended for postpartum conditions including PPA or PPD. It deters parents from asserting their leave extension rights.

Check for information on reporting processes, like hotlines, that may not create a clear written record.

Companies like you to report to a hotline because then you are not writing an email reporting illegal conduct like discrimination, which is always the cornerstone piece of evidence in our cases.

If that's the case, create your *own* written record. Any time your company expects you to report something in a conversation or a phone call, they are actively trying to avoid a track record, as it may become a body of evidence. Document, document, document!

Examples you might see:

"Employees are to call the hotline to report any issue related to a manager." → Who is (wo)manning that hotline? Can we trust this person? Is this person impartial? Is the call recorded? Do you receive a recording of this call?

"Issues may only be reported to your direct lead." → Companies write this to insulate upper management and protect themselves from liability. Companies are liable only when issues related to unlawful conduct (like discrimination) are reported to someone who has a fairly high level of supervisory authority. Often your direct lead may not even be considered a supervisor. Issues should certainly be reported up the chain, but employees are free to report issues in the way that is most conducive to the situation, including to upper management directly.

Note down every deadline, requirement, and process for using your benefits.

Part of helping HR do their job is providing what they need promptly and entirely—so learn what that means. Keep a master list of deadlines (a spreadsheet is great, so that you can rearrange it into chronological order, and even fill in specific calendar dates using a formula based on your due date) based on what the handbook requires. And if any of those dates are inconsistent or conflicting, note that too—and immediately get clarification from HR.

Examples you might see:

"Employees should submit a medical note at least thirty days prior to the need for medical leave." → Ideally, you provide your notice much, much sooner. Thirty days is not enough for an employer to prepare for your absence. The FMLA provides that notice of leave has to be given at least thirty days or as soon as feasible, so you will see this language reflected in handbooks. However, to make it easier on yourself, your team, and your employer, you'll want to give much earlier notice.

"Employees should provide a medical note when requesting a leave of absence or accommodations." → Many employees feel frustrated that they have to disclose private information to their employers, but there is no way to get the protections of your rights without your employer having any ability to understand your needs from a medical professional perspective. It is actually too late to request your note from your provider and request your accommodation at the same time. It is true that some employers do not ask for the note, but they may, and if you don't have access to a medical provider, you may get stuck on waiting lists or you may get stuck trying to figure out who is in your network and whether they accept new clients. Especially with mental health conditions such as PPA or PPD, it is vital that contact with a provider is made as soon as possible. In fact, I counsel to establish a relationship with a mental health provider during pregnancy so that you go through all the time-consuming intake and onboarding processes when you have the time. When you have to go back to work in a few days but you are still experiencing symptoms, it's often too late to get a note.

What If I Don't Have an Employee Handbook?

Many smaller employers do not have a handbook. In that case, you'll want to make sure that every conversation you have is confirmed in writing, because you're essentially crafting the policies and the handbook with your managers while you are preparing for your leave. In fact, you can even suggest that your leave can form the blueprint to systemize leave administration.

Many employees assume they have no rights if there is no handbook. That is not true. Employers are not legally obligated to provide a handbook. They have to provide notice of certain laws, but they may do that by putting signage in the office room, or sending a company-wide email.

What If There Is No HR?

If you work for a company that does not have a designated HR person, your company still has to follow the law. Often, the person administering your leave will be your direct manager. This can be frustrating, as medical information can be discussed. However, your employer does not get any excuses or passes if they don't know the rules. Lack of understanding of the law is not a legal defense. When there is no HR, ask your manager who will be administering your leave. They may ask an office manager or someone else to step into the role. With smaller employers, it's common that you will be the first person to experience a pregnancy. It is also extremely likely that your employer simply assumes they are exempt from *everything* because they are a small employer. The reality is more complex. Your employer may be exempt from some laws, but not all. What I often see with smaller employers is that they will consult with an outside HR professional that is connected to their payroll provider (like ADP). If they go that route, request to be cc'd on the conversations. If they don't, prepare to do a lot more of the legwork. This can be frustrating, and it can be an opportunity. When your employer does not know the law at all, you can explain it to them, and they may just follow your lead because you'll be the only subject matter expert. Embrace this opportunity.

Persistent:
Pregnancy Project Management

Being persistent doesn't mean being annoying, but it does mean taking full ownership of every last deadline and due date—and not just the big one at the end of forty weeks. Again, don't rely on HR to keep track of when paperwork needs to be filed, or count on them to remind you to submit documentation—you're project-managing this pregnancy, and you're not going to let anything fall through the cracks (because if you do, you're only making it harder on your future self and baby).

Here's an example timeline of when you'll want to take care of all the administrative tasks related to your pregnancy and recovery. However, this is just an example—you should make your own list of dates and deadlines based on your employee handbook and state laws, too, and always default to those dates over this general recommendation.

FIRST TRIMESTER

- Read the employee handbook (if you haven't yet) and immediately get clarification on any vague or confusing policies.
- Announce your pregnancy to your manager (which we'll cover in the next chapter!).
- Follow up in writing with your manager and HR.
- Request accommodations as you need them.
- Start writing up your master task list, and give access to your manager. These are all the tasks you are currently doing.
- Start working on your joint family leave plan with your partner, and understand the family's future benefits and time-off protections.

SECOND TRIMESTER

- Request accommodations as you need them.
- Contact a mental health provider, like a psychologist or psychiatrist. Even if you do not end up using one postpartum, it is essential to be in their system in case you will need support.

- Expand your task list by writing out your future project list for the next six to twelve months, and give access to your manager. These are the tasks that *should* get done in this time period and may need to be delegated to someone else. This is also when you should propose cross-training or retaining someone to integrate into the work.

THIRD TRIMESTER

- Obtain medical leave paperwork from your OB/GYN and submit to HR.
- Invite your manager to lunch and have a candid conversation about your upcoming absence, including any anticipated concerns or points of tension.
- Invite your subordinates to lunch and have a candid conversation about your upcoming absence, including any anticipated concerns or points of tension.
- Use your master task and project list to write out a more narrowly tailored maternity leave plan. This plan should lay out simply and plainly who will be doing what when you are gone and where to find what they need. Send it to your larger team.
- Provide notice to HR or management that you intend to return as a lactating employee, if all goes as planned. Start strategizing on pumping spaces. This is when any operational research should be done—such as blinds, pods, tents, locks, etc.—however, they should not be purchased yet. Set a reminder on your phone to follow up about a month before your return to work, at which time these items should be purchased.

MAGIC WORDS

The other key aspect to being persistent is following up . . . on everything. In writing.

Getting answers, ensuring they're on the record, and pursuing your requests through all the various hoops can feel like a full-time job in and of itself, but it will go a lot faster if you're specific, clear, and uncompromising in your communication. Of course, I'll provide scripts and templates for you to use throughout this book, but not every script will fit every situation perfectly. If and when you need to adapt one, or compose your own to suit your particular scenario, here are some powerful magic words that you can use to get your point across and make your intentions clear.

Clarify and Confirm

As we discussed . . .

As a reminder (on X date you told me Y, the employee handbook states [direct quote]).

To clarify . . .

To make sure we're on the same page . . .

Can you confirm?

Is this your understanding?

Cite Your Rights

In accordance with (XYZ company policy, ABC legal requirement) . . .

I am aware that (I may not be retaliated against for making this request; the law requires XYZ).

It is my understanding that . . .

As required by (XYZ law, ABC policy) . . .

Upon the advice of my healthcare provider . . .

State Your Case

I am requesting the following reasonable accommodations . . .

I will be taking FMLA.

Work Together

I'm happy to discuss these issues further.

I understand the company has to engage in the interactive process to determine if an accommodation can be made.

As an alternative, I suggest . . .

Push Back

Unfortunately, your proposal of (XYZ solution) does not satisfy the legal requirement of (specific language quoted directly from law).

In your email of (date), you said (XYZ), but the law requires (ABC). Please advise.

I made my first request on (date) and followed up on (date) but have yet to receive a response. I understand the interactive process is supposed to be timely.

I prefer to keep this conversation in writing to ensure that everything is documented and compliant.

If You're Thrown to a Leave Administrator

Many, many companies nowadays outsource some of their HR operations to what are known as "leave administrators." At first, you might think this is great news—a tailor-made specialist whose only job is to oversee your maternity leave!

In reality, you should proceed with caution.

Understand that these leave administrators are *not* your employer, nor are they fellow employees *at* your employer (like an HR department is—who may be a lot more concerned with compliance than a random contractor). They aren't the insurance company in charge of your short-term disability policy, either—although many people confuse leave administrators and insurance providers. They are third-party vendors hired *by* your employer to administer your leave. And since they obviously want to be *rehired* by your employer when their contract is up, they're actually incentivized to minimize your leave time (because less leave time = less cost to your employer). This isn't fair, but it's just how it is.

On top of that, the folks working at these companies are not employment attorneys. They are often poorly trained staff put in charge of extremely complex regulations. They are using AI more and more, which means the robots are now in charge of when you have to put down your baby. Plus, the administrator firms tend to keep their staff working as much as possible—again, to cut costs. It's a recipe for shortchanging you and letting things (well, "letting" them) fall through the cracks.

Long story short, leave administrators are *not* your advocates, even if they present themselves that way. Keep this in mind when communicating with these agencies. They are there to help and support your employer to avoid liability, so they will do what is required under the law, but nothing more—and their eye is always on the bottom line.

What do you need to do to protect yourself? First, know that the law considers these providers a proxy (an extension) of your employer; ultimately, your employer is liable for what the third-party administrator says and does, so they can't pass the buck and blame the administrator for any mistakes. However, that doesn't mean that your employer won't try to hide behind the fact that they were unaware and therefore did not mean any harm against you if you're denied what is legally yours.

With that in mind, your job is to make sure your employer stays in the loop and is in tune with the administration of your leave. While your employer may keep delegating your leave administration to these vendors, you'll just keep bringing the conversation back to your employer. After all, your actual leave request still needs to go to your employer, not the administrator (because, in the end, your employer is responsible for granting your leave, not the administrator).

You can state outright to your HR department that you want to keep this conversation internal: "I would feel more comfortable communicating directly about my leave. I understand you may need to seek some external guidance or support, but I do not wish to communicate with a third party that's not my employer, especially as this concerns private medical information, and private information regarding an infant."

If you're still rebuffed from there, then just keep your employer in the loop on *everything*. CC your HR person or your boss on all communications with the leave administrator (or forward these communications to them if you're going to some sort of portal). If you are submitting forms to the provider, also submit them to your HR. Insist that HR answers your questions if you feel confused. Do not assume that they are communicating with each other—and remember that if your leave is mishandled, your employer can still be liable for leave interference.

Personable:
Putting It All Together

When I post about HR on social media, I brace myself for my phone blowing up. Because I know that even though I 100 percent stand by what I say when I share information, even though I'm incredibly careful to qualify my recommendations and statements . . . inevitably, some HR people are just going to get mad.

And mad people leave comments. A *lot* of them.

But I do try to read them—the ones that aren't full of vitriol, anyway—because I genuinely do want to know what they need to get employees what *they* need. And one comment in particular stuck with me.

I agree, wrote the commenter. *Much more time should be spent teaching leaders about leave, accommodation, how to be flexible, and how to staff ahead of time to account for absences. But learning and development often has a low budget and it's never made a priority. So often managers make decisions without asking what's best for everyone, and HR ends up having to advocate for policies that won't completely mess things up.*

Really, in my ten years in the field, it's my experience that we are usually the ones advocating for our employees to their managers.

Look, I know, #notallHR, but most of us really do want to be partners and to do what's best.

I share this because, yes, dealing with HR can be frustrating, hair-pulling, anxiety-inducing, *especially* at such a vulnerable time in your life (and when even looking at a computer screen might make you nauseous). But, at the end of the day, they're professionals trying to do their jobs, just like you, and at the very *least,* there's no need to make their jobs harder by being snippy or passive-aggressive. Not to say you should be a pushover, but you can be *personable.* That's what a partnership looks like.

(Plus, people want to help people who are pleasant to deal with. Think about it: If your HR manager has ten different employee requests on her desk, all equally urgent, but she knows you've been responsive and respectful throughout the process, while everyone else has been disorganized, dismissive, or taken out their anger on her? You can be sure she's going to tackle your request first.)

So, here's a basic outline of how to write an email to HR (and yes, you want to do everything over email, so that you have your conversation in writing).

Take action as soon as possible. The further in advance you ask for something, the more likely you are to get it in time.

On the email itself, include your direct supervisor(s) as a cc (assuming you trust them) and your HR contact. Always include your personal email address on bcc. Use specific, protected language when making a request: For example, refer to taking time off for "prenatal care" instead of just "time off" to invoke your legal protections.

Relatedly, cite any applicable laws that cover your request. That way, HR knows that *you* know your stuff (and can't be strung along or manipulated!) and also doesn't have to search around in case *they* need to document the applicable law.

Confirm your understanding of any relevant company policies to ensure you and HR are on the same page. Write out what your take on the situation is in layman's terms, and ask HR to confirm if your interpretation is correct.

Emphasize your commitment and teamwork. Make it clear that your job is important to you and you want to work with them to find a solution.

Once you email HR, they may respond in one of two ways. First, they might call you to discuss. Sure, maybe they're busy and figure a chat will be quicker . . . or maybe they don't want to have a paper trail. Either way, you stay professional and cooperative.

Here's how to handle it . . .

Take the call and take notes. (It's okay to ask for a quick pause while you grab a pen and paper! Don't let them start until you're ready.)

Once the call is over, immediately follow up with an email that contains a written summary of what you discussed.

End your email with "If this is not your understanding, please let me know. Unless I hear otherwise from you, I will assume that we are in agreement here." That puts the ball back in *their* court to correct any details.

However, sometimes HR won't try to get you on the phone and will happily write an email . . . but that email will sound just a bit different than what you said. For example, they might reply to your email about setting up your maternity leave with language like "we received your request for PTO" (rather than acknowledging that you were specifically asking for a legal right) or answer your email about attending an OB appointment with more general terms like "appointment" or "time off."

If this happens, don't panic—and again, don't assume bad intent. They might just be dashing off a quick email and being a bit sloppy, they might be dealing with four other people making similar, non-pregnancy-related requests . . . who knows. Or they may be actively trying to create a record that steers you away from your legal rights. All that matters is that you respond to set the record straight.

Reply and thank them for their response.

Clarify the situation by refusing to agree to their framing language. "To be clear, I am requesting my federally protected leave, not ordinary PTO."

Reaffirm that you'll keep them in the loop as needed.

Remember, you're not alone in this journey, nor are you asking for anything unreasonable—only what is yours by legal right and what is owed to you as part of your employer's agreed-upon benefits. As we go through specific situations and issues in the chapters to come, I'll give you more detailed scripts that help you nail down the nitty-gritty of phrasing. But for now, just know that you *can* do this, and the law (and an entire community of liberated mothers!) is on your side.

If they request to meet on Zoom, they may drop in their little AI bot to take notes. If they do that, they should ask you to agree to the transcription, and you should ask at the outset if it will be shared with you. If they do not agree to share it, state explicitly that you will be recording the meeting on your phone, and turn on the recording.

Sometimes HR will try to take a de facto deposition without giving you access to the transcript. You should always have access to the conversations that occur about your own leave or accommodations. If HR won't let you record and won't turn off their bot either, conclude the meeting and explain you will provide your explanation over email.

A lot of the mothers in my community are scared of these interactions with HR. But if there is one thing I have learned from endless cases in this field, it's this: **They are actually more scared of you.** Because they know that the law demands they protect you. I'd argue this is actually a good thing: We should all be a little intimidated by our ability to create humans; it's the ultimate act of creation. Though universal, it is magical.

You embody the regenerative force of nature, and **nature cannot be stopped**. I want you to feel this power in your bones. And in a way, in modern capitalism, our workplaces can sometimes come between us and our babies when they don't respect our needs. When this goes too far, it's okay to embrace your fierce, primal mama powers.

Just see what a mama jaguar does when someone approaches her cub. She shows her teeth and her claws. Your emails will, on the surface, be professional and clean, but the woman typing it, oh friend, she is not going to let anyone stand between her and her baby.

Uncomfortable Meetings

Many mamas ask me how to engage with managers who are clueless at best and outright toxic at worst. Often, despite our communications with HR, we also need to communicate directly with managers about our pregnancies and leave plans. In fact, many of these conversations will occur in person. And while you are experiencing the miracle of life, often these jerks will just think about quarterly metrics. Remember, the health and protection of your baby is more important than your employer's business operations. Your boss may be insensitive or offensive or engage in anti-mom bias, acting as if your time off (and, by extension, your baby) is burdensome and inconvenient to them.

Let me say this loud and clear: Your baby is not a burden on your boss. In reality, your boss is a burden on your baby.

Before you walk into a meeting with someone like that, take a deep breath and remember, you come from a long lineage of strong mothers, and your strength and advocacy will also protect you, as well as your baby and the entire lineage that comes after you. It is your sacred right to be protected in your motherhood experience. Your right as a mother to have a fully embodied and supported experience is the most important. So take a deep breath and harness this strength. Own the sovereignty of what it means to be a Mother, capital *M*. Stand tall and exhale from your belly. Let it take up all the space. Now go tell them what's up and how you've already figured it out.

Because you are the Mother. Say it. *I am the Mother.* Say it again. Stand up and say it. *I. Am. The. Mother.* Yes. You are the Mother in the room. You embody souls, you make milk out of blood, you multiply, you create eyes out of bread. You can sure as hell make anything happen in the workplace too. You can birth worlds within worlds, you can create humans, and you can create a leave policy. You can change diapers and you can change company culture.

Go into the meeting with this strength. You will be calm and sturdy, without too much emotionality. No nervous energy, no nervous little laugh. Just calm, relaxed, steady, and clear. Lay out your plan and present it in a way that actually benefits your boss. No, we don't go into a room and demand things. We do not create antagonistic relationships. That is their way. Instead, you'll go in and lay out your plan, calmly and clearly. With bosses like that, we don't go into a whole story about our baby. We don't expect them to care. They don't. We just keep it short and to the point, and you'll conclude by saying, "I expect you to follow the law. Thank you for your time."

4

Exhibit A

Announcing Your Pregnancy at Work

When you announce your pregnancy at work, *don't* do what I did during my first pregnancy. Namely, don't wait until you're through the first trimester. That's how you end up nearly barfing in your boss's Tesla.

Let me explain. During my first pregnancy, I thought I was doing everything right. I waited until it was "safe" to announce that I was expecting a baby (which was, culturally, around twelve weeks), and so I went to great lengths to conceal my symptoms and play it cool in professional settings—which I soon discovered was much more difficult than I'd assumed. A legal seminar in Hawaii that should have been an energizing getaway with my colleagues turned into a week of dodging raw fish, secretly asking waiters for virgin mai tais, and eating nothing but breadsticks to keep my nausea at bay.

By the time I was three months along, I knew I was closer to my "safe" date, but I still hadn't planned out how I was going to tell my boss. Announcing wasn't even on my mind that day when we got into his fancy car to drive to a deposition, which we'd done countless times before.

The thing is, my former boss was a bit of a speedy driver, and every twist and turn he took felt as if it were sending my stomach upside down. I remember clutching my briefcase, willing myself not to lose my breakfast in this state-of-the-art electric car (this was back when we still liked Elon and Teslas were brand-new and even *more* expensive than they are now).

Finally, I had to let it out.

"I'm pregnant!" I blurted. "Can you please slow down a bit? I'm feeling really nauseous."

My boss was gracious in response.

But even though it was well-received, my haphazard announcement, and the subsequent "this will all sort itself out" attitude I adopted, started to catch up with me. I was the first pregnant lawyer at the firm, and I had not observed anyone slow down their pace or generally express any limitations. It was a full-force kind of law firm. The job was all-encompassing. I had a reputation for being a quick yet qualitative worker. I was committed to keeping up with the firm's fast pace, and instead of slowing down, I actually started to work harder and faster. I wanted—and needed—to make more money, so I started bringing in cases because that's how I could get commission. Then I pushed to finish these cases before my due date, so I'd have the money before the baby arrived. I also felt guilty about my upcoming absence, and I wanted to "make up" for the time I would be gone and showcase my value.

I also just felt weird about pregnancy in general. Pregnancy is all about the body. And when you've spent a lifetime perfecting the art of "mind over body," the body's resurgence during pregnancy was a wake-up call I was not fully prepared for. The body's needs can be loud during pregnancy, and when we're so used to not listening to our bodies, it can be a reckoning. This is one of my journal entries at the time:

> It's so weird to not be alone. I've always been alone in my body. And now I have a roommate. And he makes me so nauseous and uses my resources. Like a guy off Craigslist who eats my food and doesn't pay rent and also never cleans the bathroom. I mean how rude to move in and make me feel like shit!

Toward the end of my pregnancy, we recruited a new lawyer to take over my work, and I trained her while also working my own cases and struggling to walk up the stairs due to pelvic pain. And the whole time, I was praised from all sides for being Wonder Woman and Super Mom. And the truth is, I acted as if I were fine, as if I weren't limited, and as if creating life while litigating were no biggie. This attitude, in hindsight, was out of integrity, and I can only take accountability for this myself. I desperately wanted to be that "lean in" lawyer mom with a cute blazer, a cute bag on one arm, and a cute baby on the other, but in reality, that cute blazer ended up covered in fluids: spit and sweat and blood and breastmilk.

But more broadly, I realized I should have handled things differently from the get-go—including planning out, and documenting afterward, how I was going to tell my boss about my pregnancy. I should have taken this more seriously and accepted that a pregnancy would, in fact, change things, and it's just best to be honest about that, for everyone. Going through that first motherhood experience was like an initiation. It left me raw and broken. But I had to break. My illusion that I could control or suppress my body, my motherhood experience, and life in general—it had to break. It's only when we break that we can free ourselves, and that we can surrender to the flow, and accept the truth of our bodies. And it's from this liberated place that I can give you my advice, both based on my own experiences and those of clients.

Announcing a pregnancy is Exhibit A—the first piece of evidence in building a long, complex case for your and your baby's needs—and to present it effectively, we need to be proactive and empowered, not scared, shaky, unsure, or in denial about our needs.

This chapter will guide you through the "simple" act of telling your workplace that you are expecting a baby—the whens, the hows, and the whys—with scripts, timelines, and stories, plus a basic overview of pregnancy accommodations and discrimination so that you can go into the conversation informed. No matter where you are in your career, whether you're new at the job or at the top of the food chain, whether you're an hourly worker or a high-powered C-suite officer, if you tell them as soon as possible, you are truly going to set yourself up for success, not stress.

Why Sooner Is Better

I'll cut to the chase: If you're pregnant, and your workplace doesn't know, you need to change that ASAP.

Now, trust me: I get it. For a conversation that doesn't take more than a few minutes, announcing your pregnancy to your workplace can take up *so* much of your mental and emotional energy. I've seen countless women in my program come into group calls with anxiety, assumptions, and procrastination around this point in their pregnancy and their career. These women are executives and housekeepers, teachers and finance lawyers, nurses and engineers, yet they all feel those same vague fears of *I need to play it cool* and *It's better to wait* or *I'll tell them when it's safe to tell them.*

But pregnancy is a marathon, not a sprint, and announcing it to your workplace the right way is how you start off on the right foot. You need to announce your pregnancy prepared and on purpose—and probably earlier than you think. (When I was pregnant with my second child, I basically told my boss before the pee stick was even dry.)

So I'll tell you what I tell those women: I hear you, but it's in your and your baby's best interest that you do this as soon as you can. (Seriously— just a few weeks ago, I told a woman who was sixteen weeks into her pregnancy to get off our membership group call *right that instant* and go tell her boss.) Here's why.

REASON 1: YOU'RE NOT LEGALLY PROTECTED UNTIL YOU TELL THEM

As a pregnant employee, you are entitled to certain legal rights, protections, and accommodations under the PDA and PWFA.

But you can only claim them—or take your employer to court, if it comes to that—*if your employer knows you're pregnant.*

Pregnancy, at least in the early stages, is not like other physical conditions that qualify you for legal protection. Unlike (for the most part) race, age, physical disabilities, or gender identities, early pregnancy is effectively invisible. There's no way for anyone at your job to know you're expecting a baby. If you are not yourself, maybe slightly underperforming, they could take action they couldn't otherwise take if they knew you were pregnant. Basically, if you underperform due to pregnancy symptoms and your employer does not know you are pregnant, you can be legally terminated. And that's a *way* worse situation for you and your new baby.

Yes, this might sound unfair, but think about it: If your boss *did* discriminate against you for something related to your pregnancy (like needing to sit during long shifts, or taking lots of PTO back-to-back for doctor visits), what argument could you make in front of a judge? "Your Honor, they should've just picked up on my fertile goddess vibes"?

So, in order to cover your own bump, you need to tell them. And once you do? You can be honest. You can speak up when you experience pregnancy-related symptoms, and you can request accommodations to your job, such as a change in your schedule, a hybrid schedule, or additional time to complete projects. You don't have to awkwardly dodge work happy hours or hem and haw when it comes to work travel plans eight months from now. You'll have more time to plan your maternity leave, prepare for your leave of absence, and train your replacement.

Many mothers fear getting fired for announcing their pregnancy, but that would be illegal. But it's only illegal if they *know* you are pregnant.

REASON 2: WAITING RISKS
RESENTMENT FROM YOUR TEAM

The second reason it's better to tell your office sooner rather than later is . . . your team.

Many pregnant women wait to announce their pregnancies at work because they fear retaliation. Yet by waiting, they often inadvertently cause a counterproductive effect: There will be a higher chance of retaliation if you wait. Think about it: The first trimester is when the pregnancy symptoms often kick in. Nausea, exhaustion, dizziness . . . plenty of things make it hard to keep the same pace at work during the first trimester. If your colleagues or managers notice you slowing down for (what appears to them) no good reason, they're likely going to stew.

Holding the news under your hat can cause friction when you *do* finally tell everyone, from seething and grumbling "why did she hide it from us for so long?" to genuine logjams when there isn't enough time between your announcement and your leave to work out a smooth plan for covering your job duties while you're gone (more on that in chapter 6).

Granted, telling your workplace you're pregnant doesn't mean people *won't* resent you or retaliate. Sometimes people are just . . . bad at being good people.

Sometimes they may sense something is off, and they do actually want to know how to help you, but they're not given the information or road map on how to be supportive. This can also cause resentment because they may feel offended by your lack of transparency and lack of trust in them.

But preparing for a leave of absence does pose an operational challenge, and by waiting to announce, you are shortening the window of time you give to your employer to prepare for your absence. They may need to train someone, shuffle projects, or recruit a replacement. This takes time, and the more time you give them, the easier it will be to implement, which will end up benefiting you in the long run.

REASON 3: THERE'S NO "SAFE" TIME TO ANNOUNCE A PREGNANCY

You may have heard that it's only "safe" to announce a pregnancy after some point on the calendar: at twelve weeks, or after your twenty-week anatomy scan, for example. Well, as an employment lawyer, and as a mom who's suffered pregnancy loss, let me disabuse you of that right now.

There is no "safe" time to announce a pregnancy.

I don't want to alarm or trigger you, but the reality is that pregnancy loss can occur at any point in pregnancy. While it's true that the odds decrease considerably as the weeks wear on, the risk will never reach 0 percent until you're holding your baby in your arms. So any "rules" you've heard about when it's "safe" to announce are pretty much arbitrary. (We'll cover more about complications and loss in chapter 5.)

Even worse, if you *are* one of the one in four women who experiences pregnancy loss, playing it "safe" can backfire on you. Should you experience a miscarriage—or even just a complication that requires extra attention—it's going to affect your work, because it's going to affect *you*. You might need to take time away from the office to physically, emotionally, or spiritually recover. You might want some understanding and grace from coworkers if you need more time to complete your parts of a project. You might just feel lonely keeping such a huge secret and painting on a happy face with the colleagues you see every day.

Now think about how much easier all that recovery and regrouping will be if the people around you—including at work—know what's going on with you. I'm not saying you have to violate boundaries or overshare (and we'll also cover delivering this kind of difficult news in chapter 5), but simply be honest. You'll be relieving yourself of a burden and disarming the stigma around loss.

It's also a stronger legal position to tell them, because if you hide your miscarriage, and instead you take PTO or your attendance or work quality starts to decline, you can be reprimanded or fired. However, being treated adversely for being pregnant (or losing your pregnancy) is against the rules, and you could take action accordingly (which you couldn't do if they don't know what happened). That's because, again, *pregnancy is a protected class.*

You're a Protected Class, Boo

Protected classes are the heart and soul of employment law. They're the concept that keeps employers from saying "we don't hire Black people" or "we never promote women"—either out loud or implicitly.

Basically, the law recognizes that there are certain intrinsic qualities or characteristics that cannot be used to make decisions about whom to hire, fire, pay more or less, and things like that, because they are not relevant to someone's ability to do their job. These characteristics include race, national origin, religion, sex (which covers things like pregnancy, childbirth, and related medical conditions), age, and/or disability. You can think of being in a protected class as having a legal "shield" that safeguards you from unfair discrimination.

That's why it's *so* important to announce your pregnancy as soon as possible: Pregnancy status is specifically recognized as a protected class under employment law. This means employers cannot make decisions based on pregnancy status or treat pregnant employees differently. For instance, when considering promotions, assignments, layoffs, or any other employment actions, pregnant and non-pregnant employees *must* be treated equally—or else. (Or else what? Or else you sue them and take home a big fat check. And no company wants that.)

Pregnant women tend to be so scared to announce their pregnancies at work, but in my experience, companies are more scared of pregnant women because of the potential legal repercussions. The US civil justice system is no joke. There is nothing else like it in the world. Treating someone in a protected class poorly can bankrupt a company, and from the company's perspective, that risk is terrifying.

To be clear, pregnancy status isn't the only protected class that's relevant here. Back in 2010, when the Affordable Care Act (ACA) was passed, "lactating mothers" got official recognition as a protected group under US law (specifically, by making key changes to the Fair Labor Standards Act), and in 2022, things got even better with the PUMP Act, which expanded and clarified those rights, covering more workers.

However, it is important to note that simply "being a parent" is *not* a federally protected class. This distinction matters because it means that while your employer can't fire you for taking your legally protected pumping breaks during the workday, they *can* fire you for failing to have adequate childcare and missing too much work. (The only times this second instance would be illegal is if they treated male and female parents differently—for example, if moms were denied promotions because "moms aren't as reliable" while dads are promoted with no questions asked. In that case, it's sex-based discrimination—a legal no-no.)

Finally, this force field is *not* a magic get-out-of-jail-free card, and pregnancy is not a defense against getting fired for other, legitimate reasons. You *can* be fired while pregnant and it can be perfectly legal. If your job performance slips, your company can legally terminate you.

If you make a fireable mistake or commit any kind of fraud at your job, your company can legally terminate you. If there are in fact budget cuts and the company does mass layoffs (and applies those layoffs equally to pregnant and non-pregnant employees), your company can legally terminate you. And, unfortunately, if you work for a small business, you may not be covered by legal protections: While federal equal pay laws apply to businesses with one or more employees, federal antidiscrimination laws kick in only at fifteen or more employees. (Your state laws may bring this threshold down, however—another reason it's important to know your federal *and* state rights.)

How to Announce You're Pregnant at Work: Step-by-Step

Ready? Deep breath. Sip of water. You've got this.

Step 1: Schedule a meeting with your immediate supervisor to share the news.

If you work remotely, I still recommend sharing this news initially in a live conversation (e.g., not a Slack message). Yes, you want to have a written paper trail, but you'll create one with your follow-up email, and from a soft skills perspective, it's just a little more personable to deliver this news in a conversation.

When it comes to actually *saying the news out loud*, keep it simple and to the point.

Boss, I wanted to meet with you and share that I am currently pregnant. My estimated due date is [date]. I [or my family and I] are very excited.

I want to prepare for my leave as much as possible. I intend to be proactive and make sure everything runs seamlessly, so I'll be sending an email later today with some next steps in terms of planning. For now, I just wanted to let you know the news in person.

What happens next will depend greatly on your boss's personality and management style. They may gush with excitement and be thrilled for you. They might be visibly taken aback but express congratulations. Or they might blurt out something awkward or even inappropriate.

No matter what, keep your cool. If they say something that feels just a touch . . . discriminatory, write it down instantly, along with the date, in case you need to build a paper trail later. (Preferably email the incident from yourself to your personal email so you have a time stamp.)

What if My Boss Is Out of Town / Out Sick / I Can't Reach Them for a Chat?

If you expect your boss to be back within a day or two, it's okay to wait for a convenient time to talk with them in person (or over Zoom). But if they're going to be inaccessible for a week or two—i.e., if waiting for a live conversation would meaningfully delay the timing of your announcement—it's okay to skip directly to announcing over email. You can include a line like "I was hoping to share the news in person, but I didn't want to delay too long while you're out of the office."

Step 2: That same day, follow up this conversation with an email (script below). Send this email to HR with your supervisor cc'd (and your personal email bcc'd). Or, if your job does not have an HR department, send it to the highest-level manager with your supervisor cc'd.

This email serves as your digital proof that will secure your rights and protect your job, so be sure not to skip it.

> Dear [HR Rep Name] and [Supervisor's Name],
>
> As I disclosed to [Supervisor's Name] in our conversation yesterday, I am currently pregnant, with an estimated due date of [Date]. I am very excited.
>
> I wanted to give as much notice as possible so we can prepare and plan ahead together. To that end, I suggest the three of us set a series of meetings. A first meeting to discuss any long-term projects—and potential need for coverage—as soon as possible. I would also like to schedule a meeting when we are closer to my due date, specifically to discuss my leave plan. Then let's meet when I return to work to discuss the status of my work, and a few weeks upon my return to make sure the transition went smoothly.
>
> [Optional: I understand I may not be discriminated against for announcing my pregnancy.]
>
> I look forward to working together during this transition, and my return. Your support is vital for the health of my pregnancy, and for me to succeed as a working mother.
>
> Sincerely,
> [Your Name]

Step 3: Schedule your meeting and get to prepping! (More on that in chapter 6.)

Now take another deep breath. *You did it.* Though it may not feel like it, what you've just accomplished is one of the first acts of love and care you'll do for your baby (and for yourself, as a mother).

Pregnancy Discrimination 101

Your employer now knows you're pregnant and must treat you accordingly as a protected class. But just because something's written into the law doesn't mean employers are always going to follow it.

My client Briana was diligent about everything at work, and that included announcing her pregnancy. She told her work months in advance of her leave that she'd be having a baby, knowing that this placed her in the force field of a protected class.

Unfortunately for Briana, the red flags started almost immediately.

First, her manager asked her to work remotely during her maternity leave, to prevent the "massive hole" that her absence would create. This is unlawful—that leave is protected and can't be interrupted with work.

Then, just a few weeks later, they fired her, alleging "budget cuts" due to the pandemic.

Unfortunately, even doing your due diligence and announcing your pregnancy promptly—and in writing—isn't always going to be enough to avoid putting a target on your back. Yes, you're in a protected-class force field, but that doesn't mean you won't lose your job or otherwise experience discrimination after telling your boss you're pregnant.

It likely won't look like you expect it to look. Pregnancy discrimination can be incredibly sneaky. They know better than to simply fire someone for "being pregnant." Companies will treat your baby news as a starting gun in a race to find some other, "good" reason to fire you, like downsizing, budget cuts, or poor performance. And in doing so, they gaslight you into thinking your pregnancy had nothing to do with your termination. You know the timing *is* suspicious, and it just feels somehow *off*, but at the same time, you don't know how to *disprove* what they're claiming—especially as you don't even have access to their internal finances.

That's where I come in. When pregnant employees are fired for "budgetary reasons," my instinct is to call bullshit. *Especially* in Briana's case.

See, when a company is truly going through a financial crisis, you would see the following: widespread cuts across departments (usually of the most recent hires), operational savings measures such as sharing office space, elimination of "extras" such as company retreats or holiday parties, managers who are taking on staff functions in addition to executive functions, and the top-level executives working extremely hard to promote the company and create revenue.

None of that was happening at Briana's job. But that was just for starters.

At this point in the pandemic, lots of businesses were receiving PPP loans. As a result, many companies actually had *excess* funds beyond what they needed to make payroll. Sure enough, when we researched Briana's employer we discovered thousands of dollars in loans transferred from the government to the company. Their cash flow was just fine.

With that evidence in hand, we were able to prove that their "budgetary cuts" were nonexistent and Briana's firing was illegal, and I was able to secure a sizable settlement for her.

A fabricated reason to cover up a wrongful termination is called "pretext." My client Millie was also fired for "budget cuts" right after she had twin babies. However, a quick Google search revealed that the company was actually opening up and hiring for new positions. That is not how a company behaves when they have to cut costs. Another client, a nurse, was fired right after announcing her pregnancy, allegedly due to a lack of work. However, her coworkers all confirmed that the hospital was overwhelmed and understaffed.

Activating your protected-class force field is just half the battle here. The other half is knowing what pregnancy discrimination can really look like and keeping your eyes peeled. Here are some forms of discrimination you'll want to be on alert for both during and after your pregnancy.

Being fired or forced out after announcing a pregnancy: Again, this is why I always recommend announcing your pregnancy early to your employer. Waiting too long can increase the chances of being fired, as some employers might feel blindsided by a late announcement and react negatively. Even if you are able to successfully pursue a legal remedy, it'll take months for you to receive any settlement, and you'll need to float expenses for healthcare (at the least) in the meantime.

Facing retaliation after announcing a pregnancy or after returning from leave: This is like the opposite of demotion, and it's in many ways worse. Some employers may develop an attitude of "we've done enough for you" and place extra pressure and workload on expecting and new moms, which can be considered retaliation. That's neither fair nor legal. Often employers know they cannot outright terminate a pregnant or postpartum employee, so instead, they will create working conditions that make it impossible for her to succeed. Whether being overworked or ostracized, they are putting their bets on the fact that you'll get overwhelmed, want to "save face," and quit. Many mothers do this: quit to save their dignity. But by doing that, you've actually helped them win. Even though they caused the tension, leaving the tense environment may result in you potentially forfeiting your rights. So you'll always want to call an attorney before you quit, as they can help you negotiate an exit package. Companies only pay to relieve tension or mitigate risk. If you quit, you've removed both.

Being passed over for promotions or good assignments: Your employer should be treading very carefully when it comes to work assignments once they know you're pregnant . . . but unfortunately, there are often discriminatory assumptions that pregnant women or new moms will be less committed or capable at their jobs, leading to them being overlooked for promotions or key assignments. That is *not* legal. If you're the rock star of the sales department and you're suddenly yanked off all big-ticket accounts after sharing your pregnancy (and losing the commission that goes with them), you might have a discrimination case on your hands. Note that you don't have to be fired to be experiencing discrimination. Massive negative hits to your professional advancement count as discrimination, especially if you lose out on money as a result.

Being demoted or having your hours cut while pregnant: Both of these things *can* happen for reasons unrelated to pregnancy, but if either happens to you suspiciously close to your announcement to your boss, it's time to keep a close eye on whether these demotions and cuts are occurring across the board . . . or just to you.

Not being reinstated to the same job after maternity leave: Moreover, it's illegal for an employer to shuffle a new mom into a lesser role or different job when she returns from leave. You have the right to be reinstated to your exact same position or a "virtually identical" one.

Inappropriate comments about pregnancy or pumping: Hearing weird stuff from your managers about your pregnant body or pumping needs is more than just awkward: It can create a hostile work environment. A hostile work environment means more than just "a workplace where people are sometimes mean to me," but means specifically a workplace where protected classes are treated demonstrably and consistently poorly. Not legal.

Being denied reasonable accommodations: Emilia worked in a warehouse as an assembler. When she was seven weeks pregnant, she notified her employer. They started treating her awfully. When Emilia was experiencing severe morning sickness, including throwing up, they told her she was using the restroom "too often," and made her throw up in a small trash can near her work area. On another occasion, Emilia asked a coworker for assistance lifting a box that weighed more than twenty pounds (against her doctor's restrictions). Her manager ordered her coworker to refrain from helping Emilia. Often managers will not fire a pregnant woman, yet make the workplace impossible or unhealthy for her, hoping she will quit. However, Emilia did not quit. Eventually, they fired her, telling her her position was "overstaffed," but the very next day, they replaced her with a male employee. This scenario is illegal on many different counts.

Weird or inconsistent timing: Another way you can detect a discriminatory motive is when there is just something off about timing. One of my clients announced her pregnancy, and was fired for a mistake she made a year prior (when she was not pregnant). If the mistake was actually a fireable offense, they would have fired her at that time. In another case, my client was terminated right before her leave, allegedly due to performance, even though she had been performing the job in the exact same way before her pregnancy.

Non-pregnant employees are treated better: Lastly, pay close attention to how they treat others. Yoshira was fired after returning from leave, even though they kept her male peer who had less experience and less tenure. Another client was paid less than the man who replaced her during her leave.

REPORTING DISCRIMINATION

If you are experiencing pregnancy discrimination, you have to report it. Many mothers will get scared when I tell them because they don't want to "rock the boat." But **a boat is meant to be rocked**. If you are on a boat that cannot survive a little rocking, you are on a bad boat.

When you report it (in writing, of course), make sure to call it what it is. If you do not state explicitly that you believe the conduct is discrimination or unlawful, your complaint is not protected. If you feel too nervous using legal language, you could also say, "I feel treated differently on the basis of my pregnancy." However, if you report only that you feel treated "unfairly" or "unethically," you did not make a legally protected complaint. You are only protected from retaliation if your underlying complaint is legally protected.

If you sense you are going through discrimination or retaliation, here are some more tips:

- Make sure to keep notes of all the important events that are happening to you. I like the practice of emailing myself notes I don't want to forget, because then there's a time stamp and no one can accuse you of writing them after the fact. You can email yourself: "Today my boss took my most lucrative client from me and gave it to a guy who was hired two weeks ago. I feel very frustrated."
- Make sure all of your communications with HR or your managers are in writing. During meetings, take notes, and immediately email the attendees after the meeting: "This is my reflection of what was discussed during the meeting [you said this . . . I said that . . .]—let me know if you have a different understanding."
- Keep in mind that your work emails are owned by the company. If you get fired, they will block access to your emails. Always forward important emails to your personal email or make copies of the emails to keep in a file.
- Make sure you keep doing your job. Don't give them a reason to fire you.
- Start saving all your accolades, and make sure your "brag bank" is complete. This is in case you need evidence to disprove that you were a poor performer.
- Don't sign anything they give you without consulting an attorney.

How to Work While Pregnant:
The Wild World of Pregnancy Accommodations

Samira was just five weeks into her pregnancy when the nausea hit. And when it hit, it was like a freight train.

Suddenly, everything sounded gross, from her favorite happy hour snacks (potato skins) to her beloved morning cup of coffee. Even plain water was enough to turn her stomach. She was surviving, in her words, on "dry toast and the coldest water I could find."

Then came the migraines. Already feeling queasy, Samira would get a pounding, rolling headache at the slightest exposure to bright light . . . which made logging on for her mandatory, cameras-on Zoom stand-up meeting every morning at 8:00 a.m. sharp nothing short of torture. She muscled through the first few, but by Thursday she'd already had a close call ducking for the trash can. On Friday, she took a (very deserved!) sick day to put a cool cloth on her head, lie on the couch, and think about quitting.

Deep down, Samira didn't *actually* want to quit. She loved her job, and she was still doing pretty solid at meeting her targets despite the rocky starts in those morning meetings. *And* she needed the benefits. Still, it was clear she couldn't keep working like nothing had changed . . . because *everything* had changed.

Lucky for Samira—and for all of us—a beautiful new law was passed in 2023 called the Pregnant Workers Fairness Act, or PWFA. This federal law allows you to ask for changes (legally called "accommodations") to your job to make it easier to complete your work duties during your pregnancy. Your employer is required to make those changes for you as long as the accommodations don't cause an undue burden (significant difficulty or expense) on their end. The request has to be realistic and actually possible—no asking to telecommute to your waitress job, I'm afraid. If your employer *doesn't* follow the law, you can enforce your rights by filing a legal case and seeking money.

ADA vs. PWFA vs. FMLA:
What's the Difference?

Let's start with the first two. You can think of the Americans with Disabilities Act and the Pregnant Workers Fairness Act as, essentially, siblings. The ADA is the older sibling and is a bit strict and by-the-book, and the PWFA is the younger sibling with a bit of a rebellious free spirit.

If you call the ADA to hang out, they will tell you that they can only fit you in on Saturdays at 6:00 p.m., and only at their select choice of fine restaurants.

If you call the PWFA to hang out, they will be at your door in five minutes ready to go to Burning Man (even if it's midnight).

In other words, it is much easier to use the PWFA than the ADA.

This is because the ADA has a higher standard to meet in order to enforce your rights. Under the ADA, you need a qualified disability, which requires medical attention. Under the PWFA, however, you simply need to have a pregnancy-related condition, which is defined much more broadly and allows for more flexibility. (Though a lot of pregnancy-related conditions also qualify as disabilities, not all do.)

So, while there is overlap, the PWFA is much broader than the ADA, and many scenarios that weren't previously covered are now covered (like garden-variety morning sickness).

The PWFA also lets you suspend the essential functions of your job, while under the ADA, an employer is not required to suspend essential functions. This renders the PWFA a de facto leave law, as "not working at all" is one of the types of accommodations that can be requested.

When it comes to the PWFA and the FMLA (Family and Medical Leave Act, which we first met in chapter 2), they're more like unrelated coworkers at a big corporation. They're working toward the same general company mission but doing completely separate day-to-day jobs. They may see each other occasionally in the office kitchen where they share ideas and a donut, but most of the time they do their own thing. In short, they serve different purposes.

The FMLA exists to give you time off work for medical or family reasons. Your right to take leave is protected under the FMLA.

The PWFA exists to help you feel supported at work while you are still working. Your rights at work before and after birth are protected by the PWFA.

Because these are separate and distinct rights, you can use your rights under both laws as long as you are eligible for both. (The one time these laws work well together is when you use PWFA to ask for a leave extension of FMLA, which we will explain in a bit.)

There are a number of conditions you can use the PWFA for. In fact, the PWFA can be applied to situations postpartum too. But for now, we'll discuss it specifically in the context of pregnancy accommodations. You can get accommodations for any condition that affects your ability to do your job and is related to your pregnancy. The condition does not need to be an official "disability" and includes (but isn't limited to!) both the normal physical changes of pregnancy and childbirth *and* complications of pregnancy and childbirth.

Some Conditions That Might Cause You to Need Accommodations:

- excessive fatigue
- extreme morning sickness
- depression
- insomnia
- migraine headaches
- sciatica
- pelvic pain
- abnormal placentation

This is not an exhaustive list—your medical provider is in the best position to assess your condition and whether it's actually limiting your life to the point of being considered an impairment.

Later that Friday, once Samira's head had finally stopped throbbing, she was scrolling through Instagram with her toast and water when she saw a post I'd made about the PWFA. It sounded like *exactly* what she needed.

Well, if *I'm eligible*, Samira thought. (As a longtime Mamattorney fan, she knew establishing that up front was key!)

Fortunately, Samira's job and employer—a medium-size medical supplies company with seventy-five employees—ticked all the necessary boxes, and she immediately got to work brainstorming some accommodations.

Eligibility Check: PWFA

While the PWFA is a federal law, meaning it covers all states in the United States, it applies only to those who work for *covered employers*. However, there are some states that have their own additional rights that build on PWFA. Here's a checklist to make sure you're eligible for these labor protections:

Your employer has fifteen or more employees, unless you're in . . .

Alaska, Colorado, DC, Hawaii, Illinois, Maine, Michigan, Minnesota, Montana, New Jersey, New York, North Dakota, Oklahoma, Oregon, South Dakota, or Vermont—no small employer exception (meaning *all* employers must offer accommodations!).

Connecticut: Your employer has three or more employees.

Delaware, Iowa, Kansas, New Mexico, Ohio, Pennsylvania, or Rhode Island: Your employer has four or more employees.

California or Idaho: Your employer has five or more employees.

Indiana, Missouri, or New Hampshire: Your employer has six or more employees.

Kentucky, Tennessee, or Washington: Your employer has eight or more employees.

Arkansas: Your employer has nine or more employees.

Your employer is in either the private or public sector (including Congress, federal agencies, employment agencies, and labor organizations).

You are a W-2 employee (and *not* an independent contractor, a.k.a. 1099 worker), working either full-time *or* part-time.

Your employer can't claim a religious exemption to the PWFA.

An accommodation is an adjustment or change to your job that allows you to continue working during your pregnancy. The list of possible accommodations is, technically speaking, endless—the law allows for creativity and ingenuity. Remember: The goal is to keep you employed *and* on payroll with benefits before, during, and after your pregnancy. The process is flexible, case-by-case, and intentionally open-ended to allow you to find a solution tailored to you.

Here is a list of accommodations. This list is not exhaustive, and you (and your doctor) can come up with your own alternatives.

- **Telework** to help symptoms of morning sickness.
- **Schedule flexibility** so you can go to your doctor's appointments without losing pay.
- **Time off** for prenatal anxiety or depression.
- **Lifting restrictions** in a physically demanding job.
- **Additional time** to finish projects to account for medical care or nausea breaks.
- **A different office space** so you don't have to walk up the stairs.
- **Remote or flex work** to address any pregnancy discomfort you may be experiencing.
- **Ability to go home** during the day to get comfortable.

- **Be excused from company travel** requirements due to pregnancy needs.
- **Extra bathroom breaks** to accommodate the way your body changes during pregnancy.
- **A temporary suspension** of one or more essential functions of your job.

In Samira's case, her nausea and headaches were specifically triggered by the light of her computer screen (and ring light), the discomfort of sitting for prolonged periods of time, and having to be alert and productive during her worst window of morning sickness. If she could join by phone and listen in off-camera, she knew she'd feel a lot better (and could take the call lying on the couch with her eyes closed, if she needed to). She also realized she could just listen to the recording of the meeting at a later time and offer reflections as needed.

That seemed pretty reasonable to her, and it wouldn't meaningfully change her output. Still, because she was a little nervous about speaking up—and because she had an OB appointment the following week anyway—she decided to go the extra mile and get documentation from her doctor.

The following Tuesday, after some saltines, Samira drafted an email to her boss, Tim, and the HR director, Sheila.

Hello Tim and Sheila,

I am seeking accommodations for my pregnancy-related limitations. Please find my medical note attached.

The accommodation I am seeking is:

1) the ability to attend our morning meetings via voice only, with my camera off, to avoid triggering my symptoms;

2) the ability to listen to the recording of the meetings (and offer reflections through email), as needed, if my symptoms prevent me from being alert and proactive during the meeting. I estimate

> needing to listen to the recording instead of attending the call live once or twice per week.
>
> Please let me know if this can be accommodated.

Thank you,

Samira

After a quick proofread and some nail-biting, Samira sent the email.

It's normal to be nervous about asserting your rights. That's okay! But remember you are doing this for your baby, and for your body, so let's commit to having NO SHAME IN YOUR GAME. All you are doing here is asking your employer to follow the law. That's it. Just like we all have to stop at the red light when we are driving, employers all have to follow employment law when they employ pregnant employees.

And that's exactly what happened for Samira. A few hours later, Sheila from HR responded:

> Samira, We understand and are happy to accommodate. Please let us know if there's anything else you need.

This isn't to say that it always goes 100 percent smoothly, however. Maria, a warehouse associate at a large shipping facility, was midway through her second trimester when discussions started to pop up about mandatory overtime for the upcoming holiday rush. This particular peak season was expected to be especially busy after supply chain disruptions the previous year, so her company was essentially planning their staffing from scratch, and Maria quickly realized that the unspoken assumption was that she'd work twelve-hour shifts, six days a week—even though it meant being on her feet constantly, repeatedly lifting packages up to fifty pounds, and working in an area of the warehouse where temperatures often fluctuated.

Maria had had no problem announcing her pregnancy to her supervisor, but this felt different, and more fraught. While googling "can I avoid heavy lifting while pregnant," she stumbled upon my Instagram and learned about pregnancy accommodations. She drafted an email to her supervisor and HR, including documentation about her doctor's recommendation for limited standing, lifting, and overtime.

The response was quick and not exactly what she'd been hoping for:

> Maria, Thanks for this. Can we set up a meeting to discuss?

The Interactive Process Meeting

If your boss requests a meeting with you to discuss your accommodation, you need to go. This is the "interactive process" meeting that's required by law—in fact, if your employer does not set up this meeting, your employer can be liable.

This meeting, or series of meetings, needs to occur in a timely and good-faith fashion. Specifically, your employer may not hold this meeting just to deny your request. This meeting is supposed to be a conversation. In an ideal interactive process meeting, your employer will pull up your job description and your doctor's note and discuss your ongoing and future projects.

The goal of the meeting is to figure out how to get you accommodated. If the meeting is left open-ended, it's possible that your employer may need some more information, or needs to have internal discussions before giving you an answer. Your employer should provide you with a prompt answer or next steps.

From there, and throughout the process, your employer must do the following:

- Respond promptly and work with you in good faith.
- Determine the essential functions of your position and how to work around them.
- Consult with you to determine your specific job-related limitations and how a reasonable accommodation could overcome them.
- Select and implement the best accommodation for both of you.

> Remember: The accommodation process is interactive, fluid, and inten-
> tionally open-ended to allow for creativity.

When Maria showed up to the meeting, her supervisor was pretty blunt.

"We need everyone on deck during peak season," he said. "Everyone works overtime during the holidays. That's how the warehouse runs."

Maria said she understood, and that she wanted to contribute to the team effort, but reiterated that it would not be medically advisable for her to stand for twelve-hour shifts or continue lifting heavy packages that far along into her pregnancy.

"But it's part of your job," her supervisor said. "What if we moved you to a packing station instead of picking, so you'd lift fewer heavy items?"

Maria thanked her supervisor for proposing an accommodation, but explained that her doctor had specifically recommended against lifting anything over twenty pounds during the remainder of her pregnancy, and even the lighter packages at the packing station could sometimes exceed that limit.

In response, her supervisor panicked for a moment and instantly proposed that Maria start her maternity leave early. However, Maria wanted to save her leave time for when the baby was born, and she also just did not want to stop working yet. She clarified that she was seeking an accommodation, not to be excused from work entirely.

Maria then countered with an accommodation of her own: She could be moved to the inventory-scanning team during peak season, which would allow her to work seated for much of her shift, with minimal lifting. She would also volunteer to work eight-hour shifts five days a week instead of the mandatory overtime, and could help train some of the seasonal hires on inventory procedures. As a bonus, Maria pointed out, it'd give her the opportunity to cross-train in a different department, which would be helpful when she returned from maternity leave.

The supervisor contemplated. "That's an interesting idea. Let me think on it."

After the meeting, Maria quickly emailed a written summary of what they'd discussed, cc'ing HR as well. About an hour later, her supervisor replied that he liked Maria's proposal and they could agree to that accommodation, though he added that they might need her to work one Saturday a month if staffing got really tight.

This process is all about finding that middle ground that suits everyone's needs. "Reasonable accommodations" simply means changes to the normal ways of doing things in your work environment in a way that works for you and your employer. This means companies may need to change their policy—such as "everyone works overtime during the holidays"—to accommodate you. The law takes precedence over policy, and your employer has a duty to try to accommodate you. If they continually refuse to work with you in good faith to find a reasonable accommodation, they are not following the law, and you can bring them to court.

That said, while your preferred accommodation as the employee matters, your employer has the ultimate say. They're not allowed to just respond, "Nah, we don't want to," or "no" with no reason, but your request may be denied if it poses what's referred to as an "undue burden" on your employer.

An undue burden is something that is extremely difficult or expensive for the employer to set up. For example, Maria might be willing to work her regular schedule if her employer provided a personal assistant to do all the lifting for her, but hiring an additional employee just to help one person might strain the warehouse's staffing budget, and thus, it could arguably constitute an undue burden. Moving her to a different department with more sedentary work and a modified schedule, though, especially when she's willing to help train seasonal workers, is eminently more reasonable.

Reasonable Accommodations FAQs

How long does an employer have to accept or decline an accommodation after I've made a request?

As the interactive process is intentionally open-ended, there is no set time your employer has to respond to you. But they have to engage with you in good faith the whole time.

What if my boss tries to pay me less because I need an accommodation?

Nope, not allowed. The goal of the PWFA is to make it so that soon-to-be and new moms are protected at work, which means that you get full pay and full benefits regardless of your accommodations. An exception to this would be if you requested less work as an accommodation, then, naturally, you'd get paid less.

What if my employer just ignores me altogether?

If you feel you are being ignored, keep emailing them. You always want to be the cooperative and proactive party. This is especially true if you are waiting at home, unpaid, for an accommodation approval. This is even *more* especially true if you have indicated you have a high-risk pregnancy and you need the accommodations for the safety of your pregnancy.

If your employer is lingering in these scenarios, they are likely waiting you out, hoping you'll just quit. That's when you'd call an attorney.

Can my employer force me to go on leave instead of making an accommodation?

It is common for an employer to try to push employees on leave instead of engaging in the interactive process. This is not always malicious. Often they just get a little overwhelmed when a pregnant employee expresses she is experiencing restrictions, and is putting the health and safety of her pregnancy at issue. It is natural to want to eliminate any risk; however, offering that you start your leave clock early, in lieu of negotiating the accommodation, is not the purpose of the interactive process. The entire point of the process is to get to a resolution that works for you and actually improves the conditions of your life.

It is illegal for your boss to force you to take leave. If there is a reasonable accommodation that would allow you to keep working and the leave is not mandated by your doctor, your boss can't force you to use FMLA leave. The law is intended to keep you on payroll and allow you to reserve your leave rights for recovery and bonding.

Your employer might even try to "gently" force you into taking severance or resigning, using language like, "It's better for your baby and your health for you to be home. You'll have your hands full, so maybe it's better for you to resign." You do not have to do this, and this may constitute unlawful retaliation. Remember, they have an obligation to engage in an interactive process to find reasonable accommodations for you.

What do I do if my employer is punishing me for requesting an accommodation?

The PWFA protects you against any retaliation regarding your request or need for accommodations. That means it protects you from things like terminations, holding you back, formal demotions, or other adverse actions based on your need or request for a reasonable accommodation. This is true *even if your accommodation is not granted.*

If any of these scenarios apply to you, consult with an employment attorney.

When You're Pregnant . . . and Job-Hunting

Interviewing while pregnant can be scary. It is technically illegal to deny a job applicant a job on account of pregnancy, but it happens all the time. These claims are tough to prove because they will point to something unrelated to your pregnancy as the reason you weren't selected. This is why I recommend waiting to announce a pregnancy until you have received the job offer.

You have no legal obligation to disclose your pregnancy during the interviewing process. You also do not want to wait too long to announce your pregnancy, as they do not know you yet, and may find you untrustworthy, which may result in retaliation. Be strategic but transparent. The longer you wait, the more frustrated your employer will be.

However, if you disclose it too early, you are certainly putting the job at risk. We live in the real world. This means we have to try to walk the line between what is in your *and* their best interest.

Sadly, if you disclose your pregnancy too early, it may result in you not getting the job and it may be extremely hard to prove that you weren't hired because of your pregnancy. There are simply too many ways for a prospective employer to cover their tracks. For example, if many applicants were in the running, they could simply claim someone else was better suited to the role, and to prove discrimination, you'd have to prove that all those applicants were less qualified than you . . . and you'll likely have no idea who the other applicants are. Or, if you announce your pregnancy before your reference checks come back, they may comb through those references to find another (legal!) reason not to take you on as an employee.

However, if you wait to disclose your pregnancy until the job offer is secured, the employer would commit a clear violation of your employment rights if they rescinded the offer upon learning you are pregnant.

The employer has therefore no choice but to respect your pregnancy once you are given an offer letter. Any adverse action taken on the basis of the pregnancy announcement will be easily proven to be pregnancy discrimination.

Note: Even if the job offer is not rescinded, the employer may still be resentful that you did not disclose your pregnancy sooner. This may result in pregnancy discrimination down the line. This would also be unlawful— so stay vigilant.

This happened to one of my clients, who got pregnant right after being hired. Her managers accused her of hiding her pregnancy during interviews (which she didn't) and embarked on a campaign of retaliation, stunting her professional advancement.

Is it illegal for an interviewer to ask me if I am pregnant (or when I am due)?

Under federal law, no, the question is not illegal in and of itself. You cannot run to the court and file a case solely based on having been asked this question, because the employer is not *supposed* to factor your pregnancy status into their decision to hire you. However, this question in an interview *is* evidence of an employer who very likely intends to discriminate. If the job *is* denied based on pregnancy, that would be illegal and actionable, and this question would then be your Exhibit A.

However, in some states, these questions are illegal per se.

What should I say if an interviewer asks if I'm pregnant?

"I am surprised by this question. I'd prefer to focus on the interview" is the best way to avoid answering the question.

If they hire me, can I then be fired for not disclosing my pregnancy while interviewing?

No, that would still be discrimination on the basis of pregnancy. Remember, you are not legally obligated to disclose your pregnancy during a job interview process. Your employer may be frustrated with you because you withheld the pregnancy, or even accuse you of deceit or a lack of transparency, but none of that constitutes a legal defense to discriminate against you on the basis of pregnancy.

Interviewing While Pregnant: Sample Disclosure Email

Once you receive a job offer, here is a sample email you can use to disclose your pregnancy. Again, I recommend you wait until you have a job offer—*in writing*, not just a verbal confirmation—before you give notice of pregnancy.

> Dear [Employer],
>
> Thank you for offering me the position of [Job Title] at [Company Name]. With gratitude and excitement, this email should serve as my formal acceptance of this offer. Thank you for this opportunity! I am looking forward to joining the team.
>
> I would also like to disclose that I am currently pregnant, due [Date].
>
> [Optional: I am sorry for not disclosing sooner, but I wanted to make sure the pregnancy was safe before announcing it. OR: I was fearful that the job offer would be rescinded, and this is my dream job.]
>
> While I understand that we will have to work together on my leave plan, I am excited to hit the ground running and work with

the company to ensure a seamless transition between my start, my eventual leave, and my return.

Please let me know if you have any questions. Otherwise, I look forward to my start date of [Date].

Sincerely,

[Your Name]

5

The In-Between

Fertility and Loss

I f you're tempted to skip this chapter, I understand—but stay with me, just a moment.

We avoid talking about the hard parts of pregnancy. We're not supposed to complain about nausea (even if we have HG and are unable to keep fluids down). We're not supposed to express any fear or ambivalence about what we've gotten ourselves into (even though *everyone* worries about whether they're up to the task of childbirth—let alone motherhood). And we're certainly not supposed to talk about the heartaches and struggles of when our best efforts and biggest hopes and dreams don't result in the healthy, easy pregnancy we wanted.

As a result, we end up thinking we're alone. We don't realize how common what we're going through actually is, how there's a community out there for us and a system of support we can leverage. We end up short-changed at the time we need help—emotional, medical, *and* legal—the very most.

So I understand why you may want to skip this part. I myself struggled writing this chapter. I even contemplated making the topic an appendix, or a footnote, anything but shining a spotlight on the grief, the pain, the anger of failing to conceive, of losing a pregnancy.

But in the end, I wanted to make it a full chapter precisely because society doesn't. Society puts it all—pregnancy loss, fertility struggles, still-births, terminations—in the footnotes, despite the fact that as many as 20 percent of women who know they're pregnant experience loss during the first trimester. There's no etiquette for how we deal with these things beyond "avoid it." Society has made this reality into something women must shoulder alone, figure out alone, struggle through in silence during their everyday lives—including their workdays.

I think we need to pay more attention to pregnancy experiences, including the ones that do not end with a photo of a newborn baby and a smiling mama. So centering this chapter is part of my micro-revolution to make the loss experiences visible, supported, and even celebrated.

I'm one of those 20 percent of women. October 10, 2020, was my due date for my second pregnancy. It was such a cool birthday, I thought. Except the baby was never born that day. The new life that I so badly wanted left me much earlier. Suddenly, I felt lost, untethered. I had to navigate leave-of-absence emails, the medical system, the $7,000 charge from my insurance for my emergency room visit. It was an experience of adding insult to injury, navigating these systems while feeling this deep, deep grief. The workplace just didn't make sense to me at that time—I was in the realm of life and death, and I had no place to go. I didn't want to be in the office. Where was the tent full of warm blankets and grandmothers feeding me soup?

I want to give you those warm blankets. I want to build you that cozy tent full of grandmothers who will hold you and feed you soup. My promise to you is that I will make sure you learn your rights around pregnancy loss, health complications, or disability in baby, fertility procedures, and premature birth. I will give you the tools you need to be an effective self-advocate even when you feel hollow and rageful and exhausted beyond belief and you feel like you keep falling and falling in a pit of despair without a bottom or a way out.

This chapter—and this whole book—is me living out that promise to you. I want to provide that space—of understanding, of contemplation, to scream-cry or rage or just process the profound experience it is to see your body and yourself in this new light—in a way that our modern lives, and certainly our modern *work* lives, do not. There is a way out, but the only way is through.

Take Care of Yourself

I know this chapter will be anxiety-provoking and triggering for many, many people. There's simply no way around the topics we'll have to cover here, so while it may go without saying, I do want to advise you up top that we will talk about fertility struggles, miscarriage, abortion, and traumatic births, among other topics. Whether you've suffered a loss or not, whether you're pregnant or whether a baby is still in the future for you, I know it can feel so scary to look these things in the eye, no matter how strongly we feel that they are worth discussing honestly and openly. Trust me, I know that *deeply*.

I got pregnant again after miscarriage. Looking back to that pregnancy, which resulted in my second child, there was not one day that I just sat down to *be pregnant*. Not one. Not a single day watching reality TV, reading, or just resting. Not one. I stayed in my head the whole time, not wanting to feel my body, or my baby, not wanting to get attached. I was so scared that this new life would leave my body again. And my drug of choice, working out and dancing, was not available because of the never-ending lockdowns. I couldn't see girlfriends either. I just suffered.

Meanwhile, I was still showing up as a lawyer and as a mother every day. After all, I'm the strong one. I don't crumble. I don't collapse. I get up. I do my job.

Admitting there was a problem, that I was overflowing with anxiety and unexpressed grief, would have meant I'd have to do something about it. It would mean I'd have to take much better care of myself. It would also mean opening the gate to a river of fear and suppressed screams and unshed tears, and I did not want to put that on my growing baby. I worried that having a strong emotional experience would make me have another miscarriage—even though my baby was already bathing in a womb full of cortisol—so I simply didn't.

That whole pregnancy passed me by in a cloud of what I now know was prenatal anxiety, and it was a really, really hard year. Now, I feel an immense sadness for this woman pushing silently through her fears, this woman not allowing herself to be present in the fleeting moments of her pregnancy, this woman telling herself she "didn't have time" to contend with her emotions.

I want you to be informed and have the information you need to be your and your baby's best advocate, but I don't want you to end up like myself in that pregnancy, feeling like I barely exhaled for an entire year—tense, wired, waiting for the other shoe to drop.

So take care of yourself as you read. Make space for what you're feeling. Know that reading these stories and learning these facts does not make any of these situations more likely to happen to you. The only likelihood this chapter increases is the chance of you getting the most possible time and space for healing *if*, and only if, you end up needing it. Say to yourself, "Today, I am pregnant." Tell your baby, "I'm doing all I can for us, little one."

When You're Undergoing Fertility Treatments

When Rosie and her husband decided to start a family, they knew they'd be relying on IVF. A previous abdominal surgery had left Rosie with a very low ovarian reserve, and that, combined with her so-called advanced maternal age, made in vitro the strongest option for them to conceive.

What Rosie didn't know was how grueling it would be. Three years after starting, she'd hoped to have developed a thick skin, but every failed cycle still left her as frustrated and angry as the first one.

Fortunately, there was the smallest of silver linings: Rosie's employer had been flexible and allowed her to work remotely, which made the constant clinic visits much more manageable and allowed Rosie to keep the health benefits that defrayed at least a little of the cost. Her manager was personable and understanding and never felt the need to micromanage.

Then came new leadership, and with it, an RTO plan. The higher-ups proposed a new policy requiring *all* employees to be in the office at least three days a week. Or, rather, all except three employees (*male* employees too) whose jobs supposedly didn't "require" them to be on-site regularly.

Meanwhile, Rosie's kindly manager took an early retirement (presumably seeing the writing on the wall), and Rosie—who had been working remotely with zero issue for years, *and* carrying the workload of an unfilled position for the past eight months (with zero extra pay, naturally)—was commanded to return to her office desk *tout de suite*. When the announcement was made, she immediately emailed back to request a carve-out for the RTO mandate due to her ongoing treatments. The corporate attorney's immediate response? An offer to have a "conversation" that never actually materialized.

Rosie was *fuming*. This was how they repaid her? She'd been working from the hospital and through bloating pains. And what did she have to show for all that loyalty?

"You can't just cross your fingers and hope people will be sympathetic and understand," Rosie said. "Even if they are, it might end up being a one-off."

I firmly agree. Women navigating fertility treatments need to know their rights and know that they *have* rights. And the sooner you can learn them, the better.

Going through fertility treatments is physically and emotionally demanding. It will take a lot out of you, while at the same time your employer is expecting the same quality of work from you, leading to friction and possibly termination. Too many unexcused absences and poor work performance and you can be fired completely legally, after all—*unless* you disclose it to your employer.

Fertility challenges and related conditions are protected under your disability rights. To qualify as a disability, individuals need to have physical or mental limitations that affect a major life activity. Fertility challenges are generally considered to affect your reproductive freedom. Having a disability entitles you to disability accommodations and/or medical leave.

OPTION 1: DISABILITY ACCOMMODATIONS

In order to get disability accommodations, you will have to disclose this to your employer and provide a doctor's note that you are experiencing fertility challenges. If you do not disclose your disability, you will not be able to use the protections of the law.

As discussed, accommodations are reasonable modifications to your job to accommodate your restrictions. In the context of fertility treatments, this might look like a change of your schedule so you can attend medical visits, flexible hours so that you can complete your work tasks around preparing and recovering, or telework to make it easier to stay on top of your duties when you need to be physically away from the office. You can request these rights under the PWFA.

When you request accommodations, you can send the following email to your supervisor, cc'ing HR:

> Dear [Supervisor],
>
> I am writing to notify you of my need for accommodations. Please find a doctor's note attached.
>
> [Optional: I am requesting these accommodations under the PWFA.]
>
> I am pursuing fertility treatments in the hopes of expanding my family. I am nervous, yet excited. I hope I can rely on your cooperation.
>
> I may need to miss some work for treatments and recovery. Right now, this is the current schedule of my treatments:
>
> [Insert treatment schedule.]
>
> Can this time off be accommodated?
>
> Sincerely,
>
> [Your Name]

Once your employer is on notice, you can request time off for appointments, recovery, and mental health reasons. Your employer will have to try to accommodate your need for time off. However, your employer does not have to grant your request if the absences cause an undue burden on the employer—though, as we've seen, an "undue burden" is a difficult hurdle to clear, especially if you are proactive in suggesting alternatives. If you are denied an accommodation and you feel it was done unjustly, make sure to consult with an attorney.

OPTION 2: DISABILITY LEAVE

If your treatment schedule conflicts with your job to the point where you truly can't complete the duties assigned to you, you may need to go on a medical leave of absence. Your eligibility for medical leave for fertility treatments will be based on the same criteria for medical leave that we covered in chapter 2 so be sure that you qualify before proceeding (you may also be eligible for intermittent leave, which can be in smaller increments so that you can attend your medical visits).

Unlike an accommodation request, a leave request is an absolute right, and your employer has to provide you with the time off if you are eligible. This time off may be unpaid, but you can recover disability benefits if you are eligible under your state. You may not be retaliated against for taking this time off.

However, it's important to be mindful that taking leave now for fertility treatments may count against the leave you're able to take if you become pregnant. It sucks, but it's true: In many cases, medical leave of any kind draws from the same "bucket," and the more you dip into it before childbirth, the less you'll have left over when your baby arrives.

With all that said, it can be scary or uncomfortable or even embarrassing to disclose your fertility treatments to your employer. There's sadly still a societal stigma around medical assistance in achieving pregnancy, and even if your boss is a progressive type who isn't judgmental, talking about fertility is still somehow different than discussing a more "neutral" medical issue—I get it. Remind yourself that you *can* do uncomfortable things, and you'll be proud of yourself for asserting your rights once you've done it. Reducing your stress levels is more important than reducing their stress levels—there's a baby who wants to join you, after all.

You may also fear that you will experience a form of preemptive pregnancy discrimination, figuring that once your employer knows that you want to have a baby, you may start getting excluded or demoted or treated differently than before they knew. That may be illegal: If you are fired or treated adversely for going through testing or IVF, that can be a wrongful termination due to disability discrimination. Hopefully that *won't* be the case for you, but if it is, you do have rights under the law and can consult with an attorney to pursue justice.

When You Lose a Pregnancy

We've already discussed how work is not a place to go for personal affirmations, and the inverse is true too: The same way we can't expect our colleagues to celebrate with us when we announce a pregnancy, we sadly can't rely on them to give us support and comfort when we go through a pregnancy loss.

Even worse, we can't rely on our workplace to do more than the legal bare minimum in terms of granting us space to rest, recuperate, and grieve. That's what makes experiencing a miscarriage or stillbirth while working so heartbreakingly challenging.

Maya lost her pregnancy at fourteen weeks pregnant.

Maya remembered seeing a post on Instagram about other countries having miscarriage leave, but not the United States. The comments were full of angry American moms sharing their experience of going back to work after miscarriage. So Maya assumed that was just how it was, and went back to work.

The weeks that followed were a haze of grief. Maya was withdrawn, consumed by anxiety and depression, and barely functioning. She wasn't ready to be back to the office—not to the relentless pace of work or the well-meaning but awkward attempts at comfort from her colleagues. But Maya didn't know what else to do, and she couldn't afford to simply quit her job.

A few years later, Maya was pregnant again and joined my community. I asked her why she didn't request disability leave to recover from her loss. She told me she assumed she had no options because the United States doesn't offer miscarriage leave like other countries do. I explained that there is no such thing in the United States as "miscarriage leave" (just like there is no "maternity leave") but that these loss experiences fall under disability leave and disability accommodations. I explained there were actually two rights she could have used: a leave of absence right and an accommodation right. She was furious that her employer didn't tell her and that the internet—full of its outrage and sensationalism—made her feel powerless. I explained that this is common. These posts tend to get a lot of engagement, and providing accurate legal information on complex and nuanced legal issues just doesn't get any clout (trust me, I've tried). It's much easier to just get everyone riled up and angry, but when offering nothing to channel this rage, these posts are actually more harmful than helpful.

When Maya shared this story with me in our online community, I, too, ached for that vulnerable woman—the same way I ached for my own self a few years ago.

In my case, I didn't just experience a miscarriage while working in a general sense. I was literally in the middle of a day-long deposition when I started bleeding.

My first child was still small, and this second pregnancy was an exciting one and very much wanted.

Meanwhile, the deposition was extremely high-stakes. Witnesses had come from out of town, even out of state, to have their testimonies recorded. The media was following the case. My client's former employer had their super-expensive lawyers there, ticking up billable hours, scrutinizing our every move. We'd paid a videographer. We'd paid a court reporter. Thousands of dollars had gone into gathering all the right people and things into this conference room at the exact right minute. In fact, we had to do months of briefing to prepare for this deposition, so the judge was all over it too. I was in charge of the evidence.

And during one of our brief breaks, I sat, scared, alone, in the bathroom, stunned at what was happening to me.

That first moment, I managed to get a hold of myself. I reminded myself that it was normal to spot during pregnancy. I reassured myself—*That's probably it, just some routine spotting*—so I could clean up and go back to do my job.

But as the day wore on, it kept getting worse. Soon, it was clear that this was more than just spotting. For the rest of the day, I alternated between excusing myself to the bathroom and sitting paralyzed in that conference room, moving only to hand out the exhibits or do the highlighting when needed, just being a good little soldier. All the while, I was consumed by thoughts of *Oh no, this can't be happening; it doesn't make sense. But it is happening. Oh my God, this is* really *happening.* And all this while I was in that extremely adversarial space: People were yelling, lawyers were puffing out their chests, and the video camera light was blinking steadily, getting it all on tape.

Finally, toward the end of the deposition, I asked a coworker to take over and rushed out to the hospital, where they confirmed what I already knew: There was no life there. I had a miscarriage.

There's no societal etiquette dealing with miscarriage, and there is *certainly* no professional protocol. It's sad for me to look back on this experience, but not just because pregnancy loss is always painful. It's sad because, in that moment, I did not feel like my personal health took priority over my job. I felt I needed to be attentive and on point and operating at 100 percent. It's sad because I was not able to say, "Hey, I'm having a miscarriage. We all need to stop right now."

As a result, what I did, like I imagine many women end up doing, was just *keep working.* A soul passed through my body in those hours of trying to "break" the witness, but I felt like the work was more important.

Yet . . . for what?

That case is over. The client won, but not because I worked any special magic—her case was always very strong. It wasn't a career-maker for me, either, because I left the firm before the case concluded, and got none of the glory. Yes, there would have been a cost and delay if I'd had to leave in the moment, but this was an emergency outside my control. Would any of the male lawyers feel guilty if they'd had a sudden stroke or heart attack and had to leave? I doubt it.

So let me say first that if you experience a pregnancy loss, you are allowed to let that be the biggest thing in your life at that moment. Call out of work—this is absolutely an appropriate use of your rights—and get the medical, emotional, and spiritual care you need.

Then, be with yourself and the people who love you. Your friends, family, and/or partner are going to want to help but may not know what to do, so deputize them into helping you create that space away from work. They can act as your point of contact: Hand over your phone or laptop to let them set up an out-of-office responder for you and even take dictation on quick responses to any lingering emails.

To be fully sure you are protected legally, tell your employer that you have had a miscarriage as soon as you can, before taking any protracted amount of PTO. Just calling out of work is not protected time off and also reinforces the stigma that "we don't talk about this."

Because, yes, my advice is that you share with them what happened. It's painful, but the sooner you do it, the less painful it will be in the long run. Telling your boss point-blank allows you to set your boundaries firmly and do everything you can to avoid future awkwardness around pregnancy-related questions that might otherwise pop up. And it also protects your rights and your job. It is unlawful to terminate someone due to a pregnancy loss, but it is not unlawful to terminate someone for taking PTO or skipping work, or generally being out of it (which you are allowed to be).

How you tell your boss will depend on your relationship. If they're someone you're reasonably close with, you can let them know in person or over the phone, but you also don't *have* to if you think it will be too difficult to get the words out. It's also good to follow up with an email regardless (because, as with all things in this book, you do want to create a written record).

The same goes for your coworkers: If you're close with them and feel equipped to tell them personally, there's no reason not to. By the same token, you're not obligated to tell them, but if they knew about your pregnancy (which they likely do, if you followed my advice to announce early), you may find yourself in some uncomfortable conversations if they *don't* find out, so you may want to be proactive by letting them know. That said, it's not out of line to request that your boss be the one to spread the news to your team, the same way they might if you were unexpectedly absent due to a death in the family, for example.

At this point, my hope for you is that you have a compassionate, emotionally intelligent team of people at your workplace.

With that in mind, here's an email script you can use:

Dear [Boss's Name],

I wanted to share with you that I experienced a miscarriage on [Date]. [Optional: I apologize for not telling you in person / over the phone, but given the emotional nature of the news, I found it easier to write an email.]

This is difficult news to share, and I appreciate your grace and understanding as I take the time I need to heal and grieve. [Optional: I imagine my sudden absence may raise questions and concerns among my colleagues. You have my permission to forward this message internally to our immediate team so that they are aware as well.]

[I understand I can take medical leave under FMLA / state medical leave law.] OR:

[I am seeking a leave of absence / a telework accommodation under the PWFA.]

[Additionally, though I am grateful for thoughts and well-wishes, I respectfully ask that I not be contacted or questioned about this topic outside of necessary inquiries/questions pertaining to coverage and time off.]

Thank you again for your understanding. I expect to return to work on [Date].

Sincerely,

[Your Name]

Again, with any luck, your boss and coworkers will have the human decency to be flexible, gracious, and not bother you about deadlines and minutiae when you're undergoing one of the most difficult experiences a person can. Any reasonable person would allow you to recuperate and be happy to wait until you're back at work to figure out the paperwork and documentation. But, as an employment lawyer, I won't hold my breath on that. So it's important that you know what rights you have to take time off to recover from a miscarriage.

Legally speaking, if you are eligible for **FMLA**, you can take unpaid leave to recover from a miscarriage—however, any FMLA leave you use now will count against the twelve weeks you are allotted per year, which is important to keep in mind if you plan to get pregnant again right away.

You can also request reasonable accommodations under **PWFA** (you can follow the process on page 94 to request accommodations).

These rights are available for both the physical recovery and any resulting depression or anxiety. However, you do need medical certification, so make sure to advocate with your provider so you can submit a medical note.

Finally, certain states and municipalities (such as California, Illinois, and the cities of Pittsburgh and Portland, Oregon, to name a few) have specific laws that provide additional protections. Mamas in California can take four months of paid leave after loss, leading on the global scale.

It's also important to know that under the **Pregnancy Discrimination Act** (which applies to employers in every state with fifteen or more employers), your employer cannot discriminate against you for pregnancy-related conditions, *including pregnancy loss*. This is crucial because if you take time off, you should *not* be punished for it.

What About Stillbirth?

Women who experience stillbirth can take any sort of disability leave or accommodations. You also have a high likelihood of receiving extended disability time after a stillbirth due to the potential for depression. Sadly, stillbirth parents cannot take bonding leave. However, extending disability (through PWFA) can help make up for that time.

SHOULD I ASK FOR BEREAVEMENT LEAVE?

Julie, one of my former clients, experienced a second-trimester loss. She instantly texted her manager, *Hey I lost my pregnancy, can I please take some bereavement leave?* Her boss replied, *Let me take a look at the policies.* A few minutes later, he texted, *Sorry but the bereavement leave doesn't apply to you because per our policies, it's only for an alive person who died.* Julie was flummoxed and furious. I was, too, as a mother. But as a lawyer, I had to explain to her that she had asked the wrong question. She had asked for the wrong type of leave. Legally, pregnancy loss is considered a medical event, not a death. Accordingly, it falls under disability laws, including medical leave and accommodations. I'm not saying this is fair or that this makes sense, but this is how it is. So bereavement leave is actually not used for pregnancy loss. In addition, "bereavement leave" is not a legal right; it is a company policy. So, by asking for bereavement leave, you are asking for a policy, not a right. And that's a risky legal move.

Tamika experienced a pregnancy loss and asked for bereavement leave at work. However, she did not explain that she needed to take time off for pregnancy loss. In fact, she had never told her boss that she was pregnant.

Tamika took a week of company-allotted bereavement leave but was not ready to return to work. She texted her boss that she needed a few more days. Her boss responded that they were mid-launch and needed her back at work. Tamika pleaded with her boss, "I just need a little bit more time, I'm sorry." A few days later, she got a termination letter in the mail for job abandonment. Nothing illegal happened here. First, they never knew she was pregnant or experienced a miscarriage. Second, she asked for a company policy leave, which is not legally protected. Third, she did not ask for additional time off under PWFA, which would have been a legally protected request. She asked for it as a courtesy. I know this is frustrating to read. I know it is so enraging that we have to be so exact and specific with our words. I wish it were all easier. There are so many things I could be doing with my time instead of teaching mothers how to navigate this semantic maze. I could be on a jet ski, or at a drum circle, but no, instead I'm here, explaining to you that you have to be very, very careful with the words you use, yes, even now. This is why it's essential to review this chapter *before* it happens, because in the midst of a loss, you won't be able to find *any* words. (It may even be a good idea to create an outline that you can share with your partner: "If X happens, please help me send the following email to my boss." If they can navigate a fantasy league, which is full of if/then scenarios, they can navigate the legal labyrinth too.)

If your company offers a *paid* bereavement leave policy that covers miscarriage, of course you don't want to miss out on that money, but you'll be asking for your medical rights *and* the paid leave policy at the same time.

But it's vital that you use legal language.

Violet, a sales manager, worked for a company with a hybrid schedule that required three days per week in-office. After she had a miscarriage, Violet still wanted to work—it was a good distraction from her grief, she found—but her anxiety made it hard to stomach going to the office. Instead, she got approval from HR to work entirely from home for four weeks as a PWFA accommodation for her pregnancy-related mental health condition.

A few weeks later, Violet's boss informed her that because she'd missed too many meetings at the office, she'd be removed from the project. Violet was stunned and elevated the issue to HR. She explained that she'd received a protected PWFA accommodation and that her boss was retaliating by removing her from the project.

Because Violet requested an official accommodation based on her PWFA rights, and it was granted, her boss was in violation of her rights, giving Violet potential legal recourse. When HR received her report, not only was her job secured, but they also fired her manager for being a liability. Take good note of what happened here: The company did not dismiss Violet, they protected her and dismissed her manager instead. A few months later, Violet was promoted to a managerial position and received a significant raise. That is the power of your rights.

All right, enough about the law. This last part is from my own mama heart to you. After doing all the hard things and making sure your time off is protected, the last thing you can do for yourself is perhaps the hardest. It's to share.

After my miscarriage, I sat inside for three days, crying and cramping, staring at the TV. Paralyzed. I'm a to-do list kind of person, but I did not know where to start or how to move forward.

But then I started sharing. I told all of my friends, then I told people online. Friends called with offerings. Women reached out to me, telling me, "you're in the worst part," "life is tough but so are you," "this is not something you'll get over but you'll get through it," and "deep loss comes from deep love." These women, their words, are my medicine.

The event of pregnancy loss links a woman to a broader community of women who share in the transformative effects of such grief. These women know the pride of growing and feeding a child using only your body, and they know the anger of your body betraying you by evicting your child too soon. For me, sharing was a turning point. Because when grief is shared, it starts to move—and when you share, you receive too.

The following week, I spent an entire day at the Encinitas Botanical Gardens writing letters to my daughter (I was convinced it was a girl). I told her all about her brother, her father, her pets, and that there are playgrounds on the beaches where we live. I told her I would always be her mama.

The day after that, I went back there. I brought my young son and watched him have the best time in the beautiful sunshine, and I thought, *There is so much joy and life all around me.*

As we sat there, I saw a pregnant woman. At first I thought, *That should have been me.* Then I stopped myself and said, out loud, "That *will* be me." A few months later, it was.

Share the hard stuff. People can handle it. What you get in return is the key to your healing.

The Elephant in the Womb: Abortion

I have to be honest: I'm scared to write this.

I've spoken out in favor of reproductive freedom online, and I was met with everything from mild annoyance to death threats (which is a little ironic, if you're asking me). I've been at odds with the "pro-life" movement for my entire career, mainly because they fund and sponsor candidates who vote against mothers' rights, including paid leave, healthcare, and childcare, all the things that would make it easier to have a baby and also stay alive and healthy as a mother.

In addition, I find the rhetoric quite heartless, especially in the context of forcing pregnancies that will not result in a live birth, or pregnancies that harm the health of the mother. It seems like the mother's right to life is not really respected, which again, seems ironic.

I'm not going to go deeper into the morality of this issue, mainly because it is too controversial (though I personally do not believe it should be controversial). In addition, it goes beyond the scope of this book. The morality and motivation of abortion is—for purposes of your workplace rights—quite irrelevant. And that's exactly how I want you to approach it at work as well.

If you are in need of an abortion, here are my recommendations.

My first recommendation is not to call it abortion, but a pregnancy loss. This leaves open the voluntary-versus-involuntary aspect of it, which is good because, again, the workplace is not the moral battleground where this should be fought out.

"Abortion" is such a heavy and unfortunately politicized word, despite it being a medical term used for most terminated pregnancies, including a miscarriage.

When I sat in the hospital, holding an ultrasound photo of my uterus showing no life where there previously was life, sobbing and pleading and crying, my nurse thought it would be a great time for a semantics lesson.

I was scream/crying something to the effect of, "I lost my baby! I can't believe I had a miscarriage!"

And she said, calmly and clinically, "Actuallyyyyyyy . . ."

(Anytime someone starts a sentence like that, I roll my eyes.)

"Actuallyyyyyy, the correct medical term for what you experienced is 'spontaneous abortion.'"

Uhm, okay?

It was not helpful to me at that moment, but for some reason, this is stuck in my brain.

Whenever I hear someone say they had a miscarriage, a little voice in my head goes, "Actuallyyyyyy, it is a spontaneous abortion."

"Spontaneous abortion" joins other absurd and offensive terms like "chemical pregnancy" and "incompetent cervix" or "working mother."

So, when it comes to the workplace, you'll want to use "pregnancy loss" or "end of pregnancy," and leave it at that. In fact, with abortion bans in place in some states, you'll want as few people as possible to know about it.

Voluntary pregnancy terminations and involuntary pregnancy terminations are treated the same way when it comes to your rights. An employer does not have the right to ask you whether it was an abortion or a miscarriage. If they ask you, you can respond clearly, "This is a private matter," or more obscurely, "It didn't work out. I'm very sad about it. At this point I need some privacy to process the end of this pregnancy."

After a pregnancy termination, you have the right to a medical leave if you are eligible. This is another reason you should tell your employer about your pregnancy, because it is really hard to ask for a medical leave if they didn't know you were pregnant.

You can also request accommodations under the PWFA for medical visits and healing.

Post-*Dobbs*, some employers took a stand and declared they would help their employees get abortions if they wanted to. To me this is a little, dare I say it, self-serving. I appreciate the intention, but relying on your employer for their support terminating your pregnancy will result in you being way too enmeshed with this workplace. It is also a weird thing for employers to brag about.

In fact, in one of my cases, a business owner "joked" about putting Plan B pills in the ladies' bathroom after a series of pregnancy announcements.

In one of my other cases, my client Billie announced her pregnancy at work and asked for paid maternity leave. The company had a policy in place that they would provide paid leave after abortion; however, they did not have a paid leave policy for a maternity leave. Billie asked her boss, the owner of the company, if they could extend the paid leave to her, and she was met with a cold and stern "No." When Billie asked why, her boss told her point-blank, "Abortion is scalable, but paid maternity leave is not scalable." Translation: You having a baby makes me less money, because then I'll have a little screamer competing with me for your attention and labor, but you terminating your pregnancy makes me more money, because then you fully belong to me.

See, self-serving.

If you're in the place of needing this chapter, I recommend discretion in the workplace. This is not the time for your micro-revolution. The stakes are too high, especially in the ban states. Don't worry, there are opportunities for micro-revolutions every day.

But please take the time and space to recover. Don't sit at your desk, still bleeding and silently weeping. The law *does* have your back—yes, even now.

In conservative states, employers are big mad that they have to provide leave or accommodations after abortions. In fact, they even sued the federal government over it, when the Equal Employment Opportunity Commission made it clear they have to provide these accommodations. These employers argued that "they don't want to fund abortions." The EEOC slapped back and said, "Bitch, you don't have to fund shit" (in legal and more strategic terms). An abortion is just a medical event, and just like any other medical event related to pregnancy, they have to be accommodated.

I do also want to make it clear that this is a legally volatile landscape, and things shift faster than even lawyers are able to bill. What's important is that, even in states with bans, you don't have fewer rights under federal employment laws, like the PWFA. Those are separate issues. An employer—who somehow found out you had an abortion—may grumble and say, "Abortion is not allowed here, so why would I give you time off." It's just not the issue; you are using your workplace rights, not your reproductive rights.

When Your Baby Needs a NICU Stay

A few years ago, I saw a viral reel with a mother crying at work. The caption read something like, "When you have a baby in the NICU but you have to go back to work because you live in America and have to save your leave for when your baby comes home."

The entire internet was outraged. "America hates moms!" is the common response to these reels. All I wanted to say was, "Mama, please get yourself a mental health accommodation."

Anxiety and depression can form the basis for accommodation requests, such as an extension of your leave rights or a remote work accommodation under PWFA.

No one said that in the comments, and this is why it's so important to trust actual attorneys and not the internet. (I did end up explaining this in the comments, but was met with a lot of non-lawyer commenters telling me I was wrong—which is a very strange and common experience as a public expert.)

The impact of this reel is that all these mamas now assume they have no options when they have a NICU baby. And they do. But you have to know how to ask for your rights. And first, a case study in how not to ask for your rights:

In 2024, Kyte Baby—a company that manufactures high-end baby apparel—came under fire and ignited an online controversy around parental leave rights.

An employee at Kyte adopted a baby, who unfortunately was born with complications that required him to stay in the NICU after birth. The employee then asked to work remotely so that she could be with the baby as he recovered.

Instead of being granted the accommodation, she got fired.

Now, this was absolutely atrocious and horrible and abhorrent and definitely an injustice, *and* it was not illegal. The entire internet was outraged again: Paid leave would solve this problem! (The classic internet solution to every workplace motherhood problem.) No, ma'am, it would not. Let me explain.

First, she didn't ask for a leave of absence, and if she would have, she hadn't worked long enough to qualify. So the main culprit here was the eligibility obstacles, not whether the leave was paid.

Second, she asked for accommodations based on the *baby's* needs, instead of her own needs. If she would have asked for flexibility based on her anxiety and depression (protected by PWFA or, in this case, as she is an adoptive mom, the ADA), that would have been a legally protected ask, and then the company would have been obligated to engage in the interactive process with her to see how she could be accommodated.

This is why you are going to be prepared with what to say *before* this happens to you. Again, you can enlist a partner or relative to help you send the emails to management. All you have to do is send them the language or even have them read this chapter.

It's so frustrating and enraging to realize that we can be *doubly* vulnerable at times like these: vulnerable to the emotional reality of having a baby in intensive care, *and* vulnerable to job loss—yet that is the case. The last thing I want to have happen is that your baby needs this kind of medical care, and you're just in the middle of it, you don't know what your rights are, your manager is equally confused, and you're trying to research your rights on a phone screen while sitting in the NICU with your sweet, tiny baby.

While I'm not a NICU mom myself, I've helped a lot of parents navigate their legal rights in these tragic situations, and I know it's a very hard place to be—worn out from birth, worried sick about your baby, shuttling back and forth to the hospital in a haze that barely seems real. That's why, again, I advise you to digest this early so that, no matter what happens, you have a road map.

I wish there were a simple way to extend your leave just based on having a baby in the NICU. In and of itself, that should be enough, right? It's a stressful, agonizing time. Under the law, however, "having a baby in the NICU" is not a protected class. Instead, we do what we can to use the rights we *do* have to their maximum potential.

Let's go back to the example of the Kyte Baby termination case. It's not illegal to ask to work remotely to be with your baby in the NICU, but it's also not illegal to be *fired* in response to a question about working remotely to be with your baby in the NICU. That is not a protected ask. Again, it *feels* like it should be—but it's not.

What *is* a protected ask is a request to work remotely because of the anxiety and depression that is caused by having a baby in the NICU. That is an accommodation you are asking for under disability rights legislation—and those disability rights are more robust.

If your doctor can explain to your employer that you being closer to your baby would alleviate these symptoms of anxiety and depression, your employer must try to accommodate you under the ADA/PWFA by granting you the ability to work remotely. And if you can work remotely while your baby is in the NICU, then you will not be using your leave time during that NICU stay, because you are *still working*. Your leave time will be untouched.

Now, as I mentioned before, this mom who worked for Kyte Baby was not the birthing mom, so she could not have used the PWFA. She could have instead cited the ADA and requested reasonable accommodations to address symptoms of anxiety and depression that were caused by having a baby in the NICU and would be alleviated by being in closer proximity to this baby.

Either way, requesting the accommodation to work remotely is *not* based on your baby's medical needs. This is the key thing to understand. Your baby does not go to work in a tiny suit, carrying a tiny briefcase. There are no rights to claim on behalf of your baby. These rights are yours to claim, because you're the one with employment rights.

You are asserting *your* medical condition, *your* disability limitations, and your baby's medical status is not the core issue; yours is. You're *not* saying, "My baby needs me; it's critical to their health that I'm with them!"

You're talking about *your* needs—because only you have disability rights at your workplace.

That said, requesting these accommodations successfully is contingent on your actually being able to work remotely while your baby is in the hospital. Some parents have jobs that are easily portable, and they actually appreciate the distraction of having something else to focus on. But not all jobs can be accommodated this way (for example, if you're a construction worker working on-site, I'd have a hard time finding a good argument for how you'd still be doing your job remotely).

That brings me to the second option, which is to actually go on disability leave and use that leave to be with your baby. Then, at the conclusion of your disability leave, you can ask for an extension of that disability leave—again, not based on your baby's medical needs, but based on *yours*: in this case, due to symptoms of anxiety and depression that were caused by having a baby in the NICU, because having a baby in the NICU is a *traumatic experience*. From there, if you still have some bonding leave available, you could also add that to the end of the disability leave extension.

You will want to lean on your disability rights as much as you can during the NICU experience, and shortly thereafter, because that is when you have the highest chance of actually getting your disability rights granted—when the situation is acute and your own doctor can speak most clearly and accurately to your mental health. You also want to begin by leveraging your disability rights rather than your bonding leave, because while it's difficult to go from bonding leave to disability accommodation (since arguably you *weren't* disabled if you were able to take bonding leave), it's a lot easier to establish a disability accommodation, extend that accommodation, and *then* go to bonding leave.

This is also good news for dads or non-birthing parents. I've helped dads receive accommodations to work remotely based on their anxiety or depression caused by having a baby in the NICU or even witnessing a traumatic birth. These dads are using their legal rights—not under the Pregnant Workers Fairness Act, but under the ADA, because their disabling mental health condition is alleviated by the accommodation of being able to work remotely and support their baby (and/or partner).

Parting Words

I learned many lessons from losing a pregnancy.

That a positive test does not equal a baby.

That a soul can pass through my body.

That my body creates both life and death, both construction and destruction.

That my body is not always my ally. She has her own plan for reasons I will never know.

That too many people are wasting their lives. (Do you know what a gift your life is?)

That no one knows the right thing to say.

That the road to motherhood is full of challenges and that the perils don't discriminate. I don't get bonus points for being The Mamattorney. Life does not punish or reward. Life just is.

My third pregnancy resulted in a beautiful baby, and it did heal me, almost. But the transformative experience of miscarriage shook me to my core. It humbled me. It changed me permanently.

So, to the women who had a due date without a happy ending, to the women who keep waiting for a due date, to the women in the in-between of uncertainty, here is what I want to say to you:

This. Sucks.

It is unfair.

Anyone who comes to you with "silver lining" arguments (all the "at leasts," like at least you're young, at least it was early, at least you can get pregnant) deserves to be slapped in the face. I will personally come do that for you.

No one understands how deep the well of grief is after miscarriage, and, as far as I can imagine, fertility challenges. Not unless you've been down the well. It is a well without a bottom. You just keep falling. There is a sad comfort in knowing many of us have been down the well, but also a sadness that such a common experience is still so stigmatized and shielded behind a cloak of shame.

Death, life, we need to talk about both. Both your stories of death and life are welcome here. I am not afraid of the darkness. I have spent many nights roaming through the dark forest, wailing and raging and drowning in never-ending tears.

And here's what I can also say: The light will come back. It always does. There is one thing more reliable you can hold on to: nature. After the darkest night, the sun rises in the morning. After the darkest winter, spring always returns. It is inevitable. Life *wants* to live through you. In fact, it already is.

I want to conclude this chapter by celebrating *your* life. Your beautiful body that sustains you. Your cells that regenerate to keep you alive. Your digestive system that breaks down food and gives you energy. Your beautiful big heart that is capable of such big love and now such big grief. Grief is the price we pay for love. And just look at how big your love is. I am so proud of you for daring to take a chance. Motherhood is always an exercise in surrender. We don't have control over the outcome. The journey is full of risk. It takes a gutsy woman to look this fear in the eye and say, bring it on. I trust life enough to catch me if I fall.

Now allow me to get a bit spiritual here. If you believe a soul was embodied within you (which I did), I am convinced that this soul never actually leaves us. I have two theories for what happened after my miscarriage: One, that soul just wasn't ready (it was 2020, after all) and checked out, but came back a few months later and became my second son.

My second theory is that this soul is here to guide me and liberate me, to send me whispers from the "other side." I have actually felt a female spirit with me since I had this event. A bridge to the other world was built. I don't know if this is just my own inner knowing, the collective voice of my ancestors, or this spirit that I lost, but either way, it's brought me a lot of comfort to listen to these whispers. I don't have any proof for these theories, but no one can disprove them either, and that's good enough for me. It is a much better story than assuming this was lost forever. No, I did not lose anything. In fact, I gained so much. And the most important thing I gained is a profound appreciation for life itself.

My greatest love story has been the one between me and the current of life that moves through me. I trust it, even if it brings me to my knees in despair. I trust that life and my body act in my best interests, even when I cannot understand it. If this sounds a bit too "God has a plan" and "everything happens for a reason" to you, I say, that's some bullshit. There is a randomness to life that can be very scary to accept. One day there is life, then it is gone. It is also the most natural cycle: The life/death/life cycle is the most primordial thing there is. Sometimes, the cycle is just much shorter than we would like it to be. And yet, life happened. And that's worth celebrating. This being will always be with you. You shared a body. You shared cells. This being still lives through you. Embrace both of you with the fullness of your heart. Love yourself and this being like only a mother can. Allow your heart to break. That's how the light comes through. I got you.

6

Babyproof Your Job

Preparing for Your Absence at Work

When I first met my client Aimee, her career had completely unraveled.

Aimee was hardworking, extremely competent, and had in-demand skills in a niche role: a software engineer at a big tech company. Her job was her whole life, so when she got pregnant, she told her coworkers, HR, and supervisor fairly early on, with a plan to, basically, "work up until birth, then take leave."

But, this being tech, Aimee's coworkers were mostly men, and all without kids themselves. So when Aimee started experiencing prodromal labor three weeks before her due date, *and* contracted an infection, her decision (at her medical team's insistence!) to take her leave early took everyone by surprise. Her team then had to scramble to figure out her projects, and because they were not allowed to contact her while she was on leave, *and* because her work was so specialized, they were left clueless on how to finish her projects, which dealt a huge blow to their deliverables for a big-ticket client.

Aimee's baby arrived happy and healthy, but she ended up being replaced by a man during her leave and ultimately fired.

I took Aimee's case because it was obvious that what her employer did was illegal—and, happily, through our representation, she walked away with hundreds of thousands of dollars. Companies never admit or apologize when they do something wrong, but when we get these big payouts, it's because they know they messed up. Employers may not punish women who go on leave due to medical emergencies, including pregnancy—full stop. Moreover, this company had done absolutely *nothing* to cover their tracks. Once court proceedings were underway, I subpoenaed Slack transcripts between two managers, and the things they said during that period were just horrible:

> She's not looking out for us. She's just looking out for herself.

> Seriously, how can you bounce like this? You're not an immature 23 year old. You're a mother.

> She's just gonna do an extended paid leave, and she's gonna say, "Oh, an opportunity I couldn't refuse came up. I wasn't even looking!" We really should just let her go now.

Even in deposition, I was shocked at what the HR rep was willing to say on the record. "Aimee clearly lacks common sense," she told me. "How could she not contact her team as soon as she knew she was leaving?"

It was all I could do to stay cool and respond, "Ma'am, she was *in labor*."

However, while I was cross-examining her direct coworkers, they told me a slightly different story. They recalled having to work through the night to finish her projects. One of the coworkers started crying as she recounted how much stress she'd been under.

In hindsight, I can see that, while the legal blame for her unjust firing lies with the company, there were some valid frustrations among her coworkers. After all, Aimee didn't leave any instructions or a transition plan for her projects. Both she and her managers assumed that conversation would take place closer to her actual planned leave date—and even scheduled some major, unmissable client calls the week she was originally due to deliver.

Pregnancies are not predictable, schedulable, or movable like project due dates. We can lose the pregnancies. We may need to go on leave for a little while and then come back. Or the baby may come early. We just don't know. (You may be shocked to learn that people in your workplace do not understand that your due date is not an actual due date—I made the mistake of placing my due date on the law firm calendar, which led to a colleague emailing me the day after my due date saying, "I hope you're enjoying your new bundle of joy!" Except the baby was still in my belly . . . awkward.)

This is why the leave plan must be created almost immediately after announcing your pregnancy: Because while pregnancy is inherently unpredictable, you *can* (and should) make plans for how your workplace will handle your absence.

To be clear, as a pregnant woman, you have a right to an uninterrupted leave, and as an employee, you do not have an obligation to plan out your own leave coverage. The law does forbid your employer from bothering you during leave—but it's silent on your employer's duty to provide enough coverage while you're out.

In other words, the law protects your job, but it does not necessarily protect your *work*. If they let your projects die out, there is little you will be able to do about that. I have talked to too many women who had to go back to work sooner because the company simply did not account for enough staff to bridge the gap in labor, or who came back to work only to find their work projects abandoned, languishing, or even detonated, and their professional reputation along with it, or to find others had stolen their ideas and ran with them, causing a major unfair career setback.

In Aimee's case, her company was unequivocally in the wrong for firing her—she was victorious in her case. The company was far too nonchalant and lackadaisical around planning for coverage and ultimately retaliated against *her*, which is not allowed. At the same time, though, Aimee's job was a very technical, specialized role. It's not surprising that her sudden absence left so many coworkers in the lurch and stressed out of their minds . . . to the point of crying just thinking about it. And while she won her case, the months of legal proceedings weren't stress-free for her either and took up time she could have used to progress in her career.

No matter what you do for a living, *you* are in the best position to know what your job entails. Planning for your leave is really a "both/and" situation, where you and your employer team up to make sure things go as smoothly as possible. Actively participating in your own leave transition will not only minimize the risk of discrimination down the line, but also put everyone's minds (including your own!) much more at ease because you'll all be prepped and primed for the disruptions of pregnancy (which, as we know, can come at any time). Plus it allows you to showcase your value to the organization, as most managers are clueless as to what their subordinates *actually* do all day. Pregnancy is a great time to remind your employer how essential you are.

A clear plan for how things will get done during your leave from work is a necessity—and your responsibility—and this chapter will help you make one. I'll give you a step-by-step timeline of how to prepare one, build it out, share it with your coworkers and managers, and set everyone's expectations up for success.

Timeline and Preparation

My recommendation is to start your leave plan right after giving notice of pregnancy, because you just don't know what will happen—or when—and it's better to be overprepared than underprepared. Plus, operationally, it's easier on your team if they have a lot of notice to prepare for your absence, chime in on your coverage plans, and all get accustomed to their temporary roles and responsibilities, instead of scrambling right at the end.

Create a Google Doc and make sure you give access to your manager, subordinates, and whoever needs to be kept in the loop.

Documenting Your Work
and Writing Your Plan

There are two main elements to your documentation: your job task list and your projects list. The former is for the stuff you do routinely, regardless of what specific projects you're working on. The latter is for all the ongoing individual projects you're a part of and what your specific role and responsibilities are within that scope.

Let's start with the task list. Writing out what you do all day might seem like busywork, but I promise you, it's not. Because I also promise you that no matter how closely you collaborate with your colleagues, no matter how frequently you're in touch with your manager, the people around you at work don't actually know what you do, and they definitely don't know everything it involves.

I know this because when I made my own task list for my first maternity leave, my boss was stunned by all I'd been taking on. I know this
because I've taken countless depositions of managers who were clueless
about their subordinates' day-to-day tasks. And I know this because I'm a
business owner and constantly reminded of how many little things go into
someone's job when my team sends me reminders and jumps on things
without me even knowing until they're done—I don't track their every
move because I trust them, they're capable professionals, and because I'm
too busy doing my own damn job.

Plus, writing out this task list not only helps with the transition during
your leave, but also showcases your value to your employer. It's an opportunity to highlight your successes and contributions, which can be beneficial for your career in the long run—it's essentially an audit of your work
and how amazing and successful you are at it, with an implied undertone
of YOU CAN TRY TO REPLACE ME BUT I DO SO MUCH I'M
BASICALLY IRREPLACEABLE SO YOU PUNKS BETTER SUPPORT
ME!! (Except, you know, in professional language.)

And, finally, remember how, legally under FMLA, your employer must
give you back your job, or one that is nearly identical? Well, it'll be a lot
easier to make sure that happens—or prove that it isn't, in a legal case—if
you have an in-depth, detailed list of what, exactly, your job is.

By starting early, you're already ahead of the game, and you don't have
to draft the whole thing in one session. You can collect tasks over a series
of days or weeks simply by observing what you do and writing it down,
kind of like a reverse to-do list. Ultimately, though, your task list should
be broad and deep. Get as granular as you can.

It can help to break down your job duties into categories. Start with
daily tasks and then the weekly or monthly tasks. Next, jot down anything
you do irregularly, ad hoc, or on an as-needed basis (such as providing
feedback on drafts or meeting with potential clients). You'll also want to
include all your meetings and your expected contributions to those meetings (such as organizing the agenda, taking minutes, preparing a specific
status update, etc.).

Sample Task List

Daily Tasks

- Check emails and respond to client inquires as needed.
- Daily check-ins with sales reps to address any immediate issues.
- Review sales dashboard and benchmark against quarterly goals.

Weekly Tasks

- Weekly strategy meetings (Wednesdays @ 10 a.m.) with senior management to discuss sales strategies and performance → prepare summary notes from field reports.
- Organize and lead weekly brown-bag lunch sessions for Women in Tech affinity group.

Monthly Tasks

- Review and approve expense reports and time sheets for sales team (by last Thursday of the month COB).
- Compile monthly sales reports for upper management → template on server, email to director of sales, cc'ing CFO.

As-Needed Tasks

- Provide feedback on marketing materials, product documentation, etc. (aim for 48 hours turnaround to Sara).
- Market research on emerging trends/opportunities.
- Event participation/on-site client meetings as arranged.

With those written out, you're basically done—but you don't have to stop there. Next you'll SOP your work. This is corporate speak for "standard operating procedure."

Do you know one of the reasons McDonald's is so successful? Because you could start working there any day, follow their SOPs, and know what to do by the end of your first shift. Their highly systemized and optimized process of labor means they only have to spend a little time training new people.

A good SOP would be a step-by-step guide that gets extremely specific (including which buttons to click). You should SOP not just your processes, but also relationships with clients or customers. For example, "Katy does not respond to email. I communicate with her by texting her cell, asking her to call me. Her husband often attends calls and may chime in. He appreciates directness, but Katy is the one paying for the services and nervous about the costs. I always make sure Katy understands the value she is receiving, where we are going, and why patience is an essential ingredient to this service succeeding."

You probably tackle these tasks or conversations in a particular way, in a certain order, or with different priorities at different times. Your job isn't just doing these things, but knowing which to do when, and the person covering for you might not have that same experience, intuition, or institutional knowledge. So go ahead and categorize things accordingly. You might assign stars or color codes to top-priority (or low-priority) tasks, write in suggested time allotments (e.g., "don't spend more than ten minutes on this"), or note down coworkers who can pitch in if need be. You could even break down your list by day of the week if certain tasks need to be done on certain days. This is where making a spreadsheet or document can be really handy—it's easy to rearrange and reformat as you go, or add redlines and tooltip notes without overcrowding the list itself.

Next, you'll want to map out all your work projects. Whether you're leading the charge or you're just one of several contributors, you definitely want your projects to keep humming along smoothly while you're on leave (because, otherwise, you'll be coming back to pandemonium).

Create a list of projects and what needs to happen to your projects during your absence, including all relevant deadlines, milestones, and specific deliverables. It's fine if you don't have firm dates for some of these yet—even writing something relative (like "two weeks after delivery of final proofs") is helpful.

Sample Project List

Rebranding for Earthly Delights Natural Foods (logo, business cards, brand guidelines document)

Deadlines/Milestones

    Finalize logo design: September 28

    Logo concepts presentation: October 1

    First draft of the brand guidelines: October 5

    Business cards and stationery: October 10

    Brand Guidelines Document: October 15

    Specific Deliverables:

- 3 logo concepts
- Final logo in multiple formats (AI, PNG, EPS)
- Business card design template
- 20-page brand guidelines document

Annual Report for Turner-Whitman Foundation

Deadlines/Milestones

    Initial layout draft: September 22

    Final copy and art due from client: October 5

    Final layout: October 12

    Client approval due: October 15

    Submission to printer: October 19

    Specific Deliverables:

- 30-page report in PDF format (hi- and lo-res versions)
- Print-ready files for the printer

Next, I highly recommend you draft a suggested coverage plan for each project: who of your colleagues will do what in your absence. True, technically this is not your responsibility. But, to be frank, it's often easier to come up with a solution ahead of time than it is to deal with the fallout once you're back. Proactively delegating also protects against your work, or career, being impacted because no one felt specifically responsible for anything and your projects weren't kept on track.

That said, it's important not to *assume* that you can give someone a responsibility. In the end, we don't have the authority to shift our work; we can only make recommendations. So first the plan has to go to our immediate managers, that is, the people with the authority to assign tasks and work.

Communication and Sharing

Once you've gotten that plan together, you'll want to share it with your immediate supervisor, make any necessary adjustments with their input, then loop in HR (as an FYI), and then get it out to your colleagues and coworkers. I recommend having your boss send it out to the larger team, because then they can assume the responsibility for it. (No one likes to receive extra work, and it can exacerbate coworker resentment if we are sending it out ourselves.)

Sample email:

> Hello [Boss],
>
> I've created a maternity leave plan with the intention to make the transition easier on everyone. You can find it here. I'd like to get together to make sure we can be aligned. These shifts are what made the most sense to me in the context of the specific projects and the talents on this team. But I don't want to shift any duties or responsibilities to anyone who is already maxed out, and I'm not fully aware of everyone's workload. It would help getting your bird's-eye view on this plan so we can anticipate and prevent the potential of anyone having too much on their plate. It may also help us prioritize these tasks and decide whether anything can be put on hold until I return.

Once the plan has been distributed, set meetings with the people who will be taking over your work. Record these meetings. You can also create a series of screen recordings and save them in your drive folder. Instead of talking about the task or project, show people how you do your work and have them shadow you. Ideally, more than one person would be trained on your job, to prevent burdening one person and also to protect yourself (because that one person may also leave).

You'll also want to decide on a liaison. You need one person who will be listed in your out-of-office email. That person doesn't necessarily need to do the work but needs to be most intimately aware of where to funnel people. Ideally, this is an admin support person who can filter these messages. Tagging in a peer can cause a lot of overwhelm if that person also has to take over some of your tasks.

Another key aspect is to ensure that the plan is communicated across the larger team—this is such a common mistake and can result in some unfortunate misalignments: for example, an upper manager finding out from a junior that you gave them a certain responsibility, and that junior is now using that responsibility as an opportunity to ask for a raise, even though you never cleared that with the upper manager, or a junior always going to the same peer-level person to ask questions they would ordinarily ask you (because, ideally, the work is spread out to avoid burdening one specific person). If everyone has one source of directives, and everyone knows the plan, then there will be fewer surprises for everyone.

The other mistake I see moms making is just not making information accessible. Think ahead (*way* ahead) about who'll need access to certain Google Docs, files, or servers, and ensure they have it (or have a way to get it when they need it). Having your team wait to be granted access while you're not checking your phone because your baby is cluster feeding can be so frustrating for all parties involved (including your baby).

With all that taken care of, I now need you to *resist* the urge to write, "If anything comes up, don't hesitate to call me!" Don't be complicit in your own leave interference. You'd be violating your own rights! The plan is supposed to allow everyone to know what to do without your involvement.

Finally, remember that you can only do so much. If they are not cooperating with you or are actively obstructing you, then you have to just take your time and let the chips fall. In the end, the success of your birth and postpartum experience is more important than your employer's operational needs.

Setting Expectations

People don't know that you're not allowed to contact people on leave for work-related tasks. It should be common sense, but it is not.

So, to prevent the ubiquitous "hey, I know you just had a baby but . . ." messages you may receive, you have to make that clear in your plan. I suggest some version of the following:

> Thank you all for your cooperation, and please come talk to me in the next two weeks if you have any questions or concerns. While I'm on leave, I will not be accessible or available to work, as I'll be in recovery and tending to a newborn.

Yes, this can be an anxiety-inducing boundary to set, but take it from me: You've just gotta let that shit go. Work comes and goes, but that baby is only little now. In a few years, you won't even remember what you were stressed out about in Q3 of whatever year. But you'll always have your child in your life. There will be times to balance motherhood and work, and put a movie on for your kid while you jump on email. But this is not that time.

In addition, I recommend you thank those who take over your work. I actually threw a pastry party to thank my team. These are just little gestures that go a long way. A leave of absence *does* have an impact on operations— it's best not to be naive or flippant about that. Responding to the support you received with reciprocity is vital in preventing resentment and also allows your team to feel like they are a part of the village raising this baby.

How to Handle Insensitive Comments

Daniela was seven months along when her firm held its annual holiday party. Even though standing around drunk executives was the last thing she felt like doing, she squeezed herself into a cute maternity cocktail dress and turned up with her husband.

Mocktail in hand, she was slowly circulating the room when her coworker Ron sidled up, smiling broadly. After giving Daniela's husband a firm handshake and hearty congratulations on his impending fatherhood, he turned to Daniela with a smile.

"And I bet *you're* looking forward to a three-month break!"

Daniela was too stunned—and too exhausted—to do anything but laugh politely and wait for Ron to drift back into the party. *Dude, it's maternity leave, not a fucking break*, she wanted to scream.

Work isn't just where we get shit done and make bank—it's also, for better or worse, a social environment. And, unfortunately, that means that part of preparing for your leave is preparing to field a bunch of awkward and insensitive questions and comments from your colleagues.

To be clear, I'm talking mainly about those offhanded questions and observations that don't *technically* rise to the legal standard of unlawful conduct (mainly because he's a coworker, not a manager), but are still just . . . way off base for the workplace. Ron's remark to Daniela was certainly tone-deaf, but unless he was a manager and it was part of an escalating pattern of discriminatory behavior, it wasn't anything to sue over.

The best practice here is to just *learn your lines.* Have canned, polite responses ready, and then quickly change the subject. And fortunately for you, I've got a whole host of scripts you can arm yourself with.

PEOPLE WHO JUST DON'T GET WHAT
MATERNITY LEAVE IS

- *Wish I could take a three-month vacation!*
- *Must be nice getting a break . . .*
- *Enjoy catching up on Netflix!*

Whether they're coming from a place of genuine ignorance or mere passive-aggressiveness, these kinds of comments are maddening. Maternity leave is nothing like a vacation . . . unless your idea of a relaxing time involves five hours of broken sleep, wearing an adult diaper, and smelling like old milk.

If you're feeling polite, here are some good responses:

Yes, I'm looking forward to bonding with the baby.
We're very excited to have time together as a family.

Yes, I'm proud that our company/state values mothers.

If, on the other hand, you're not feeling quite as charitable, you could answer:

I'm not going on vacation. I'll be recovering from a major medical event.

I'll actually be quite busy caring for a newborn baby around the clock with no breaks, but thank you for the well-wishes.

I'll enjoy it just as much as you enjoyed your hip replacement surgery, Kenneth.

PEOPLE WHO ARE WEIRDLY CURIOUS ABOUT YOUR SYMPTOMS

- *Any puking?*
- *Any dilation yet?*
- *Wow, look at you—you sure it's not twins?*

Pregnancy has this tendency to get pretty visible, especially toward the end, and some people seem to take your growing belly as an invitation to ask questions about your personal health they'd never dream of otherwise. Again, it can be from a place of good intentions . . . but that doesn't mean you're obligated to answer. Of course, if it's someone you're close with and don't mind sharing details, then there's no reason not to (provided you keep it PG). But if you'd rather not, you can brush them off a variety of ways, from polite to . . . less polite.

Can't complain! Taking it one day at a time!

Thanks for your concern, but if I need accommodations, I'll be sure to ask.

I'd prefer not to discuss my physical symptoms while I'm at work.

PEOPLE WHO ARE WAY TOO INVESTED IN
YOUR BIRTH/PARENTING PLANS

- *What's your birth plan?*
- *Make sure not to eat when you're in labor in case you need a C-section!*
- *I recommend an unmedicated homebirth. Epidurals are bad for you. Homebirth worked best for me and it's also best for your baby.*

These questions tend to skate closest to the edge of appropriate office talk, simply because childbirth and infant care by nature involve at least one body part usually covered by a swimsuit . . . and that's really not something you're likely going to want to discuss around the office Keurig.

You can always make an exception for your office bestie, but for the rest of the Curious Karens out there, the best move is honestly just to shut them down—quite firmly, if need be.

I'm not sharing that information publicly.
I don't discuss that with anyone besides my family/doctor.
That's personal.
That's a strange thing to ask. Or: *Why do you need to know?* (Then watch them sputter and flounder.)
I don't think that's appropriate for work.

Harmless or Harassment?

When does something cross the line, though?

Let's reimagine Daniela's holiday party. Say her boss had come over and made a remark to the effect of, "A three-month break right when the busy season starts? You sure planned that well!"

This one crosses the line. Why? Because anything referring to your absence as an inconvenience on the business can amount to gender harassment. So would any comments that play into gendered stereotypes about mothers not being committed, reliable, or dedicated. If you hear anything like the remarks below, start documenting ASAP.

- Back in March? We'll see about that. You know how moms always say they want to come back to work, but it's a different story when the baby's here . . .
- You're applying for the lead? That role requires a lot of dedication and commitment, you know. Won't you have a six-month-old baby by then?
- I'm putting Sandra on this big account since her kids are all grown.
- Well, your husband works, so you don't really have to worry about earning an income, do you?

The Baby Bubble

What to Expect When You're on Leave

fter my first baby was born, I wrote the following entry:

He's two weeks old today. Latching and healing and sitz baths and witch hazel pads. I'm so thirsty and tired and everything hurts but my heart is so full. I want to hold him all the time but I also need a moment to myself and alright I'll go take a minute . . . oh no he's hungry again!

We're out of breath and out of bread. Is he constipated or cluster feeding? There are so many fluids . . . The newborn stage is messy and humbling and totally consuming. It's work. But it's peace and bliss too.

You are up at night. I am tired. The nights are long. While the world snoozes through the dark winter pause, we are awake. I look outside at the darkness, with nothingness staring back at me. I walk around the room, rocking you. An eternity between the minutes. Tick . . . tick . . . tick . . . Time has never passed this slow. I feel both bored and overwhelmed.

And I'm overwhelmed with gratitude too. Because oh my goodness you're here! And you're here because I made you. While I was working, cooking, laughing, and crying. And now we rest into each other. You came from my warm belly and went straight to my warm arms and you haven't left. I don't know where I stop and you start.

I am his home. My body's embrace is the medicine. It's all he wants.

I have never been needed this much. It's 24/7 giving. His needs surpass what I can give, yet I do. I give, I give, I give. I go into the dried-up well of my patience and generosity, and I keep digging for more water. With every step, step, step, with every tick, tick, tick, my heart expands. Here baby, here's a little bit more love, here's a little bit more comfort, here's a little bit more milk. I did not know before, how much of myself I could give.

So I keep walking, rocking, comforting through the long nights. I envision our family when we are all older. Big family gatherings filled with joy and belonging. And I know that I will forget about the long nights, and that it will all be worth it.

A day will come when I will have all of my time and my body back, and maybe then, all I'll want . . . is one more long night holding you. My sweet son, I'll always be your home.

This is what I call the *baby bubble*—that wondrous, unique, unprecedented stretch of time after your child arrives, when your life shifts to a very specific focus and society gives you some space.

Any mom will tell you that it's hard to describe the shift into motherhood, that you have to *feel* it to understand it, but in this chapter, I'm going to try.

In the baby bubble, you might not be at work, but you still have work to do. The work is *hard*, too, but it's also simple: Keep your baby alive. You need to be on call for anything and everything the baby needs . . . but there are no performance reviews, no standing meetings, no set schedule at all. Nights become days. Time becomes stretched and infinite. There is one project and one project only: the repetitive and monotonous labor of tending to this new baby. The stakes are high, there is no handbook, but also: You have one job.

You see? Simple, but hard.

To many mothers, it is the hardest phase. To me, it was my favorite phase, precisely because of the baby bubble. Once your baby is no longer a newborn, the bubble bursts, and though your baby will still have intensive needs, the world will no longer cut you any slack.

It can be an incredible phase, a golden phase, a one-of-a-kind experience, and it's one we need to cherish. Yet too often, we don't.

It's surprising to many new moms how *strange* it feels to cut the cord (as it were) from work when they take their postpartum leave. Even if you've fought hard for your rights, are adamant about taking the time you need to recover and bond, you'll still likely feel that tug of *Wait, isn't there email I need to check?* Or maybe you might just want to share the joy and cuteness with everyone you know—including your colleagues—and find yourself hopping on to send around a photo, or even visiting the office to show off your bundle of joy.

The shift from your job to being on leave and taking care of a newborn can be so major: not just in terms of the physical changes to your body, and the arrival of a new family member, but in terms of your mental framework. Having strong boundaries with your employer, manager, and coworkers is important, but just as important is that mindset shift from being a go-getter at work to being a 24/7 caregiver (not to mention recovering from a major physical event).

That's why I invite you to embrace the baby bubble: not just because it's your legal right to take that time uninterrupted by the demands of work, but because it's simply a time unlike any other. Children only get more complicated as they grow—take it from the mom of a eight-year-old (from library visits to in-depth interrogations about animals, there's a lot of mental stimulation required) and a five-year-old (how dare you forget to use his blue cup!). Your job, with all its complex challenges and demands, will be there when you get back. The baby bubble, while not easy, is simpler. It's a focused project where you're primarily feeding, caring for, and monitoring this new human being.

In hindsight, I'm so grateful to (and impressed by!) my past self for writing down journal entries like that. The days themselves were such a blur, and the sharpest emotions that stick out in memory aren't always the most pleasant ones. Yet, as Past Daphne knew, even within the seeming chaos and upheaval of life with a newborn, there is genuine peace to be found. When we can truly disconnect from our work lives, embrace our role of mother-in-chief for the next few weeks or months, we move with grace into a new way of being.

You might feel uncomfortable as you enter the baby bubble, questioning if this is *really* all you're doing, if there isn't something more, something important, you're needed to do, but I'm here to reassure you: You don't need to take this time to learn new skills, accomplish major tasks, or stay in the loop. You don't need a handbook. In fact, the guidelines are written on your bones. In the baby bubble, it's truly okay to just sit there, take your time, and care for your child.

It may feel unproductive, but it's actually the most productive thing. There couldn't *be* a more important job. Welcome, new mother.

The Mom's Bill of Rights

When I was a few weeks postpartum, I experienced a strange feeling: I missed my baby. Even though . . . he was always on my body. But I missed living together in the same body. Always being together. And always having aligned needs.

Once the baby was there, my body was no longer his home. Instead, while I was still his primary home, other arms also became his home. My husband. My mother. Different caretakers. And now that he's older, it's school and friends.

And as his primary home, it was really hard to witness others tend to him differently or in a way I believed to be harmful.

My first birth was traumatic. I don't really remember much, honestly, other than a feeling of total powerlessness.

I was like an egg that had to be cracked for the little chickie to get out. And after he was out, I was shells on the floor. And yet, no one puts you back together, because there's a new little chickie!

I was so out of it after birth, from the drugs and the interventions, that I had a hard time breastfeeding. He just wouldn't latch. Ow. This was all wrong! Meaning, I was so used to achieving and accomplishing things if only I tried. And then motherhood came and said, "Oh, you think you have control. That's adorable!"

Suddenly, the most dominant factor in my life was my baby's temperament. Whether he wanted to come out of me (he didn't), whether he wanted to latch (he didn't), whether he wanted to sleep (he didn't). Turns out, you can read all the books you want, you can do affirmations and meditations, but you can't make anyone—including, and maybe especially, a baby—do something.

Suddenly, we were no longer aligned. Ouch.

While I was getting sewn up, I tried desperately to get him to latch to my breast. After all, I'd read all about that golden hour and the baby crawl and colostrum and how it would help shrink my uterus. Except . . . he just didn't latch. Point of no contact.

I didn't have that immediate wave of love because I was too drugged out. I didn't really feel anything. But that night, when everything was quiet, and I saw his little body and his beautiful face next to me, it came. I was overwhelmed with love. The love was so strong that I didn't just feel it; I became it. It was the strongest feeling I'd ever experienced. "Okay, baby, we can do this," and that night he latched and took in a few gulps. What a relief.

Then a nurse walked in, and he unlatched. The sweet moment ended. Lights went on.

She asked, "How many dirty diapers has he had?"

I had no idea. I wasn't mentally capable of counting anything. I probably didn't even know how old I was that day. So I said, "I don't know." And it concerned her.

And then the interference started. Donor milk. Formula. Syringes. Nipple shields. Breast pumps. It was so overwhelming. Nurses, lactation consultants, doctors walked in and out of the room and grabbed my boobs. It's so unbelievably weird. Suddenly, everything you learned about consent goes out the window. There's people all up in your vagina and basically honking your breasts.

All I could think was . . . I failed. I already failed. At birth. At breastfeeding. How is this possible? I am so used to being good at things.

And I felt like a failure all while being poked and prodded, while not being able to walk or sit, all while having flashes of the traumatic birth, all while applying witch hazel pads and numbing spray and sitting in a sitz bath trying to keep my stitches clean.

Birth had *broken* me, and I felt like I had failed it.

How sad, right? The cultural conditioning is so strong. There is such a perfectionism and performatism in motherhood, as if we rank births from best to worst: "unmedicated, calm, serene, meditative music, GOOD" to "medicated, industrial medical complex, beeping sounds, flashy lights, BAD!"

When truly there is no good or bad birth. There are as many expressions of birth as there are humans.

And.

You can't fail birth. For an event that is objectively not without risk to our health and lives, we are putting *way* too much pressure on ourselves and each other.

And yet . . . there are ways to have a more protective birth. Did you know you have birthing rights?

We are so focused on our birthing "plan" that we forget to bring the most important document to our birth: a list of your rights. Here it is, your Mom's Bill of Rights.

Keep these rights in your back pocket when you arrive to give birth. Take a screenshot or print it out and attach it to your birth plan. These are federal rights and apply to all patients in America, pursuant to 42 CFR § 482.13.

1. INFORMED DECISIONS: You have the right to refuse treatment even if a medical professional recommends it, and the right to request treatment.

2. INFORMATION: You have the right to be informed of your health status.

3. PARTICIPATION: You have the right to be involved in your plan of care, including development and implementation.

4. PRIVACY AND SAFETY: You have the right to a private and safe setting, free from abuse or harassment.

5. CONFIDENTIALITY: You have the right to confidentiality of your medical records.

6. ACCESS TO RECORDS: You have the right to access to your medical records, upon request.

7. NO ABUSE: You have the right to be free from physical or mental abuse and corporal punishment. You have the right to be free from restraint, which includes drugs or medications used to restrict your freedom of movement (as long as it is not a standard treatment or dosage for your condition).

8. VISITATION: You have the right to be informed of family visitation policies.

9. CHOSEN FAMILY: You have the right to receive visitors of your designation, including a spouse, domestic partner (including same-sex), another family member, or friend. You have the right to withdraw consent of a visit at any time.

10. NON-DISCRIMINATION: You and your visitors have the equal right access to visitation privileges, which may not be restricted based on race, color, national origin, religion, sex, gender identity, sexual orientation, or disability.

The Emotional Shift:
From Hustle to Nurture

Motherhood is a transformative, sacred experience that should be celebrated.

It's also, in many ways, a complete lack of control. And that can be terrifying.

Suddenly, you're thrust from a working world where duties are defined, roles are prescribed, and schedules are (more or less) honored, to one where you don't know what to do, you don't know how to do it, and you have to do it around the clock.

All that, and you're recovering from a major physiological event, one that might be the biggest and most disabling physical experience you've ever had. On top of *that*, if you're breastfeeding, you're relying on that healing, aching, *tired* body to be the food source for a tiny, ferociously hungry being who doesn't know how to eat any more than you know how to feed it.

The weekdays you used to spend tackling a to-do list, using your brain to crunch numbers or synthesize information or coordinate meetings, turn into boundless, shapeless stretches of time, with no real distinction between a Monday and a Saturday beyond what flashes on your phone screen.

This is normal. It's scary, but it's normal.

The fact is, taking care of yourself during your maternity leave isn't just about tending to your (and your baby's) physical needs. Nor is it just about doing what you can to maintain firm boundaries with your employer without risking getting shunted to the "mommy track." It's actually about reframing your mindset around productivity—about *doing things*—entirely. That reframe can be one of the hardest parts to prepare for, simply because it is so transformational (and because it's happening on broken sleep and a deluge of hormones) that there's almost no way to describe it accurately until you feel it, let alone give good advice for how to navigate it.

But I'm going to do my best. I want to guide you from hustle culture to nurture culture—and these are my best pieces of wisdom.

Leave the world of time: As a new mother, you're leaving the structured "world of time" that you're used to in your professional life. This transition can be difficult, especially because you can't really prepare for it in any meaningful way—one day you'll be pregnant, eating and sleeping and going about your life on a more or less regular schedule, and the next day (or a few days later), you'll have a baby in your arms. All that matters is to recognize—and radically accept—that your relationship with time is changing. You are no longer working a nine-to-five (or eight-to-seven, as many of us are used to). You're not really keeping *any* kind of regular schedule, and that can be disorienting even before sleep deprivation comes into the mix.

My advice is to shift your mindset from one of by-the-clock *schedules* to one of instinctual *rhythms.* You may not be able to set your watch by when your baby (or you!) will want their next meal, but you can anticipate that if it's been a few hours since anything's gone in that tummy, it might be time for a refill. Pay attention to their cues—those little hands rubbing eyes, a tiny pout, or extra squirming could mean it's time to eat, sleep, or cuddle. Trust that you'll learn their signals over time, even if it feels overwhelming in the beginning.

Granted, this sounds simple, but in practice it can be frustrating—especially because the *rest* of society, including even the most well-meaning of family and friends, is all still spinning around in the world of time. It's all well and good to follow the rhythms of your and your baby's needs . . . until your mother-in-law declares she's coming over for a visit at 10:00 a.m. sharp, or you have to get to a pediatrician appointment at 3:15. Just remember: Flexibility is your friend. Some days will run smoother than others, and that's okay. You're both figuring this out together, one day (and one snuggle) at a time. If others outside your baby bubble aren't getting the message, you can always gently remind them: "Baby Silas is so excited to meet you, but he's still mastering the art of managing his calendar! Can we set a tentative window for you to stop by, and I'll text you on the day of to let you know when exactly would be good?"

Also, remember that this intense period is temporary. It's okay to have a different relationship with time and productivity right now—things will eventually shift again. I know it's hard, verging on impossible, to believe that at 2:00 a.m. when your baby is wailing, your arms are aching from rocking her, and nothing will calm her down, but that will not be your life forever.

Let go of KPIs: New babies come with a surprising number of things to monitor, track, and even chart. From the first hours in the hospital when they announce the length and weight, to the inaugural pediatrician visit when you're instructed to track wet diapers, to ounces in the bottle, weighted feeds with a lactation consultant, and the endless, exhausting calculus of newborn sleep, you may feel the impulse to bust out a spreadsheet.

My advice, as a seasoned mom and your fellow recovering "yes girl," is try to resist that impulse—at least as much as you can. Obviously, some of these metrics are important to keep on top of: You do want to see that your baby is gaining weight in those first few days, for example, and staying hydrated by producing enough wet diapers.

After that, however? Short of doctor's orders, there's no need to obsess over numbers. Really.

Our achievement-oriented culture—especially at work—is driven by metrics, measurements, key performance indicators. But that mindset doesn't translate well to parenting. Babies don't have job descriptions or quarterly targets! They just need to *be*—and so do you.

Now, intellectually, you probably understand this. Yet so many moms (and dads) get pulled into these tracking routines, armed with all the latest apps and gadgets that can keep a record of everything from when the baby last pooped to how many minutes they spent in a "deep sleep" versus "light sleep." My theory is that, in doing all this tracking, we're trying to prove ourselves, and we're trying to establish control. Deep down, the logic we're operating on is something like, "I'm a good mom because my baby slept," which is a logical fallacy. The numbers we attach to our baby don't say anything about us as parents or even the baby as a baby. "Good" numbers (long stretches of sleep, a robust high-percentile weight) really just mean we're lucky, and "bad" numbers (zillions of night wake-ups, endless hours of cluster feeding) just mean . . . we have a baby, and it's babying.

The bottom line is that trying to control and measure everything about a baby's development can lead to unnecessary stress and anxiety. Again, if you truly *need* to measure something—because your doctor or lactation consultant or other professional has asked you to—then do. But beyond that, allow yourself to let go.

Lower your expectations. No, even lower than that: You've just spent several months reminding everyone in your working life (implicitly or explicitly) that maternity leave is *not a fucking vacation.* But in spite of that, you may still be harboring some notions of, you know . . . knocking out a few personal projects. Finally learning to knit. Picking your Duolingo streak back up. Going to postnatal yoga every week. Cooking from scratch. *Making use of your time.*

I'm not here to burst that bubble, but I will say that I thought many of those same things before I had my first baby, and so did plenty of my mom friends. Now we can only look back and laugh.

It's not that you *shouldn't* be using your leave to focus on things that matter to you. You absolutely should—rest, recover, and take care of the baby, absolutely, but also those small activities and rituals that give you back your sense of self. If doing your makeup or making a bougie latte every day makes you feel good, then by all means, go for it.

But you also should recognize that new mothers make plans and their newborns sabotage those plans. The same way you've left the world of time, you've also crossed over into a realm where your day-to-day energy, motivation, and mental bandwidth will be unpredictable, to say the least. Expecting that you'll be able (or willing) to do these kinds of things—even ones that are enjoyable, restorative, fun, enriching—during your leave is more than likely going to set yourself up for disappointment.

So I encourage you to take a step back and remind yourself that this is a time to embrace a new rhythm. If you're able to tackle a cross-stitch project or reorganize your pantry, then hell yes, girl, go for it. But if all you can manage is ordering DoorDash and scrolling through romantasy books on your phone during a contact nap, that's fine too. Really, it is. No one's going to show up in a few months and demand why you didn't "make better use" of this time. *It's not a fucking vacation.*

Beyond that, try to emphasize reflection and contemplation over achievement. Rather than knock out some of your long-standing personal development goals, use this time to rest and get to know this fresh human. The best plan is no plan.

Practice some radical acceptance: I wish I could say that you won't miss out on exciting opportunities while you're away from work on leave . . . but I'd be lying. I'd be misrepresenting my own career experience, even.

When I was on maternity leave, a particularly exciting case came to the law firm where I worked at the time—the kind of case I'd have jumped at the chance to work on. But since I was on leave, I wasn't there to do the initial intake or start-up work on it. I did end up contributing to the case somewhat, but it was never really *mine*.

To be clear, this wasn't an opportunity withheld from me in retaliation or anyone consciously "mommy-tracking" me. It was just crappy timing. The intake needed to be done ASAP, and I wasn't on hand.

Being away from the workplace—for any reason—means risking missing out on a big fish or a juicy project. And . . . yep, that sucks. Especially when your world has contracted to the four square walls of your house and the relentless cycle of change-feed-burp-play-sleep, it can feel devastating to know that your colleagues are out there, rolling up their sleeves and digging in like nothing has changed.

Instead, try to reframe those feelings with compassion—for yourself and the situation. Yes, you're missing out, but you're also gaining something irreplaceable: time to nurture your baby, recover, and recalibrate. While the work will move on without you for a while, your career isn't going anywhere in the long run. Projects come and go, but opportunities have a way of circling back when you're ready to engage again.

It's also worth remembering that taking this time isn't a weakness—it's an investment in yourself, your family, and your long-term ability to thrive in both your personal life and career. The work will still be there when you return, and you'll rejoin the fray with new insights, empathy, and resilience. In the meantime, trust the process: You can't be everywhere at once, but you are exactly where you need to be right now.

Embrace the new facet of your identity: Being away from work can be downright strange. Our culture puts work and workplace roles in the foreground: The second question after "What's your name?" is almost always "What do you do for a living?" after all. (I despise the framing of "What do you do for a living," as if "living" needs to be earned. Barf.)

Your job is important to your identity, yes, but it's a part of your identity that will shift. The workplace shifts, the economy shifts, our needs shift, and suddenly we've got something else on our business card. Me, I've been a trial lawyer, a Zumba teacher, a business owner, a law student, a library admin, a solopreneur—the list goes on. And yet we still attach so much weight to this inherently shifting identity, even when we don't even know if we'll care about this job in a few years. Maybe we'll want something more expansive, maybe we'll want a smaller role, maybe we'll up and quit and start our own business, maybe robots really *will* take over our industry and push us all out of work.

Embracing your identity as a mother is a way to untether yourself—and your sense of self—a bit from work. It's an ego death of sorts. You're not fully letting go of your ambitions, and you're not resigning yourself to being "just a mom" (even though parenting 100 percent of the time is the hardest job). You're simply recognizing that whatever your day job, whatever your role at work—it's not permanent.

Being a mother, however, is.

You can move through your career with "mother" as your primary identity—the one that is timeless—in a way that no other job ever can be. And that, my friend, is an extraordinary thing.

Do Not Disturb:
Rights and Boundaries While on Leave

When it comes to the question "Can my employer contact me while I'm on maternity leave?" the answer is going to be one of those classic lawyerly ones:

It depends.

Basically, we put workplace communication during leave under two key categories: rights and boundaries. Legally, if you're taking job-protected time off (such as FMLA or a state-level equivalent) there are limits they need to respect while you're on leave. Those are your *rights*: what the law says is, and isn't, okay.

But even if a quick message, update, or phone call doesn't break any laws, it can still be an overstep, creating unnecessary stress when you're meant to be focused on your recovery and your baby. These edge cases are more a matter of *boundaries*—what norms you establish (and uphold) for acceptable forms of contact (even if the only acceptable form is "none whatsoever, thank you").

Navigating this balance is about knowing what's allowed and also having the confidence to establish what feels reasonable. Just because an employer *can* text you for a password doesn't mean they should. Your time away is meant to be yours—both by law and by right of the new season you're stepping into as a mother.

RIGHTS

Under FMLA, a leave of absence is a leave of absence: You have *left* work (temporarily) and you cannot be asked to *do* work while you're absent. That is the law.

However, there are *some* exceptions. Your employer is allowed to contact you with certain requests known as *de minimis* (legalese for "basically doesn't count"). *De minimis* requests are small, low-effort asks from your employer—like forwarding a document they don't have access to, answering a quick question, or sharing a password—things that are, all told, minor and nondisruptive. Ideally, you've set up a coverage plan that foresees, and avoids, these kinds of requests by making it crystal clear where, for example, the quarterly budget spreadsheets are stored on the server, or who the point of contact is for each major client. But there might be the odd detail that slips through the cracks, so if the request is a quick one, and you're truly the only person with the answer, your employer is in the right to reach out.

Legally, these types of requests are generally allowed because they don't rise to the level of interfering with your maternity leave. Think of it this way: If a *de minimis* request is asking you for the key so someone else can unlock the storage closet, a non–*de minimis* request would be asking you to unlock the door yourself, walk inside, and start reorganizing all the Post-its. In other words, it crosses the line when the ask requires you to actively engage in the work, forcing you to invest time, energy, or decision-making that pulls you back into the flow of your job. The key (pun intended!) distinction is that a *de minimis* request leaves the heavy lifting to others, while anything beyond that shifts responsibility back to you, thereby interrupting your leave.

If you do find yourself with requests that ask you to do work while on leave—either up front, or on a more slippery slope level starting with an acceptable ask and falling downhill toward actual work—you can remind your colleague (or boss) that you're on leave and not actually working.

For example, say you're contacted about where to find a particular client proposal on the server, you respond with its location, and your manager responds by asking you to give it a quick once-over for some feedback before it goes out. You can write back something like this:

> Hi [Boss],
>
> Glad you were able to locate the proposal. I'm not engaging in any work while on my maternity leave, so you can reach out to [Backup Person], who I've cc'd here and who will be handling tasks like this while I am on leave (as outlined in my coverage plan), for feedback.
>
> I'll let you two take it from here, as I will not be available to check emails regularly.
>
> I look forward to reconnecting on my return.
>
> Best,
> [Your Name]

Outside of strictly *de minimis* requests, there are a few other reasons your employer could contact you and (probably) be legally in the clear. For example, if your boss wants to reach out to discuss a promotion or encourage you to apply for an internal opening, they're probably legally clear to do so: There isn't a real material benefit to the employer (i.e., they're not getting "free" labor out of you) and you don't *have* to take any action if you don't want to (the exception being if applying requires you to attend interviews or take tests that interfere with your leave). Or if you are a witness to an urgent safety issue and your employer needs you to participate in a workplace investigation, they arguably *could* require you to come into work to do so . . . but they should really exhaust all other options (like a phone call or a written testimony) first.

Finally, your employer can be in touch to coordinate on the details of your return to work (because it'd be a bit absurd for you to just show back up one day, ready to dive back in) but those discussions should be limited as much as possible to logistical details and not doing actual work.

BOUNDARIES

The law can protect your right to time off, but it can't guarantee that others will respect the spirit of that leave—or exercise common sense. It also doesn't account for the subtle, unspoken pressures that come with workplace culture: the "not exactly required, but definitely expected" social obligations that can make it hard to say no. (After all, work isn't just a place where we mindlessly execute tasks in silos—it's a social place too.)

For those, we need boundaries. At least, I definitely did.

Somehow, despite still bleeding and exhausted, I found myself dressed up and ready to go at just five days postpartum. I'd put on real clothes, brushed my hair, and made it out into the real world. Cradling my baby in the office break room, I smiled and made mindless small talk with the host of curious onlookers, repeating the same short answers to the same stupid questions.

Yet all I could think was, *I got out of bed for this?*

We were visiting my husband's office, a workplace where—like many—there was this cultural practice of showing up at work with your newborn in the first week or so and, basically, showing them off. I didn't begrudge his colleagues their congratulations, or excitement—I *also* thought my son was the cutest thing I'd ever seen—but it felt like I'd barely had a chance to cut my hospital bracelet off before I was making this command performance. There were unfiltered questions about the birth—which had been traumatic—and older parents telling me their birth and baby stories unsolicited.

The greetings and well-wishes wore on. My son started to fuss. My breasts started to ache—my *everything* started to ache, honestly. I don't know how long we'd been there at that point, but I remember in particular one of his colleagues who arrived toward the end. This guy showed up eating a messy meatball sub, wiping his fingers on his pants, and then suddenly grabbed the baby—*my* baby, who was tiny and scared and hadn't received any shots yet. That was it—our cue to go home. I cried on the way back home, feeling fragile and disoriented. *Why the hell did I do that?* I felt terrible.

All in all, that seemingly innocent check-in with the workplace was overwhelming. And for what? All I got out of it was more stress, and I certainly don't think my baby enjoyed the experience. And yet, a few days later we did another baby tour, this time at my office. I was a mess and yet I smiled, one of the first smiles at work that would mask my real experience of motherhood.

It's natural, even thoughtful, for your coworkers and work contacts to want to hear how you're doing once the baby arrives. They're excited for you, or eager to hear you're happy and healthy, or maybe a little bit nosy. Technically—legally—there's nothing that says they can't text, call, or send a fruit basket. But just because something is allowed doesn't mean it's, well, not annoying.

And even though these kinds of visits or "how are you feeling?" messages aren't *work tasks*, per se, there is still a kind of nebulous career-related pressure to respond to them: We don't want to seem standoffish, rude, like we're not a team player, even though our new baby has absolutely 0 percent to do with our job description.

So what do you do?

Well, for starters, I'd say skip the office visit. Skip *any* kind of in-person visiting you don't want to do. If a firm "no" is too hard to deliver, you can fob the blame off on your pediatrician ("Baby's doctor doesn't want her out and about for a while—we'll let you know when it's time!").

Beyond that, decide in advance how you're going to answer certain questions and stick to your script. Make it almost automatic. Yes, this might mean simplifying, glossing over, or omitting gory details—that's fine. Your coworkers aren't actually reaching out because they want a blow-by-blow or an in-depth answer; they just want to express that they're thinking about you and have that care acknowledged.

An easy way to get ahead of this is to have a premade "the baby is here!" email announcement drafted. Once your newborn makes landfall, just fill in the blanks with the details (or hand your phone to your partner) and send it office-wide. In that email, you'll also state (politely!) that you won't be answering individual texts or calls.

> Hi Everyone,
>
> We're thrilled to share that [Baby's Name] arrived on [Birth Date] at [Time]. Both baby and I are doing well, and we're excited to start this new chapter together.
>
> As I'm officially on maternity leave, I won't be available to respond to individual calls, texts, or emails during this time, but trust that I appreciate all your well-wishes from afar! If you have any work-related questions or needs, please reach out to [Backup Contact] at [Backup's Email and Phone]. I look forward to catching up with everyone when I return.
>
> Warmly,
> [Your Name]

Optional, but often appreciated, is to include a photo (of you and the baby, or just the baby—with everyone clothed, please!), but you do not have to share that if you're not comfortable doing so. In fact, these baby photos have come up in our cases when a company tries to prove they are family-friendly (Yes, there is a "the moms love us" category of evidence). So think twice before hitting that send button, because you may be giving your company ammo to use your baby's face as the poster child of their PR campaign.

Things get a bit more complicated if you experience any kind of medical issue—not just for your and your baby's recovery, but because people are that much more likely to want to pry into your business. In that case, you can send something like this:

> Hi Everyone,
>
> I'm happy to share that [Baby's Name] arrived on [Birth Date]. Unfortunately, we've had some unexpected medical complications, and both the baby and I are focusing on rest and recovery right now. For those wondering, the prognosis is positive—we just need space to focus on healing and adjusting.
>
> Because of this, I'll be fully offline during my leave and won't be available to respond to messages or calls. Please know that I still value all your kind thoughts and well-wishes. If you have work-related needs, please contact [Backup Contact] at [Backup's Email and Phone].
>
> I appreciate your understanding and support during this time— we'll be in touch when we're ready to share more.
>
> Best,
>
> [Your Name]

Sometimes, however, the issue with unplugging from work isn't a demanding boss or a nosy coworker weaseling their way into our maternity leave. Sometimes, the issue is . . . ourselves.

You might *know* that maternity leave is a precious, fleeting time to bond with your baby, rest, and recover—not a time to be haunted by work emails or Slack notifications—but when you've poured so much into your career, really and truly unplugging can *feel* impossible, to the point of being anxiety-inducing. Even if you've done an amazing job of prepping for leave and setting your coworkers up for success in your absence, the FOMO (especially through the lens of postpartum hormones and sleep deprivation) can drive you to "just check in" with your workplace. Before you know it, you're answering emails, offering feedback on projects, and fully self-sabotaging.

The best offense here is a good defense. Protect your future mother self by setting up boundaries with yourself and creating systems that put a firm, unshakable wall between you and work. Here are some ideas.

Delete Work Apps from Your Phone: Yes, it might feel a little scary, but trust me—delete those apps. No Slack, no Asana, no email notifications buzzing in your pocket just as you're rocking your baby to sleep. You can reinstall them later when you're ready to ease back in, but for now, they're only a temptation to peek (and stress). And for the love of God, no smart watches. Just remove anything in your vision that can distract you and pull you into work stuff.

Set Up a "Gatekeeper" System for Work Calls: If you're worried about emergencies, set up notification filters on your phone so that only select high-priority work contacts can get through—and only the ones you trust to contact you if it is an absolutely urgent, fire-drill level emergency.

Craft Your Out-of-Office Message Thoughtfully: A well-crafted out-of-office message can set boundaries while reinforcing your professionalism. It can look something like this:

> Thank you for reaching out. I am currently on maternity leave with an expected return date of [Return Date]. During this time, I will not have access to emails. For urgent matters, please contact [Backup Contact]. I look forward to reconnecting when I return.

This sets expectations—no ambiguous "checking emails occasionally" or "please only email me when it's an urgent matter" promises that make it easy for people to sneak through your boundaries.

Put Work Devices in Another Room: Out of sight, out of mind, right? If you have a dedicated work laptop or phone, tuck it away in a drawer or closet—or just leave it at the office. Seeing it can create mental clutter, or trigger a guilt trip, making it hard to fully unplug.

Practice Saying No (Even to Yourself): You'll likely feel the pull to "just check in" more than once. When we're so used to facing every morning with all those red notification badges, it's totally normal to be itching to clear them. Come up with a mini game plan ahead of time for what you'll do when the urge strikes. For example, "When I feel the need to check my work email, I'll get up and change my surroundings for a quick reset," or "I'll text my BFF the latest milk-drunk baby pic to feel connected with the outside world," or "I'll listen to a podcast to keep my brain engaged."

Go Nuclear: Yes—you can outsource self-control! If you've read *The Odyssey*, you might remember how Odysseus, wanting to hear the singing of the Sirens—whose music drove men to madness and jumping to their deaths—ordered his men to tie him to the mast of the ship, stuff their ears with wax, and absolutely, under no circumstances, cut him down, no matter how much he begged. Well, you can do the same thing—sort of. If you really don't think you'll be able to resist temptation, ask your partner (or a trusted friend) to (temporarily) change the passwords to your work devices or accounts, with a promise to let you back in when your leave is actually up.

Learn to Ride the Waves

When my oldest son, my first baby, was a newborn, I was completely overwhelmed by the explosive love I felt for him—it was as if he were the only thing that mattered, the only thing I could think about. I fell *so hard* for that baby. I couldn't breathe, I loved him so much. I wanted to be with him every second of the day and found myself daydreaming about quitting my job just to stay with him.

I knew that wasn't a practical or helpful thought, but I couldn't shake it. The idea of being away from him made me feel restless and empty. Just a few weeks earlier, I had felt ready to go back to work—but *now*? Now nothing seemed to matter: not my career, not my friends, not even my husband. The only thing that mattered was this tiny person I was holding.

I had thought I knew what love was—with partners, pets, family—but this was something else entirely. It was raw, primal, and consuming, and I couldn't remember what my old life had felt like. My own needs became irrelevant. Hours would go by before I'd realize I hadn't eaten or even sipped water. This love was both a gift and a curse.

Those early days, just the two of us, were some of the sweetest moments of my life. There was a quiet, easy happiness to our time together that I knew I would miss once it ended. We weren't lonely—far from it. My heart felt full in a way it never had before. Life slowed down to a peaceful rhythm of feeding, holding, and simply being. I wasn't rushing, thinking, or planning; I was just there, in my body, with my baby, and it felt like the sweet simplicity and presence I had been craving for years.

But with that peace came a creeping thought: *Could I do this full-time?* The idea of leaving him overwhelmed me. He needed me—I was the only one who could truly soothe him—and our love felt intoxicating. It was the most flattering feeling I'd ever experienced. He didn't care how I looked, what I did, if my Instagram post was too controversial, or who I voted for. All he wanted was me, just as I was. I knew I was lucky to have a supportive work environment awaiting me back at my job, even the option to bring him to work.

But how feasible was that, really? The idea of sitting through dull depositions while I could be holding my baby felt unbearable.

And yet, what other option was there? Could I give my all to both work and motherhood without feeling like I was failing at both?

I knew these feelings were normal, but I couldn't tell if they would pass or if they would stay with me forever. Thinking about our quiet days ending, about being away from him for full, long workdays, broke my heart. I'd have only a rushed hour with him in the morning, and then some time at night when he was at his most cranky. I'd miss his happy window. It felt nonsensical and unnatural.

Suddenly, the things I had cared about—money, prestige, accolades—felt meaningless. I had worked so hard for so long; couldn't I just ride it out now? Did I really need to work? Hadn't I already achieved enough? Maybe the best thing I could do with my time was to "just" be a mom. These feelings *shocked* me, because let me tell you: I am not really a domestic kinda gal. But it's not that I wanted to be a domestic housewife. I wanted to be a feral animal mother, roaming the wilderness with her cub. Motherhood had awakened the primal wildness in me, and I couldn't get enough.

Looking back, I wish I'd had more guidance through those intense feelings. I, of all people, never expected to want to quit my job, but in that moment, it felt so *right*, so urgent. Early motherhood is full of wild emotional swings, and part of surviving it is learning to ride those waves.

In hindsight, I'm really glad I didn't quit. I'm glad I didn't make any decisions of that magnitude at that moment, or in the few weeks that followed, either. What I did that day was remind myself: *Daphne, you always figure things out. Trust that you'll do so again.*

So that is my advice to you, too, new mother. Float. Gently tread water. Do what you can to keep your head up. Trust that the tide will ebb, and when it does, you will know what to do. If you feel like quitting, wait. If you feel like you can't breathe, can't think straight, can't take it a minute longer, or can't bear to ever do anything different with your life, wait. And then wait some more. Don't make a decision until that feeling is the only wave you're riding—for many weeks, or even months.

Until then, just ride those waves.

8

Childcare

Finding Your Chosen Village

When I decided to have children, I was fortunate enough to be in a position to hire a nanny. In many ways, having an individual dedicated solely to watch my kids and my kids only made things a lot easier for me, no question.

But hiring a nanny wasn't without its struggles. For one thing, a nanny is an employee. They are someone you are obligated to hire with legal paperwork, prepare tax withholding for, and offer specific amounts of paid time off and sick leave. Too many people think of childcare as an "under the table" job, a side gig, something a college student or retired person can do casually for extra cash.

But that's not the reality, that's certainly not the *law*, and that's generally just not fair. Devaluing childcare work inevitably shortchanges women of color, low-income women, and other people on the margins. It also means we are complicit in relegating caretaking to the shadows, as a type of work that is "not a real job." Moreover, if you're demanding *your* boss hold up their legal end of the bargain by giving you your full legal rights to leave, pumping time, and so on, you can't ethically turn around and attempt to deprive someone *else* of their workers' rights.

Granted, as someone who knows much more than your average mom about employment law thanks to my line of work, I was somewhat ahead of the game on this front. But the other thing I failed to realize about finding a good nanny is just how hard it is to, well, find a good one.

There was the nanny who took my credit card and ran up thousands of dollars at Hobby Lobby buying "craft projects." The nanny who put my sick toddler in her car because her boyfriend was stuck at a gas station and needed money. My child threw up in her car, and she just kept driving. Or the nanny who tried to bring my tiny baby along on her *other* gig as a dog walker. Or the nanny who straight up *stole my husband's (new, electric) bike*, never came back to work, and ghosted our many attempts to get in touch with her. I'm often surprised when mothers express that they believe daycare is "unsafe," because my experience with nannies involved a series of terrifying situations. After all, we can screen them, but in the end, we don't really know them when we start out the relationship, and just like in dating or recruiting, some candidates present really well. There's this false narrative that daycare is risky and unsafe, and I really disagree with that. In my experience, going for a more institutional space, with more rules and regulations, is the safest route. However, I never made it off any waiting lists, and the hours just did not work for my erratic schedule.

Eventually, we ended up with a nanny we love and trust, who's wonderful with our kids, but getting there wasn't without its bumps along the way. The process to get to where we are more often than not left me straight-up shocked: How could someone do that? It's going to cost *how* much? I needed to be on a waitlist *how* many months ago?

In that, I'm not alone. In my online community, in the comments of my Instagram posts, in the conversations I have with moms across all sectors and careers, the number 1 emotion I see associated with childcare is *shock*.

Shock at how much it costs. (A lot. As in, potentially as much as your take-home pay.)

Shock at how *early* you need to reserve a space or find a provider. (Very early. As in, around your twenty-week anatomy scan, if not before, depending on where you live.)

Shock at the legal requirements for hiring a nanny and surprise at the legal restrictions on things like daycare capacity. (Yes, you have to pay payroll taxes on their income, and no, you can't just pay "under the table.")

And most of all, shock that you can be fired simply for failing to have reliable childcare. In fact, I'd say that childcare—or lack thereof—is the number 1 reason my clients lose their jobs. And unfortunately, when that happens, there's no legal case. "Mom without reliable childcare" isn't a protected class the way "lactating mother" or "parent who's taken FMLA" is.

Luckily, preparation and education can save you a lot of the shock (sticker and otherwise) that comes with childcare. In this chapter, I'll lay out everything you need to know about finding the right caretaker for your baby. With the right tools, you won't have to end up scrambling, on work probation, or with a bike missing out of your garage, and can actually get back to doing your job.

Childcare Sticker Shock and Mom Guilt: A Match Made in Hell

Melissa, an accounts manager in her mid-thirties, was having a phone chat with her father, catching up about—of course—her kids. The conversation eventually turned to how her oldest son would soon be starting kindergarten, and how excited (and nervous) everyone in the family was for the big transition.

"At least we'll be saving on daycare," Melissa joked. "So that's a little bonus."

"No kidding," her dad said. "An extra $500 a month to burn! I hope you treat yourself to something nice."

Melissa couldn't help but laugh. Because surely he was joking, right? She asked as much, and it quickly became clear he wasn't.

"Dad," she explained, "we pay about $1,800 a month for daycare. That's over $22,000 a year—and that's not even including the extra fees for supplies."

It's easy to underestimate the financial burden that childcare represents for modern families. Like Melissa's dad (who, in his defense, raised his own kids in the 1980s), you might think you have a sense of what's reasonable—until you see the actual numbers.

During my most intense mommying-while-litigating years, I paid around $7,000 per month in childcare, a combination of a double preschool bill for two kids, as well as a nanny for all those school breaks and awkward in-between hours (school ended at 3:00 p.m., but my workday did not). This is a result of having no family support where we lived, living in one of the most expensive cities in the world (where preschools cost more than a college degree), and managing a law firm.

"Yes girl" or no, there's one reality that can catch even the most prepared among us by shock: the true cost of childcare. It's easy to assume that daycare or a nanny will be a manageable part of the family budget, but the numbers can be staggering. In fact, a recent research project found that nearly half of American parents are spending up to $18,000 a year on childcare, with 20 percent paying more than $36,000 annually, and to me, these numbers seem low based on the conversations I've had. Meanwhile, the average cost for a year of tuition, fees, and room and board at a public, in-state university for the 2023–24 school year was just over $24,000.

In other words, it's entirely possible you'll be spending more on preschool for your toddler than you would for a college education. That kind of sticker shock is enough to give any new parent pause.

That's why it's essential to be realistic about how childcare costs will factor into your budget. American parents spend, on average, about 24 percent of their household income on childcare costs. It's not something you can really scrimp and save for by cutting out your daily avocado toast (lol) and yet it's something that, compared to saving for college, doesn't often strike a lot of first-time moms as a major cost to be budgeted for.

And when it does, your reaction might be something like Melissa's dad's: "That's baloney!"

I get it. It's easy to feel overwhelmed when you see the numbers. You might expect to spend $36,000 for a down payment, but not on daycare.

But here's the thing: High-quality childcare *should* cost that much.

Think about it this way: In the best infant care programs, the ideal child-to-teacher ratio is 1:3. If each family pays $2,500 a month for daycare, that adds up to $7,500 per month per teacher.

To retain qualified, skilled childcare providers, daycare centers need to pay them well—at least $50,000 a year, ideally with employer-paid benefits. (And that's a bare, bare minimum, especially in a high-cost-of-living area.)

And true: If you do the math, that salary and benefits package is well under that total "per-teacher" take.

Except that $2,500 per month, per baby, doesn't just go directly to the teacher. A good chunk of it supports the other workers who make the daycare function—think about the cleaners, administrators, and assistants who keep the place running smoothly. And then there's the overhead costs of the facilities: rent, utilities, insurance, food, toys, safety equipment, and everything else it takes to keep a secure, nurturing environment for your child. (Plus, if it's a for-profit center, there's that all-important profit margin to consider.)

When you start adding it up, it makes sense. The price is high because it should be high. Your money is going toward ensuring your child is cared for by trained professionals in a safe, well-equipped space. In fact, if day-cares were not charging this much, you might start to worry about whether the staff are being paid fairly or if corners are being cut somewhere.

My son went to a "cheap" preschool once, and they often watched YouTube videos on a teacher's phone (something he was not allowed to do at home), and we once ended up in the ER due to a lack of safety measures and a lack of supervision (a result of understaffing, too much staff turnover, and old equipment).

The issue isn't that childcare is too expensive. It's that families are unfairly expected to bear the full financial burden on their own. I believe childcare should be funded through public investments, but we are not there yet.

In fact, when I speak to my mom friends in Belgium, they can't fathom how American parents pay so much in childcare. After all, they pay about €100 per month for daycare, and summer camps are €40 per week and are ubiquitous and on a "come-as-you-need" basis. Yet before we start to idolize these systems too much (which Americans tend to do), keep in mind that the folks in charge of the kids during these summer camps are usually sixteen-year-old high school kids. There is no nanny or private education culture, so the only option is public daycares. Many places are filled up, so you just have to accept whatever provider has open spots in your vicinity. In populated areas, daycare teachers are in charge of nine babies at a time. Belgian preschool teachers are in charge of up to thirty toddlers at a time. Generally, school curriculum and policy is harmonized nationwide, so there is little room for differentiation. While it is equitable and accessible, it is limiting in a different way. In contrast, Americans have a wide buffet of options and pedagogies that do not exist elsewhere. While I missed my ancestral lands when I was a new mother, I was also happy to have access to some of the childcare options available in the United States, however expensive they were. So I believe there is a happy medium.

And while I wish for (and actively work for, through the Chamber of Mothers) change on that front, if you're having a baby in the next few years, the possibility of governmental action in two years (that takes effect five years later) isn't really going to help.

So this is the reality: How do you navigate it?

One of the toughest mental hurdles for working moms is coming to terms with the cost of childcare—especially when you realize that, in some cases, it could eat up nearly 100 percent of your salary.

At first glance, it can seem as if you're working just to pay for someone else to snuggle your baby. Which is hella depressing. That, plus the absolutely astronomical costs that you can see at the bottom of those brochures, can be enough to trigger one of the most insidious yet powerful forces of modern life: Mom Guilt. (In case you have yet to experience it, Mom Guilt is that omnipresent sense that, no matter what you're doing, you're either doing the wrong thing, or the right thing the wrong way, and you should feel bad about it.)

This tug-of-war is as exhausting as it is unsustainable—but, fortunately, it's also avoidable. Before you even start sketching out your plans for childcare, I highly, *highly* encourage you to do some mental reframing around this decision.

You're not the only one footing the bill. I constantly hear moms—married moms, whose spouses *also work*—saying, "I don't even see the point in working sometimes, considering my whole paycheck goes to daycare."

Um, why is it *your* paycheck that "goes to daycare"?

Daycare (or a nanny, or any paid childcare arrangement) allows *both* parents to work and bring in an income. So if you're part of a dual-income household, it's important to consider your overall family income against the cost of childcare, and not just yours as the birthing parent. If you are still netting a positive figure after daycare costs, collectively, then you're doing great.

You're investing in your future. Beyond just covering bills, childcare allows you to stay in the workforce, and that ensures that your career—and by extension, your earning potential—continues to grow.

Think of this phase as an investment. Childcare costs won't last forever; as your children grow, they'll need less full-time care, and eventually, they'll enter school, significantly lowering those expenses. By staying in the workforce now, you're maintaining your career trajectory, which positions you for future promotions, raises, and job opportunities. Stepping away from work entirely, even for a few years, can make it harder to reenter your field at the same level. (And, equally critically, you're continuing to build retirement savings, contribute to Social Security, and possibly even profit from employer-sponsored benefits like healthcare, which are long-term financial assets.)

You're providing for your family. Additionally, staying in the workforce can provide a financial cushion for your family. Life can be unpredictable (and layoffs are unfortunately part of life these days). Maintaining two incomes means greater security if one spouse loses a job or becomes unable to work. By staying in your career, you're helping protect your family's future from potential economic instability.

You're providing your child with a natural village experience. Yes, I said it. Staying home with kids is not more "natural" than going to work. One of the lies told to mothers is that it's in the children's best interest to be with them and only them each day, every day. They tell us this is "natural" and "a good mother would . . ." Let me tell you: A mother alone in a house with children—with no support or interaction with others—is *not* natural. Humans have always lived in villages and children have always been raised in a communal setting, tended to by big groups of adults. Schools/educators/nannies are modern-day villagers. Children benefit from being held by a wide ecosystem and being exposed to different adults. What the parents know and can teach is limited. Children need more than their parents. And mothers have always worked in and outside of the home! You are re-villaging. You are providing your child with access to other adults for them to get to know, learn from, and bond with. This is not a new way of raising kids. This is actually the traditional, old-fashioned way of raising kids. A mother alone all day without support, that is actually the unprecedented model.

You're embracing your full self. So many moms, when going back to work, express a sense of guilt that they're actually *relieved*—to get a break from the incessant needs of their babies, to use their "grown-up brains" for complex tasks, to just be back in the regular world where they're not constantly in the monotony of the diapers, feedings, naps, cries, repeat cycle.

That relief is *fine*. It's *good*, even. And I encourage it.

What children need most is a happy mother, and what real feminism is all about is protecting the mother's choice and agency in setting the terms of her own life and happiness. Whether that is working, or staying at home, or a mix—as long as it works for her, it works for her kids. A child is better off for a few hours with a well-trained and loving professional who is devoted to the art of caretaking than a whole day with a grumpy, overwhelmed mommy who would rather be doing something else. A child can feel when the parent feels unsatisfied or when its needs are too much. That's okay. You don't have to love motherhood 100 percent of the time, and certainly not this version of motherhood—without the proper support and community. As a professional, you've likely built years of experience, skills, and networks, all of which contribute to your sense of identity and fulfillment. Leaving the workforce entirely, even for a short period, can feel like hitting pause on that part of your life, and the mundanity of day-in, day-out infant care can be genuinely crazy-making. For many women, continuing to work—even when childcare costs are high—is actually a lifeline to sanity. Work keeps them engaged with their passions, connected to their professional communities, and allows them to continue developing their skills. There were days that the boredom of early motherhood really got to me. After all, that baby is not a great conversationalist. For me, I can be a good mom only when I can be my full self. It's actually when I get no reprieve from momming that I am not showing up well in my motherhood. It can be good to actually miss these babies so we can be super present and devoted when we're with them.

A sense of purpose and sovereignty can be just as valuable as the paycheck itself.

You don't have to go all-or-nothing. There have never been more options and opportunities for moms to make money while still getting to spend time with their kids (and no, I'm not talking about joining some multi-level marketing scam). So, for starters, working part-time and paying for part-time childcare might be an option. So is using the time after having your baby to step away from a "traditional" job, do some gig work while raising your kids, and reentering at the same level later on. There's a lot of unnecessary fear around taking a career break, but sometimes these mini sabbaticals, or reflows of energy into different priorities, are exactly what's needed. If you're spending your time and money to achieve the balance *you* want and that makes sense for *your* family, then you are a role model. Speaking of which . . .

You're a role model. Let's not forget the power of representation for your children. If you go back to work in any capacity, you're showing your kids (both sons *and* daughters) that mommies, as well as daddies, can be successful professionals, contributors to the household, and loving, present parents. But the same is true for taking a sabbatical while raising your children: You're showing your kids what it means to have real values and live by them and embodying what the *choice* aspect of feminism means firsthand.

So, while the sticker shock of childcare costs is real, and the Mom Guilt can be strong, try to see your situation through the lens of the bigger picture. Any childcare you do pay for is ultimately a temporary cost in exchange for the long-term financial stability, professional fulfillment, and sense of self that continuing to work will provide. And any energy you put toward supporting your family's future—at work, on a career sabbatical, in a new professional direction or form—makes you a positive role model for your kids.

What If You Just Work Without Childcare?

Many parents believe they can work while they tend to a baby at the same time—especially if they primarily work from home. This may be something you believe is possible when you are still pregnant, and you assume babies sleep a lot or just lie there.

I was one of those women, and I tried, really hard, to work while tending to a baby at the same time. When I returned to work, I decided to get childcare for only four out of five workdays. This plan did not last very long.

Because it's so unbelievably hard to do both.

It sounds nice, in theory, to work with a baby. But, speaking personally, it completely took me out of my mom game. I was constantly checking my phone. I wasn't present with him. And I hated the version of myself on those days. He watched TV a lot. We weren't getting any kind of quality time. It was supposed to be a day where I could just be present with him, but when you're on the clock, you're always pulled toward work.

Or maybe you think you can work while the baby naps—not unreasonable, but again, only in theory. For me, my biggest stressor on baby-plus-work days was when he didn't nap. One day, he didn't nap at noon as planned, so he was in the crib while I tried to work, which was incredibly frustrating. Eventually, I caved and just hung out with him in the crib (thinking the whole time, *Why won't you sleep?*), and after that, we went for a walk, and he *finally* napped—three hours after his usual nap time. Other days, I remember bouncing with him in the carrier in my office or marching around the block, and he still wouldn't fall asleep. I spent hours in pure agony trying to get him to sleep so I could get some work done. That's something I learned—I could create an environment for sleep, but he could still decide not to. When I had to rush through a work project, and he just wouldn't sleep, I had to put him in the crib while he cried for me. My body ached—screaming and begging me to go to my baby—while I typed aggressively to get the project done.

The moral of this story is that, in theory, if everything is perfect and goes according to plan, you could, maybe, work some days without childcare and have your baby at home. But the reality is that things rarely go according to plan with a baby. Naps don't happen on schedule, or at all. Deadlines come up just when your little one needs you most. And the emotional tug-of-war between being a present parent and a productive professional is exhausting. I learned that trying to do both without help left me feeling like I wasn't giving my best to either.

The truth is, having some kind of reliable childcare is essential. It gives you the freedom to focus fully on work during work time and to be truly present with your baby when it's their time. Whether it's a nanny, daycare, or even a friend, neighborhood kid, or relative helping out, having a system in place to support you takes so much weight off your shoulders. You'll be able to work with less guilt and stress, knowing your baby is well cared for—and when you're off the clock, you can fully enjoy those precious moments together.

There may be days when your childcare plan falls through and you still need to work. Here are my best "work-with-baby" hacks:

- A regular desk with a yoga ball seat for bouncing (alternatively, a standing desk for wearing the baby in a carrier).

- Headphones so you can dictate your work as much as possible and prevent typing (there is great dictation software you can find online).
- Take calls while you go for a walk with the baby.
- Once your baby can sit on your lap, put up two windows on your screen, one for your work, and one for cartoons.
- Find an old keyboard for your little one to slap while you're typing away.

Childcare Options: Choosing Your Village

Mercedes—a soon-to-be mom and healthcare aide—was torn about what to do. Already in her second trimester, she knew she was going back to work at twelve weeks postpartum: She loved her job and knew that being back at work was going to be critical for her mental health. But she also knew that daycare would break her heart. She couldn't bear the idea of "strangers" raising her daughter when she was that small.

At first, Mercedes figured she'd just hire a nanny. But in her high-cost-of-living area, the cost of full-time care from a nanny was astronomical. She started crunching the numbers and thought about cutting back to just a few hours of nanny help each day, dipping into her savings to cover the gap. She even considered not going back to work at all, even though the thought made her heart sink.

Then, something unexpected happened. She received a call from a day-care center she had her eye on for when her daughter was older: An infant spot would be open earlier than planned because a family was moving out of the area. Would Mercedes be interested in a tour?

"I went to visit when I was hugely pregnant," Mercedes recalled, "and I must have looked exhausted, because they let me sit in one of their gliders as soon as I got in. I chatted with the teachers as they held the babies and I just felt so welcomed. Suddenly I couldn't see taking her anywhere else."

Just like that, Mercedes became a daycare convert. "It's so true what they say that the teachers are only strangers the first day," she said. "They're amazing with my daughter. She's thriving there. I never have to worry about whether they'll be open or available, and I don't have to do payroll myself or be someone's boss. I absolutely love daycare now."

There's an unfortunate bad rap around center-based daycare. Some combination of cultural Mom Guilt ("I could never leave my baby with strangers!") and new-parent anxiety ("There are so many babies there! How will I know she's safe?") has led many of us to believe that daycare is basically baby jail. But, as Mercedes's story shows, the *right* daycare is more than just a solution to a problem—it can be a real gift.

DAYCARE

Daycare—a dedicated facility where professional, trained, and licensed caregivers watch a group of children—has a number of pros that might make it work for you.

Structured environment: Daycare centers are known for their routines and structure, which can be incredibly beneficial for children. They follow set schedules for meals, naps, and activities, which helps kids develop a sense of routine and stability.

Socialization: One of the biggest perks of daycare is the social aspect, especially once your baby gets older. Your child will be surrounded by other kids their age, giving them the opportunity to develop social skills, learn to share, and interact in group settings—all of which are important for their emotional and cognitive development.

Educational activities: Many daycare centers offer educational programming—yes, even for infants. Age-appropriate learning activities, like arts and crafts, music, and physical play, give your baby new experiences they wouldn't get otherwise.

Reliability: Unlike nannies, who may need time off for illness or vacations, daycare centers operate on a consistent schedule. You don't have to worry about finding backup care at the last minute because of a sick day.

Affordability (compared to a nanny): Comparatively speaking, full-time daycare is cheaper—usually. Although costs can vary widely depending on where you live, the average cost in the United States for center-based infant care usually ranges from about $1,000 to $2,000 per month (though urban areas and high-demand locations may charge significantly more, even up to $3,000 or more monthly).

That said, there are some drawbacks to the daycare setup too.

Sickness: Ask any daycare parent and they'll tell you their biggest frustration is *all the damn colds*. Because your child will be interacting with a group of other kids, they're just more likely to get sick (and to get *you* sick). Once my kids were in preschool, I often felt like I was just paying for the entire family to get ill with the sickness du jour. This can mean missing work (to care for them, or yourself, or both!) and having to wait for a clean bill of health before taking them back to daycare.

Less individualized attention: Daycare centers typically have a set ratio of caregivers to children (usually 1:3 or 1:4 for infants), and that means they simply won't get the same amount of one-on-one time that they would with a nanny.

Lack of flexibility: Daycare centers operate on set hours, which may not always align perfectly with your work schedule. If you need to work late or have early meetings, you'll need to figure out backup care, or be prepared to pay extra fees for extended hours.

Waitlists and availability: Let's be clear: There's a childcare shortage in America, and daycares are feeling the crunch. You'll want to be on a waitlist as *soon* as possible—as in, pee-barely-dry-on-the-stick soon. So, even if you're just considering daycare as an option, get researching right away.

What About In-Home Daycares?

In-home daycares can be a nice middle ground between a larger daycare center and hiring a private nanny. As the name suggests, these are typically run by individuals in their own homes (sometimes other moms in the neighborhood) and tend to have smaller groups of children than a center does. The feeling can be much more "going to a friend's house" than "getting dropped off at school," and the cost is usually lower than center-based daycare.

That said, while all in-home daycares *can* be licensed (and therefore subject to safety standards), depending on where you live, there may be loopholes where licensing is not required—below a certain number of children, for example, or if it's a drop-in model. Caregivers also may not be required to complete background checks or be CPR-certified. And if there's only one caregiver in charge, you could end up with the same illness- or vacation-related gaps in coverage when they take a day off.

Bottom line, it's important to do your research and—honestly—trust your gut. Don't hesitate to ask a ton of questions (see the checklists at the end of this chapter), and if anything doesn't align with your values, keep looking. Nothing is more worth your time than the safety of your baby.

As manager at a large chain retail store, Akari was used to tackling logistical challenges and managing people, but finding a nanny for her first baby was putting all that experience to the test.

With four weeks left of maternity leave, she was especially worried about balancing her return to work with exclusively breastfeeding—she'd gotten the hang of pumping, but Sadie, her three-month-old, did *not* care for bottles. And she would only sleep on Akari's body. "I probably interviewed twenty people every week," Akari recalled. "I felt like I'd started work already, just from being on the phone so much. But then we found Tricia."

Tricia was a seasoned nanny with what seemed like endless patience. She figured out how to get Sadie to accept the bottle. She helped her through the rough nap transitions. And now, each morning, Akari gets to watch Sadie's face light up as Miss Tricia walks in.

"She's just better at entertaining a baby than I am, and I'll totally admit that," Akari said. "At first it made me feel worried that I was a sucky mom, but then I realized it makes sense that Tricia's better at baby play—it's her *job*. She's a pro. Plus, Sadie definitely still prefers Mama at the end of the day."

NANNIES

A nanny—a dedicated caregiver who comes to your house and watches your baby one-on-one—can be a wonderful option and a years-long trusted relationship for your child. There are some excellent pluses.

It's all about you, baby: A nanny provides focused, individualized care for your child, in a familiar environment (your house!) so they can adapt to your baby's needs and routine instead of the other way around.

Schedule flexibility: You and the nanny can work out a mutually agreeable schedule, which can be helpful if you work part-time or otherwise don't need the standard nine-to-five, Monday-through-Friday coverage.

Light housework: Many nannies are willing to take on extra tasks like washing bottles, baby laundry, and even meal prep—agreed upon in advance, of course.

Transportation: Nannies can also take your baby out and about, whether that's for stroller walks or to sing-alongs at the library.

But there are also reasons a nanny might not be ideal for you.

Cost: Nannies simply tend to cost more than other options. Expect to pay at least $25 per hour, depending on your location and the nanny's experience. You'll also likely need to agree to a guaranteed minimum number of (paid) hours per week.

Time off: Nannies are individual humans with human lives, and they're going to take vacations, spend holidays with family, and (probably) get sick once in a while—which means you may need to have backup care lined up.

You're an employer: Hiring a nanny means being an employer—not just in terms of being in charge of the job description, but paying taxes and doing payroll as well. (More on that later.) This can also add additional costs.

What About Nanny Shares?

A nanny share is a way to, well, share a nanny. In this arrangement, two (or more) families hire a single nanny who will watch both families' children. The parents get to split the cost, while the kids still get lots of individualized attention.

That said, this option can be more complex to coordinate, as you'll need to align schedules, parenting styles, and logistics with the other family or families involved. (And that's on *top* of all the legal and payroll paperwork.) You're also not simply dividing a nanny's salary by two—most nannies will charge a higher rate to watch multiple children, so *that's* what you'll be splitting with your co-boss family. Still, it can be a great solution if you're set on having a nanny but want to mitigate the cost a bit.

FAMILY CARE

Bitna had thought she'd struck the perfect balance. With both Omma (her mom) and Nana (her mother-in-law) eagerly offering to watch her daughter twice a week, she and her husband found themselves saving a small fortune on daycare costs. They hadn't even asked for the help—both grandmas had retired early and volunteered, a gesture that seemed almost too good to be true. Full-time daycare in their area was more than their mortgage, so this setup felt like a blessing, especially with the flexibility each grandmother allowed when the occasional schedule shift was needed.

For the first few months, the arrangement worked beautifully: Both Bitna and her husband, Ha-Joon, took care to express their gratitude to Omma and Nana alike and coordinated their own work schedules to avoid either grandma feeling overwhelmed. But then came a curveball: Bitna's mother began planning a series of vacations and doctor's appointments, nearly wiping out their carefully balanced schedule for an entire month.

Bitna, hoping to avoid overburdening her mother-in-law with extra days, tentatively asked her mom if she could pick up an additional day here and there at the end of one of those disrupted weeks. The reaction was . . . not great. "It's very tiring to watch a baby at my age. I already raised you all and now I'm doing it again. I'm going to need to rest now and then," she huffed. "Honestly, I think you're acting ungrateful, Bitna."

Even though Bitna hadn't said anything critical when her mom first announced her unavailable dates—she consciously kept her tone *incredibly* polite and deferent—the sudden intensity of her mom's response left her wondering if their arrangement was creating more friction than it was worth.

After that conversation, Bitna and Ha-Joon began to consider other options, even looking into daycares again, especially considering their daughter was almost one and would get the (slightly, slightly) cheaper rate for the toddler room. In the end, Bitna appreciated the savings and the value of family time while it worked out, but over the long term, the juice of free childcare wasn't worth the squeeze of all the tension with her mom.

Before the days of the nuclear family, it was almost a given that the senior generation would contribute to child-rearing, and a doting grandparent who wants to spend time with your baby and has the flexibility to watch them while you work can be an incredible blessing . . . or, as Bitna's story shows, an additional stressor. The pros are fairly obvious—family bonding, lower or no costs—but the cons can weigh heavier than pretty much any other option—from squabbles over parenting techniques to reopening old trauma. Ultimately, only you know your relationship with your parents (or in-laws) and whether the dynamic you have with them is well-suited to this kind of arrangement or a ticking time bomb.

Even in the best and most solid relationships, the blurred lines of child-care can make navigating family dynamics a delicate task. When planning to rely on family members, especially grandparents, for childcare, it's worth preparing in a way that preserves both your relationships and the quality of care for your baby.

Start with open conversations . . . : Before the childcare arrangement begins, take some time to talk about how things might shift between you and your parents/in-laws. Get ahead of anything you know will be a hot-button issue.

. . . and firm boundaries: Establish what are deal-breakers clearly, and attach real consequences. The key here is being willing (and able) to follow through. If you've told your MIL that letting your baby cry it out for naps is not allowed, then you need to be prepared to proceed with alternate childcare (even if it means paying more). Waffling on core values like this will only make things stickier.

Agree on some ground rules: Working together to establish clear poli-cies or agreements about the childcare arrangement helps everyone get on the same page. Be specific: For example, if your mom's agreed to watch the baby on Tuesday mornings, and you have a standing Zoom at 9:00 a.m. sharp, make it clear that you'll need your mom to arrive *before* then, not just "anytime before noon."

Borrow from professional norms (even if it feels strange): On that note, sometimes it helps to approach parts of the arrangement like an employer–employee relationship, even if it's family: for example, setting up a shared calendar or task management board (if you have tech-savvy parents) rather than relying on ad hoc texts and calls to schedule.

Be direct and specific: Don't assume that family members automatically understand what you want, and don't take for granted that they'll have the same assumptions as you. Instead of leaving everyone stewing in their own interpretations of what it means to be "watching the baby" (or "working," for that matter), spell out some policies. Does "no screen time" mean "don't park the baby in front of an iPad for hours," or does it mean "don't even have the TV on in the background"?

Address issues right away . . . and the right way: The sooner you address an issue, the less chance there is for resentment to build. But sometimes intervening can be interpreted (fairly or unfairly) as a referendum on Grandma's parenting skills—which is not usually welcome. My pro tip is to frame those corrections as a favor to *you*, and you'll likely get a much better response. "Mom, I noticed you had Charlie in his swing without the harness fastened. Can you make sure it's buckled when he's in there? I know you're keeping a careful eye on him; it's just really important for my new-mom peace of mind."

Check in regularly: Life changes, and so do people's availability and capacity. Even if things are "going great," make it a point to check in every so often about how the arrangement is working for everyone. Some grandparents (and moms!) can be *overly* polite and accommodating and may not even set their own boundaries. This was the case for my client Amira. She noticed the demands of childcare started to impact her mother's health, but her mother was devoted to Amira and her baby and just kept showing up. Amira decided to request a lateral shift to a remote job that opened up in her workplace so that she would lose less time on commuting (giving her mother a later start time) and be more accessible to support her mother during her work breaks. This was an effortless solution for both of them, as they now were raising the baby together, which was their common dream.

Have an exit strategy: Don't necessarily assume this arrangement will work for everyone until your baby is in kindergarten. If there's a built-in end date (your MIL's a snowbird who'll be jetting down to Florida, you're starting a nanny share when baby turns one, etc.) then be sure that everyone knows it, and you've got a plan for childcare after then. Even if you're all agreed on an indefinite granny-nanny situation, life happens (especially considering older folks are more prone to medical issues that might slow them down), so it'll serve you well to get a read on local daycares, nanny costs, or whatever alternative you'd turn to.

Show genuine appreciation: Finally, don't forget to express your gratitude. Family members who provide childcare are giving your child love and care that truly matters and are literally saving you thousands of dollars. It's a form of generational wealth that only a lucky few have access to. Parents who do not have access to this privilege experience significant grief, financial stress, and logistical and mental overwhelm. Family support allows you to save for a down payment or a college fund. You won the family lottery. Say thank you. Try not to micromanage (key word being "try"). Perhaps prepare some kind of special memento for Grandma (a handprint picture, a photo book) that she can treasure even after your kid is off to school.

Do not avoid the money conversation: Nadia's mother was set on being the one who would tend to the baby while Nadia worked. She felt uncomfortable with the idea of a non-relative tending to the baby. It was just not her culture. However, Nadia's mother worked at the local grocery store to supplement her meager retirement payouts. Leaving that job would mean substantial hardship for her mother. Nadia decided to pay her mother for the labor of childcare, in an amount slightly higher than her store job (but still less than a private nanny). I often see parents rely on the grandparents too much, using them as free on-demand labor. Watching little kids is hard, tiring work. Our elders are not supposed to be our entire social safety net, and if they do show up for us consistently, allowing us to work, it may come at a cost for them. That is just the nature of capitalist modernity, which exploits everyone at the margins, including mothers and the elderly (all without proper support). If parents do support you, how can you share your resources and make sure there is a flow of support (including money) reciprocated their way?

How Should I Pay My Parents (or In-Laws) to Watch My Baby?

There's no reason a family member can't be paid to provide childcare (it is, after all, real work). However, bear in mind that family members should technically be subject to all the same requirements as any household employee (i.e., tax withholding and any applicable labor laws—see below) and they cannot be claimed as a dependent on your tax return.

Additionally, if you plan to pay your parents using funds from a dependent care FSA account, then you'll need them to prepare a receipt, including their tax ID number (SSN), just like any other childcare provider, that you can submit to your claims administrator. In that case, too, the care must be for the purpose of helping you work (e.g., not for date nights) in order to qualify for reimbursement and should be paid at a competitive rate (your FSA provider likely won't reimburse a $1,500 receipt for three hours of childcare, for example).

There are also tax benefits to hiring family members. For federal taxes, paying a grandparent for childcare while you work (or look for work) could make you eligible for the Child and Dependent Care Credit, which covers a percentage of qualifying childcare expenses. California residents can also make use of the state's similar Child and Dependent Care Expenses Credit, provided they don't exceed the income thresholds. Consult with a tax professional to learn more.

Paging Mary Poppins: Hiring a Nanny

After I graduated from law school, my husband and I did a bit of a pendulum swing: Rather than jump on an extremely tempting job offer at an oil company (one that would've almost wiped out our student debt *and* helped me get my green card), we headed to Oregon with a dream of becoming environmental lawyers.

Yes, quite a 180. This meant racking up more debt, another master's program (for him), and working for free at a local civil rights and environmental law firm (for me). I worked on Sierra Club cases as well as other civil justice causes, doing prestigious and important work, including appellate briefs, but it was unpaid.

To support myself, I took odd babysitting jobs. One of those jobs was for a family with a new baby. It was an easy baby, and a good gig. It started very early in the morning, but I enjoyed going for walks in the green neighborhoods of the Pacific Northwest.

Still, it was a strange time of my life. I got paid for wiping bums and wrangling naptimes, while I got *nothing* for working on these high-profile environmental cases . . . yet I never thought of the *paid* work as "a job" (never mind that working as a babysitter was infinitely harder than legal work). I didn't particularly enjoy babysitting, but I needed money, and the jobs were ubiquitous and reliable—especially considering babysitters (particularly French-speaking ones like me) were in high demand. Watching kids felt like something I did to support myself in my actual dream, ambitions, and passions. Temporary, and ultimately not *that* important.

In hindsight, my attitude and behavior were pretty typical for a lot of the younger women who end up as nannies. They look at childcare as a "whatever" kind of job. I remember one of the other nannies who had a shift after me often showed up with a red sweaty face and a hot pink tongue. "Too many Jell-O shots last night, huh?" I'd ask. She'd just moan and say, "Don't tell the mom."

For better or worse, there are a lot of people—mostly young women— who will take these jobs because they are "easy." They are caring for kids to afford Jell-O shots or their "actual" careers, and while they may be perfectly competent (I was a pretty good nanny, after all), you don't want them watching your precious baby. They may present well (like I did!), but ultimately their hearts aren't in it. And why would you settle for someone whose heart isn't in the most important work there is?

There *are* some really good nannies—they're just hard to find. But you *can* find them.

Your ideal candidates will usually be career nannies who have made childcare their mission. This will be obvious if you look at their resume and see other childcare jobs, but experience as educators, camp counselors, or youth leaders can also fit the bill (I've found that anyone who's worked at a church childcare center has really good skills).

I also ask them about their family constellation. To me, being an older sibling (or responsible cousin-in-charge) is worth just as much as official babysitting experience. Don't write off college students entirely, either: They can be a wonderful option if you don't need full-time care (because they'll have to work around their class schedule), and if you find someone who is actually studying education, you have stumbled upon a unicorn. Treat them well—anyone who *wants* to devote their lives to the well-being of children is an absolute hero.

Also, don't limit yourself to only women caretakers, either. Personally, as my boys are getting older, I've been doing an intentional job of trying to find boy babysitters. After all, I don't want my kids to learn that only women take care of them! So don't count out male nannies, or the boys in your neighborhood, for the occasional sitter. Equality requires that men do more caretaking, and it needs to start young. This may sound scarier, but trust your instincts. As a mother of two energetic boys, I really needed other boys to match that kind of energy. There's a set of twin teenage boys that occasionally come to my house while I work from home. I have them play soccer outside and I keep an eye on them. It's different from the women sitters I've employed (not to reinforce stereotypes, but with the girls, there are more arts and crafts activities, and, of course, no wrestling). It's really great. I do actually need sitters to wrestle and play sports with my kids, and hiring teenage boys as sitters has been a wonderful addition to our family experience.

As for finding these nannies, you'll want to cast a wide net. Directory websites like Care.com, Sittercity, and the like are always a good place to start your research (and some will even handle payroll and paperwork for you—more on that later). But to be honest, the top place my mom friends and I have had the most success networking for childcare is Facebook. Local "seeking childcare" groups attract parents and potential nannies alike and allow you to browse candidates, ask questions, and get a bead on things like going rates and expectations. More general classified websites can work too—I suggest ones that are geographically specific (or, even better, tied to a local college or university so you can reach out to students).

When interviewing your nanny, ask for references and pay attention to how she connects to your children. Before agreeing to move forward, set up trial days where you are home and able to observe and guide her. Be explicit that these are trial days, and that she will get paid.

If you are returning to work, make sure to have your nanny shadow you while you are still on leave. You may actually want to move her start date up a week or two so your baby can learn that this is a person Mama trusts and enjoys having around. It will also make the handoff easier and allow you to feel less stressed on your first day. Do not wait to onboard your nanny until the end of your maternity leave.

Unless you have a flexible job with flexible hours, make sure to have a primary nanny, and a backup nanny, and then put them in a group text together with you. If there are any shift changes or updates, you can communicate them there.

Then create a one-page list to "explain" your baby's needs and wants. I tend to write this from the perspective of the baby.

> Hi, I'm Matteo. I'm so excited to get to know you! Thank you for agreeing to take care of me. Here are some things you should know about me:
>
> I can already roll over, so please don't leave me on the couch or changing table because I may roll off.
>
> I drink a bottle at 9:00 a.m. After that, I like to take a nap. Usually I will fall asleep while drinking my milk. If I'm not asleep, please rock me to sleep. My mama lets me sleep on her, so you're free to hold me while I sleep too. Or you can try to put me in my crib but only once I'm asleep. I'm not able to put myself to sleep and need a warm body to help me fall asleep.
>
> I'm sensitive to light and sound, so while I sleep, please close the blinds and turn on the noise machine; otherwise, I will wake up quickly and be very cranky.

. . . and so on.

A letter like this can be a huge help. When I was having some communication issues with a nanny, I emailed her a schedule and some policies, and she ended up being really grateful. She said she was really struggling to understand the baby's sleep/awake rhythm and explained that she needed an "orientation" to know how to meet my baby where he was.

Mom Boss:
Your Legal Responsibilities as an Employer

Our culture tends to devalue childcare instead of viewing it as a legitimate career. But yes, childcare is an actual job, including for tax purposes.

Yes, "everyone" seems to accept that childcare is an under-the-table kind of job. But the public acceptance of this practice doesn't make it legal. If you have a nanny on a schedule, you have to put them on payroll, pay income taxes, and do all the other formal things you do when you employ someone, including giving paid sick days, depending on your state.

If you fire your nanny, they can claim unemployment, and if they are injured on the job, they can recover disability benefits.

I believe this to be right—morally, legally, and ethically.

However.

Many nannies will still ask to be paid under the table. Some even insist—and walk away from a job if you won't pay off the books. What do you do then? To me, this was always an indication that they did not intend to file taxes, and it was something I did not want to be a part of. I have spent too much time in the land of government investigations to take these kinds of risks. So my recommendation is to find a nanny who wants to be on payroll, even though it is harder and more expensive.

And also.

It's very hard, as a single person or a couple, to be a full-blown employer. Being an employer is serious! There are responsibilities! Which sucks, because you just had a baby and you're vulnerable and exhausted, and now you somehow also have to be a goddamn boss and everything that comes with it.

So here's what you need to know.

Most nannies are legally considered household employees, meaning you (as the household owner) are the employer. They cannot be legally classified as 1099 independent contractors. This means you're responsible for withholding certain taxes, reporting their wages to the IRS, and following any applicable local or state labor laws. At the end of the year, your nanny will get a W-2 form (just like you get from your employer) from you, and you'll file a Schedule H form to report household employment taxes.

Specifically, you have to withhold **Social Security and Medicare (a.k.a. FICA) taxes** from your nanny's paycheck (typically 7.65 percent of their gross pay) and *also* contribute a matching amount as the employer (also typically 7.65 percent of their gross pay). And since that employer contribution is coming out of *your* pocket, you'll need to budget for that on top of the nanny's hourly rate. You'll also be responsible for—as applicable—state and federal unemployment taxes. There can also be other items (like disability deductions and paid family leave!) deducted, depending on your state payroll system.

And you'll need to keep records of all this so that you can file your own tax forms appropriately at the end of the year.

This is a lot—and honestly, it's something I highly recommend out-sourcing as much as possible. There are payroll services and apps specific to household employees that can take care of the details for you (for a monthly fee), and tax professionals (not just software) can advise you on the specifics of your own withholding and filing. What's crucial for you to understand is that following the law here matters—not because it elimi-nates risk and gives you peace of mind, but because *not* doing so is, frankly, hypocritical. Advocating for yourself at work, insisting on your legal rights as a mother, and then turning around to deprive someone of theirs as their employer (because, again, as a nanny parent, you *are* an employer) isn't right and doesn't help the cause of motherhood in capitalism. Paying under the table might allow you to pay "less," but at the expense of your nanny both contributing to and having access to her share of the social safety net: unemployment insurance, Social Security, and all the societal benefits supported by tax dollars.

Sample Timelines and Checklists

Here are some timelines and checklists you can use to complete your child-care prep.

NANNY TIMELINE

First Trimester

- Research your local nanny scene online: Browse directory websites, join Facebook groups for parents in your area, ask around to any parent friends.
- Learn what the going rates are for your area and start to save or budget accordingly.

Second Trimester

- Draft a job description, including specifics on times, days of the week, and your expectations for baby care.
- Post your job description.

Third Trimester (ideally)

- Interview candidates on the phone.
- Interview candidates in-person.
- Conduct reference/background checks.
- Draft a contract in advance, and discuss terms during interviews.

Fourth Trimester

- Complete the retention process, select the nanny, and sign the agreement.
- Create a "baby handbook" to introduce your baby to the nanny and include all relevant care/house details.
- Set up the payroll system and onboard your nanny.
- Trial days (nanny watches the baby while you are home).
- Off to work!

NANNY INTERVIEW CHECKLIST

Childcare Philosophy and Experience

- What's important to you in a nanny-child relationship?
- How do you approach a nanny-parent relationship? What's your ideal dynamic?
- What's your typical day like with the infants or children you care for? What kinds of activities do you enjoy doing with them?
- How many first-time parents have you worked with, and how do you help them adjust to the nanny-child dynamic?
- Can you give examples of unexpected issues that have come up in previous jobs? How did you and the family work through them?
- Can you provide us with references we can contact about your previous work?

- What system do you prefer for daily updates on feedings, sleep, and diaper changes?

Health, Safety, and Comfort Levels

- Are you CPR certified?
- Are you okay with us submitting a background check (on things like childcare clearances, driving record) for you?
- Do you smoke?
- Are you okay with taking the child for walks or outings? If so, do you prefer within walking distance, or would you be comfortable driving?
- If so, would you be comfortable sharing your location on your phone during work hours? (Alternatively, you can provide an old phone for them to use.)
- Are there any activities or requests (like feeding certain foods or doing household tasks) that you would not feel comfortable with?
- (If you have pets): Are you comfortable with dogs/cats?

Employment Terms & Responsibilities

- Are you looking for a minimum weekly guarantee of hours?
- Overtime: Are you available for overtime? If hours exceed your weekly guarantee, how would you prefer overtime to be handled?
- Do you understand that, as a household employee, taxes will be withheld, and payment will be "on the books"? (Share any payroll service plans you have.)
- How would you like to approach vacation time and sick days?
- Are you open to handling additional tasks, like tidying up the baby room, the baby's laundry, or baby meal prep?

NANNY CONTRACT CHECKLIST

When writing up a contract, you'll want to include the following:

- Start date and work hours: Specify the date they'll begin working, their regular work hours, and any flexibility needed.

- Guaranteed hours: Specify how many hours you will guarantee your nanny on a weekly basis.
- Responsibilities: Including any non-baby duties like meal prep or light cleaning.
- Communication expectations: How you will communicate with the nanny and mutual policies for giving notice of sickness, emergencies, cancellations, etc.
- Payment terms: Stipulate clearly what the hourly rate is. Include the payment frequency (weekly, biweekly, or monthly).
- Paid time off: Offer details on paid vacation days, sick days, and holidays. Include how far in advance you'd like to receive notice.
- Sickness policy: Have a plan in place for what you'll do when you / your baby, *or* the nanny is sick.
- Benefits: Stipends for healthcare or cell phone, reimbursement for mileage/gas.

Want a solid place to start? Download my Nanny Contract Template at themamattorney.com.

DAYCARE TIMELINE

As soon as possible:
- Research local daycare providers.
- Get on waitlists.

Prior to going on leave:
- Tour centers.
- Make your final choice and pay the deposit.
- Confirm the start date.

Two to three weeks before returning to work:
- Prep daycare bag (bottles, changes of clothes, diapers, wipes, solid foods, any medications plus printed directions and dosing

schedules if applicable, printout of family contact numbers and essential info).

- If your baby is exclusively nursing, start practicing with bottles to acclimate them.

At least one week before returning to work:
- Do a "trial week" before going back to work so Baby can get acclimated to daycare. This should just be a few hours so your baby can ease in, and make sure you are available and accessible if anything comes up.

DAYCARE RESEARCH CHECKLIST

- Review your state licensing website to confirm active licensing and to search for any complaints or violations.
- General vibe of the center: Is it clean, tidy, and well-maintained? Are there any obvious hazards?
- Facility safety: Everything is appropriately babyproofed, entry points are secure, outdoor spaces are fully fenced.
- Hygiene: Hand-washing and sanitizing routines (especially around diaper changes) are in place; breastmilk and food is stored appropriately.
- Staff qualifications: All staff should be certified in CPR and first aid and up to date on any required licensing.
- Staff interactions: Are the staff members interacting with the babies and toddlers in a friendly, engaging way? Do they generally seem caring and kind? Are babies held and played with more than they are put in swings or bouncers?
- Toys and equipment: Are all toys and equipment clean and safe? Are babies and toddlers given screen time as part of their care?
- Feeding: When do they feed babies and how do they track feeds? How will they accommodate your feeding setup (whether that's pumped milk, formula, or a combination)?

- Sleep: Where and when do babies nap during the day? What will they do if your baby has trouble napping away from you / in a crib?
- Communication: How do they stay in touch with parents during the day? Text, phone, an app? Are there cameras parents can use to check in on their babies?
- Confirm their rates, payment policies, and any penalties or extra fees for late pickups or absences.
- Confirm their sickness policy (e.g., how long will your child be required to stay home after a fever or vomiting?).
- Confirm their closure dates (holidays, etc.).

9

No One Puts Baby in the Corner Office

Going Back to Work

Jaya, a customer service representative at a local bank, joined my online program when she was five months pregnant. Although she was well into her second trimester, she wasted no time in diving in.

A week after she joined us, she'd told HR about her pregnancy: first in person, and then in writing.

Two weeks after joining, she'd started mapping out her work duties, major projects and milestones, and key contacts and support people.

A month after joining, she jumped on childcare research and got on a waiting list for a daycare just five minutes from her office.

So far, so good . . . and then the third trimester hit. As her baby grew, Jaya started experiencing intense pelvic pain when walking, standing, or even shifting position. It was a "normal" symptom of pregnancy—as in, majorly uncomfortable, but not a danger to her or baby—but still made just going into the office excruciating. After the birth of her healthy baby girl, Jaya was still in considerable pain, and now needed to somehow find time for physical therapy appointments on top of her busy commute—a long drive that was actively aggravating her injuries.

She knew how key her role was, and she knew how badly they needed her to do her job to keep things going. Fortunately, since she'd been proactive in planning ahead for her leave, she also knew that she didn't need to be in the office every single day. She could just as easily conference with customers from home. She just needed a good headset and a solid internet connection. So she took that pre-leave preparation and used it to write up an accommodation proposal for a new schedule—one that would let her rest her body while still achieving her work targets. She laid out how it would save the company money if she could work from home, the ultimate power move.

She even included research on teleworking efficiency and documentation from her doctor for her physical therapy treatments, but didn't end up needing it: HR was so impressed with her suggested schedule that they signed off on her plan right away.

It gets better: When Jaya was ready to return to work, she asked to stay on the hybrid schedule, and they agreed because she had already proven that the job could be done just as well from home.

"Because of what you'd taught us, I felt motivated to request a hybrid schedule," Jaya recalled later. "And I not only kept that hybrid schedule even when my leave rights expired, but helped my employer set up a task force with a focus on supporting moms. Overall, my new work setup has allowed me to be more comfortable *and* more productive."

I believe that working while having a baby is the hardest thing a human being can do. Period. Your baby doesn't become less needy when you go back to your job, you're going through a massive identity transformation, and you're just *So. Damn. Tired.* It's an incredibly vulnerable time in your life, both as a professional and as a mom, and it's easy to feel like everything is an edge case, like there is "no right answer" and that you're failing someone, somewhere, no matter what you choose to do or how hard you try.

What I want you to remember, though, is that a sense of ease is your birthright. You do *not* have to resign yourself to feeling stuck. Yes, you have rights that can be protected—such as rights to reinstatement and rights to be free from leave retaliation—but on a grander, more personal scale, you have a right to step into this new reality of who you are, and to do so with grace. Like Jaya, you can face the challenges with an attitude of "what if it all goes *right*?" When you know your rights, feel confident in your abilities, and trust yourself to speak up for what you need, you can make that transition comfortable and productive for yourself . . . and maybe even forge a path for the moms that follow in your wake.

With scripts, stories, and troubleshooting help, this chapter focuses on going back to work: understanding/navigating reinstatement rights, the nuts and bolts of your first days back at the workplace, and similar topics. But it also contains many stories from working moms, like Jaya, across career stages and industries to empower readers to see that while there's no one "right way" to go back to work, there are common threads to what keeps us going as working moms when we finally jump back in. I'll also cover the crucial steps to finding accommodations (like extended leave, telework, or a flexible schedule) around postpartum anxiety or depression—one of the top reasons women come to me.

Reinstatement Rights:
Knowing Your Legal Protections

Employers are often fairly careful with pregnant women—they know better than to mess around with the bumps or risk being sued. Yet, for some reason, once the mom comes back from maternity leave, many employers think it's all fair game and start discriminating. Maybe it's that a lot of pent-up frustration is bubbling to the surface after covering for her workload, maybe someone's resentful that the company's paying you for your leave (even if it's a benefit given to all employees), maybe it's just ol' school misogyny. In any case, whether you are excited to head back into the office, or you're feeling heartache over the transition back, it is important to know your rights, because this can very much be the danger zone.

When it comes to reinstatement, you'll actually start asserting your rights before you even set foot back in the office (or sit down for your first Zoom). At least thirty days before you return to work, you should inform your employer of your intent to return, and mention that you do, in fact, know your rights (because you do!). Send an email like the one below to HR and cc your immediate supervisor. If there is no HR department, send this email to the highest level of management, and cc your immediate supervisor.

> Hello [Name],
>
> The last date of my leave is [Date]. I am excited to return. Please let me know if there have been any changes I need to be aware of, and who to talk to about returning to my work and projects when I return.
>
> Please confirm that I will be reinstated to my job. [I understand this to be my right under 29 U.S.C.A. § 2614.]

[If you want to pump at work, add this:

Upon my return, I will need lactation accommodations. Is there a space and policy set up for lactation? I understand I should have access to reasonable break time as well as a private room free from intrusion, whenever I need to pump. I have learned these rights from 29 U.S.C. 207 and the PUMP Act.]

I'm happy to return to work and your support is vital for me to succeed as a working mother.

Thank you,
[Your Name]

As for the rights themselves, we've already touched on these a bit when discussing legal protections, but: In short, the law is there to protect your job after your leave. Following either a pregnancy or postpartum disability leave or family bonding leave, you're entitled to be immediately reinstated to the same or an equivalent position.

An equivalent position means employment in a position that is virtually identical to your position held prior to your leave: virtually identical pay, benefits, working conditions, responsibilities, skill, authority, jobsite, and schedule. In other words, when you return, you may *not* be returned to a subordinate, lower position, and your responsibilities need to be returned to you. One of my clients, Joy, returned to work and was placed in a position subordinate to a coworker who had been a peer prior to her leave. They also transferred Joy's support person, leaving Joy with more work and more stress but also less authority. This is not an equivalent position.

Some women return to work and are offered the "same" position, but only part-time, and can even lose their healthcare as a result. Or the reverse can occur. One of my clients worked a flex, part-time job for many years. After her leave, they wanted her full-time at the office.

That is not an equivalent job, and is essentially a termination from the original job, and an offer for another job. If this happens, call an attorney.

They also can't say, "Oh, Roger took over your responsibilities, and he's doing a pretty good job, so we're just going to have you assist him." Illegal. If you were in a managerial position before, you need to be in one upon your return.

They can't say, "We're going to keep Roger in your job, because who knows, you might get pregnant again!" Illegal. If someone is doing your job duties during your leave, those duties have to be returned to you. They can't just keep Roger in your position because that's more convenient to them and they're worried you will leave again soon.

They can't say, "We really need people who are more reliable here, and you're just too unreliable." Illegal—all these are examples of discrimination and leave retaliation.

There is one exception: If your job disappeared or changed for reasons unrelated to your leave, in a way that it would have even if you *hadn't* been on leave, there's likely little you can do. For example, if the whole department disappeared and your job was eliminated, that sucks—but it's probably legal. During those big tech layoffs, thousands of workers got laid off while on leave. They all called me, assuming their job was protected because they are on leave. It's not. Your job is only protected to the extent that your job actually still exists (meaning someone is doing those job duties). If you're part of a reduction in force, your job is not protected.

Just make sure the employer is not trying to cover up, pushing you out of your job because they want the replacement Roger to keep performing your functions. For example, if there is a reorg and you're out of a job and Roger is not, that may be suspect. "Reorg" is a common employer defense to hide behind, when what really happened was a strategic and wrongful termination.

SQUEEZED OUT

Often, employers will not outright terminate mothers, but they will make it really hard for them to succeed, sometimes to the point where the mothers just end up quitting. For example, they will change your shift from the daytime shift to an evening shift, knowing it would be really hard to combine with a baby.

In yet other cases, they'll find a way to fire a mother but cover their tracks, trying to circumvent the rules.

Alejandra had been a star performer at her bookkeeper job, where she had successfully supported a few high-profile clients thanks to her sharp attention to detail. So she was blindsided when, three weeks into her return from maternity leave, she got a weird reply-all email from her boss, chewing her out about a formatting issue in a spreadsheet (a matter of styling preference, really). Meanwhile, her male colleague had sent out a spreadsheet with the same formatting style as Alejandra, a few days earlier, sans issues.

Then, the following Monday, her boss informed her that her "performance was slipping" and she'd be put on a performance improvement plan (PIP) to address her "attention to detail." Alejandra was absolutely stunned—but, in the moment, she swallowed her pride and apologized profusely to her boss. "I genuinely wondered if it was just mom brain and I *was* making mistakes," she said, "even though I couldn't remember any and small stuff like that had never really been an issue before—it was a fairly casual workplace."

It wasn't until two days later, during an all-staff meeting, that Alejandra connected the dots. Open enrollment was approaching and HR was explaining that the company had been labeled "high-risk" and they were investigating new health insurance vendors. The team was fairly young and healthy, so one of Alejandra's coworkers asked, not unreasonably, what had happened, because suddenly insurance was going to cost a lot more.

The HR director said, "When you have a premature baby in the NICU for an extended period of time, that's going to raise your premiums."

Alejandra felt the air leave the room. She was the only employee with a NICU baby, and everyone knew it. Afterward, people told her they were shocked to hear her called out like that—it was almost cruel.

The PIP wasn't about performance. It was punishment for taking leave—a leave on which she birthed, in their eyes, an "expensive" child. In that moment, Alejandra realized that this organization she'd once loved had reduced her to a liability, and this "performance issue" was just a flimsy way to cover for firing her.

What happened to Alejandra was illegal. Drumming up a made-up reason to eventually fire her after she took leave (and had a premature baby on the company health plan) doesn't make this okay. As discussed earlier, this made-up reason is called *pretext*, and it's against the rules. When I speak about my work, people often say, "Well, don't companies just make up fake reasons to fire people illegally?" to which I say, yes, always. They are not dumb and will not write "She's a mom" on the pink slip. Part of my job is disproving that the false reason is the real reason. We do this by poking holes in their defense, for example, by highlighting that the male coworker acted in the exact same way as Alejandra and was not impacted like her, or by explaining that Alejandra acted just like she did before she was pregnant and that she was never scrutinized before. The adverse treatment also happened right after returning from leave, and this temporal proximity creates a strong argument that the motivating factor for their poor treatment of her was her taking leave. Lastly, these offhand comments about her baby are also a window into the state of mind of the employer: They were frustrated because her motherhood experience was costing them. These are all signs of leave retaliation.

BENEVOLENT DISCRIMINATION

Another category that crosses the line is in the form of what we call "benevolent discrimination." This is discrimination that is intended to be helpful (if that's a thing), but truly what it is, is them making decisions for you and robbing you of agency.

When Annika, a pharmacist, returned from leave, she found a very different landscape than the one she'd left. The organization had expanded, with four new pharmacists on board since she'd been out, and Annika's boss "encouraged" her to ask for a ramp-up schedule, a plan that would help her transition back gradually rather than jumping into a full caseload of patients each day. Her boss had even "helpfully" worked it out so her first week back would start at four patient calls per day, then six—still challenging with charting and pumping breaks squeezed into every shift, but a way to build up her full-time workload.

And maybe that wouldn't have been so bad had it not *also* come with a sudden shake-up. For almost four years, Annika had been the lead pharmacist at her branch and had formed relationships with doctors, staff, and patients alike. She really cared about those people and valued them as part of her work—and now, just as she prepared to return, she learned that they'd been reassigned to Cheryl, the pharmacist who'd covered during her leave. The reason? Something about a need for a "quick impact on quality gaps."

Reading the email, Annika felt gutted. She knew these new assignments—small clinics with no established relationship with a pharmacist—would make it hard to meet her productivity metrics or referral targets. More painful, though, was the feeling that all the work she'd poured into her previous office had been wiped away overnight. She wasn't being given time to "ease back in" as much as she was being pushed out of the office relationships she'd worked years to build.

Annika's case, I'd argue, is *benevolent discrimination*—when an employer is voluntarily changing up your work assignments, thinking that's what you want. Benevolent discrimination usually comes from a well-intended place but is still based on the assumption that you can't handle your job now that you're a mom and need things rearranged for you. If you want to take a step back, that's fine, but that has to be your decision. Staying (or not staying) on your same professional track is your right, and they can't simply decide on your behalf. Just because you *had* a child does not mean they're now allowed to treat you like a child!

Another client—an educator—asked for maternity leave. A few weeks later, the administrator told her they canceled her class roster for the entire next year, and then tried to have her agree that this was in her best interest because it would mean she could take a full year off. However, she did not want to take a full year off, and also could not afford it. She wanted to take her regular leave and just come back to work.

Lucy worked for a nurse staffing company. When she gave notice of her pregnancy, her manager said, "If I were you, I wouldn't return and I would just stay home to take care of my baby." When Lucy returned after leave, her manager demoted her. When Lucy complained and reported the demotion, her manager said, "Maybe it's best to appreciate your role as a new mother and take it slow." The woman who demoted her was also a mother, but older, and shared her own motherhood experiences, which were unrelatable. Lucy felt like she was being subjected to outdated perspectives of motherhood, that is, that she should no longer be ambitious or seek professional advancement.

Here are some more examples of benevolent discrimination:

- "Isn't it better for your baby if you don't come back to work? My wife stayed home with our kids and it really benefited them to have their mother at home."

- "To give you more time for breastfeeding and pumping, we'll just go ahead and take you off this project."
- "This promotion will cause too much stress and I'm worried about the health of your pregnancy."

The only appropriate response is, "Thank you for your concern. I trust my own instincts when making decisions for my own career advancement, and I believe this is the best direction for my family."

Inform your employer, kindly but firmly, that this is not what you want or need, and that you would like to simply do your job at your usual jobsite. In Annika's case, she could also explain her reasoning (i.e., she's invested years into the relationships at her office and that it would be disruptive to her *and* the patients, and possibly cause an operational challenge for herself and other staff).

If that does not work, remind them that, by law, you are supposed to be returned to your job after leave, which includes the same jobsite.

To be clear, discrimination happens only when your employer takes an adverse action that you do not agree with. Managers foreshadow, consciously or unconsciously, "Oh, she's going to be leaving," or "She won't be as reliable," and promote accordingly. Moms, meanwhile, are grateful for what are essentially crumbs. We think, *At least I have an income* or *I'm lucky just to have a job.*

However, you are free to decide yourself that you want to slow down your work pace through an accommodation request, and no, it does not make you less dedicated or committed.

That is the mentality I am challenging. Not just that mothers are somehow less dependable and capable (if anything, it's the opposite), but that work, productivity, and the almighty dollar do not need to be the center of your career 100 percent of the time for you to be successful at what you do, and you should always be grateful for that "gift."

No. It's okay to step away from work and step into life. You'll get back. The work will be there. And with the right support, you will thrive. That's why I'm dedicated to my skills and my knowledge about employment law to give concrete tips and strategies—so that women are no longer penalized for procreation.

But the bigger truth is, jobs, employers, work relationships—these will all come and go, but a baby is something else entirely. Bringing a new person into the world will happen only a few times in your life, maybe just once, but in every case, let me tell you, it is the most magical and transformative ride. It is work at the dimension of the souls. I feel a deep desire to protect this experience for you, and for all mothers. Because, I'm sorry to say, no matter how kind your manager is or how warm your company culture may be, they don't really care about your baby. Inevitably, there will come a time when your boss's demands and your baby's demands will conflict. Your boss will want you to choose work, and you will feel like you are failing everyone. When that happens, you really need to know your rights so you can make an informed decision.

BACK IN MY DAY . . .
HANDLING PASSIVE-AGGRESSIVE COMMENTS

Zoya's return to work after leave was going mostly as planned . . . until the comments started.

Randomly, during a team meeting, a manager looked pointedly her way and said, "Well, we were supposed to finish this last year but were delayed for many months . . . but back in my day, there *was* no such thing as maternity leave, so we were just expected to jump right back in." Another colleague, seeing her leave the lactation room, informed her that it "must be nice to have that cozy little room . . . I had to switch to formula when I went back to work." Then her boss's boss, a middle-aged dude, asked how her husband "enjoyed" his "little vacation," saying, "I don't understand how this generation of dads gets away with it. What are they doing at home? Playing video games?"

Every time, Zoya cringed. The first few were maybe coincidences, but after a while, they started to pile up into a real mental load.

Zoya was being barraged by the kind of passive-aggressive "back in my day" commentary that many moms will recognize—I've certainly had my own run-ins with them, like the time I was stuck in a deposition until 8:00 p.m., my boobs almost exploding and my hungry baby at home with no milk, only to have opposing counsel sneer that "We *all* have kids we need to get back to." (Then she informed me that if I wanted to suspend the deposition, so be it, but I'd have to have my client pay to get everyone back for another round.)

These are remarks that don't *seem* to constitute gender harassment in a vacuum, but which aren't exactly warm and friendly, either. And what's surprising (or was to me, anyway) is how frequently these comments come from other moms—moms who didn't have the support, rights, or benefits newer generations of parents do: Zoya's manager, who apparently returned back to work right away, or the opposing counsel at my deposition, who *also* had kids to get home to.

In those cases, it's best to try to absorb these comments with empathy, as much as you can (as unfair a burden as that is on you). The truth is that many moms *didn't* get the support or time off they deserved when having their babies, and they might still be carrying feelings of grief, resentment, or sadness about that time in their life. This doesn't excuse the comments, of course, but understanding where they come from might help you bounce back.

Of course, navigating these remarks requires more than just understanding where they come from. Legally, how these comments are treated depends on who's saying them. For Zoya, her boss's remarks could cross a line if they were accompanied by some adverse action, like a denial of a promotion. In that case, these comments might fall under retaliation if Zoya could point to the adverse action and a specific reference to her taking leave. Comments from coworkers, on the other hand, are mostly just annoying—until they reach a point of being so frequent and severe that they could be considered unlawful gender harassment (and only if you have reported the conduct to your higher-ups, and the harassment continues or gets worse). Either way, it's helpful to document what's happening—so that's what Zoya did.

As a practical step, she decided to email a record of each instance to her personal email, noting who said what and when. Although it felt a tiny bit petty to be doing so, Zoya reassured herself that it was about creating a record, not writing out a Burn Book. Fortunately, she never encountered any adverse action, and gradually the comments faded with time. "But I'm proud that I did that," Zoya said later. "It was like sending a little reminder to myself that I have rights, and that I don't have to take people's shit if they cross a line."

Your First Days Back:
What to Expect When You're Expected
(to Start Working Again)

So you've set up your childcare plan, you've found clothes that still kind of fit, you've gathered your pump and your supplies, and you're headed off to work like a champ. Ready or not, here you go . . . and you're probably feeling more "not" than "ready."

It is not easy to reenter the workforce after having a baby. Not only are you still a bit mentally and physically worn out, but the work may also have piled up in your absence, your coworkers may be slightly irritated with you, and you may be really missing your baby (and your yoga pants).

I wish I could tell you that your employer will reward your loyalty by welcoming you back with a plate of pancakes and a team of assistants, but they won't. Returning to work is a difficult experience, period. Babies do not stop needing their parents when the leave time ends. At the same time, your professional obligations don't stop churning onward either. And on top of that, you're just *So. Damn. Tired.*

Just like you had to leave the world of time behind when you entered the baby bubble, you now have to make your way back to that world of time . . . only instead of an easy, slow transition where you can wear sweatpants all day and don't need to muster the energy to wash your hair, you're now expected to jump back in with both feet and *without* missing a beat.

Personally, when I went back to work after my first baby, I was . . . tired. Except "tired" feels like such a small word for it. Like a lot of "yes girls," I had reasoned—prior to giving birth—that I could handle being tired and working. *I've been tired before, after all,* I told myself: from long all-nighters cramming for the bar exam, from sixteen-hour days doing motion work, from exhausting conference schedules and unfortunate shoe choices.

But this was something different. At a mediation, I was so delusionally exhausted that I forgot how to speak English (which, in my defense, is my third language). I felt like I was about to faint. Once I was done, I had to ask a bunch of old white dudes where I could go pump (because in my haze I hadn't given earlier notice of my accommodation needs) and they had to put a space together quickly, where I almost dozed off, still attached to my pump. While I was on leave, my baby and I had been going to bed really late and waking up late, and unfortunately, that schedule conflicted with the attorney schedule . . . so now I needed to get my baby to adapt to the hours of the litigation world. He did not take that well (which he shouldn't have; the pace of litigation is berserk). Shifting our rhythm and routine turned out to be one of the most exhausting and stressful parts of the entire motherhood experience.

I share this not to scare you (although if sleep deprivation is causing you severe anxiety and depression, there *are* accommodations for that—more in the next section) but simply to reassure you that if your first few days back in the office feel like an absolute haze, like you're swimming through soup and picking up only every fifth word that people say to you, that's okay.

The best-case scenario is that you simply pick up where you left off. At the same time, in a lot of ways, the first days back at work can feel like your first days at a new job entirely—you'll likely have to get up to speed on a lot of things, fast, you'll feel a bit out of step with the rhythm of the workday, and you might start questioning your sanity, your competence, and your path. The intense pace can feel aggressive, almost violent, to your tender animal body.

The most important thing I urge all new moms returning to work to do is to give things time. You know that saying about how you shouldn't make any major decisions in your marriage in the first year of parenthood? I'd say much the same thing about your job and your first six weeks back at work. There is just so much going on—physically, emotionally, mentally, hormonally—for you to get a clear read on how things really are at your job now that you're a mom, let alone how they'll be in the future.

So give yourself grace and recognize that this transition stage is temporary. You won't always cry at daycare drop-off, you'll get in the habit of packing and unpacking your pump every day, you *will* get real sleep again. You haven't lost your mind or your professional edge or any part of your brilliance—you've only added to it. And if you're struggling, make sure to request a ramp-up schedule, gradually increasing your days to full-time. You can do this as a PWFA request.

Getting Down to Business:
Picking Up Where You Left Off

With all that in mind, how do you actually just . . . start working again? After weeks wrapping swaddles and changing diapers, the world of work can feel like it's on another planet—full of urgency and machines. And then, when you do, it can feel like drinking from the fire hose—hundreds of emails, zillions of pings and chats, and a whole quarter's worth (or more) of progress to debrief on.

This (loose!) schedule helps you break down that first full week back at work into manageable, discrete, but still *flexible* chunks. Every company, every team, and every role is different, but my hope is you can adapt these general guidelines to your specific circumstances and use them as a way to take care of business *and* yourself in your first days back on the job.

DAY 1: CONNECTION AND CATCH-UP

Make sure your first day is *not* a Monday. Ideally it's a Thursday or Friday. It's too overwhelming to start with five days in a row.

Beginning of Shift: Start with a bit of gentle, collegial socialization. (Yes, there's work waiting, but you can spare a few minutes to reconnect with people.) Say hello to your supervisor and coworkers. Keep it low-pressure and casual—these are just informal catch-ups to hear about how things have been since you left, not official updates. Be prepared for questions about the baby (and requests for pictures): Come armed with simple answers if you don't want to go too deep.

Early in Your Shift: Check in with your supervisor about any changes to procedures, equipment, schedules, or safety protocols that happened while you were gone. If you work with machinery, take time to refamiliarize yourself before diving in. For retail, warehouse, or service workers, get updated on any new products, policies, or systems. Don't stress about being instantly up to speed—just take stock of what's different.

Mid-Shift: Have your "welcome back" check-in with your supervisor. Keep this one more of a "listening session" if you can, aiming to get the overall picture of what happened during your leave, but not yet taking on your full workload. Ask about any schedule adjustments you might need for pumping breaks or childcare pickup.

End of Shift: Reflect on the day. What emotions came up for you? What were unexpected moments of joy or tension? Take a few minutes to think about it on your commute home or jot down some quick notes. Then get back to your baby for some cuddles!

DAY 2: REVIEW

Beginning of Shift: Take time to review any posted schedules, shift rotations, or task assignments. For those in manufacturing, construction, or skilled trades, check the status of ongoing projects or equipment you typically work with. Use this information to mentally prepare for what your work will entail this week.

Early in Your Shift: Build a little momentum by easing into one or two familiar tasks. If you're in food service, maybe it's prep work rather than running the line. If you're in manufacturing, perhaps it's a routine task rather than something requiring split-second timing. The goal is to get back in the flow of "work time" and rebuild your muscle memory.

Mid-Shift: Chat with the coworker(s) who covered your position while you were on leave for a status update. If you're in healthcare, retail, or service work, ask about any regular customers or situations you should be aware of. For factory or warehouse workers, get updates on inventory levels or production goals.

End of Shift: If possible, check in briefly with your supervisor about how the day went and any areas where you might need support. For hourly workers who can't stay after their scheduled time, consider sending a quick text or having a brief conversation during a break. They'll appreciate the communication, and you'll feel good about being proactive.

DAY 3: FINDING YOUR RHYTHM

Beginning of Shift: If possible, try to focus on one of your core job responsibilities today. For construction or maintenance workers, this might be a specific type of repair. For healthcare aides, maybe it's focusing on patient care rather than paperwork. Reengaging with the heart of your work will help you feel more confident.

Break Time: Schedule something to look forward to during your break, whether it's enjoying a hot meal uninterrupted or stepping outside for fresh air. Find small moments of pleasure and self-care, even on the job. This is vital; otherwise, you will just find yourself giving endlessly.

Mid-Shift: Settle back into your work rhythm. Don't push yourself to work at your pre-baby pace—just get comfortable with a steady, sustainable work pace that allows you to be thorough and safe.

End of Shift: Take a moment to reflect: You're over halfway through your first week back! What's going well? What's challenging? If you're on your feet all day, how is your body holding up? Consider what adjustments might help (different shoes, compression socks, etc.) and make notes about what to bring tomorrow.

DAY 4: RECALIBRATE AND REENGAGE

Beginning of Shift: Three days down! If you work in a team environment like a kitchen, production line, or construction crew, focus today on rebuilding those collaborative relationships and communication patterns.

Mid-Shift: Now that you've had a chance to immerse yourself back in the work, reflect on your energy levels and physical stamina. Are you able to maintain focus throughout your shift? For physically demanding jobs, are you pacing yourself appropriately? Check in with your body and adjust accordingly.

End of Shift: Reflect on what you appreciate about being back to work—even if the list is short. Maybe it's using skills that feel like part of your identity, interaction with adults, or simply the satisfaction of completing tasks. Even "I get to have conversations about something other than wake windows" counts as a win!

DAY 5: YOU DID IT!

Beginning of Shift: You've almost made it through your first week! Focus today on settling into routines that will sustain you going forward. If you need to pump at work, make sure your break times are working well. For those with variable schedules, confirm next week's assignments.

Mid-Shift: Take note of what went well this week and what might need improvement. Maybe you need more comfortable workwear, different shoes, or to request a specific accommodation. For shift workers, consider if your current schedule is compatible with childcare arrangements.

End of Shift: Have a quick check-in with your supervisor about the week. This is a good time to address any issues with break times for pumping, physical limitations, or schedule needs. For hourly workers who can't extend their shifts, consider arranging a brief meeting during your break time or asking to speak with them before you clock out.

Weekend Prep: Do your "future self" a favor by preparing what you'll need for next week. Pack your work bag with extra breast pads if you're nursing, prepare easy-to-grab lunches, and lay out work clothes or uniforms. Consider meal-prepping for your family to make weekday evenings less hectic.

Return-to-Work Pro Tips for All Workers

Weekly Planning: Before I was a mother, I made daily to-do lists. After becoming a mother, I switched to weekly planning. It's much easier to complete tasks by the end of the week than by the end of each day, because your energy levels will fluctuate. This approach works especially well for those with physically demanding jobs—save more challenging tasks for your higher-energy days.

Physical Recovery: If your job requires standing, lifting, or repetitive movements, be honest about your physical limitations. Your body is still healing, even months after childbirth. Ask for help with heavy lifting or take an extra minute for tasks that strain your body.

Childcare Backup Plans: Always have a plan B (and C) for childcare. For shift workers who can't easily leave in the middle of work, identify who you can call if your primary childcare falls through.

Communication: Keep lines of communication open with your supervisor, especially if you're in a role where missing a shift impacts others. Most supervisors would rather know in advance about potential issues than be surprised by a last-minute call-out.

Self-Compassion: Accept that you're not at pre-baby productivity yet, and that's completely okay. That pace was probably unhealthy anyway. Your weekly goals should account for lower energy days—they're to be expected and necessary as you adjust to your new normal.

The Ultimate Power Move: Extending Your Leave

Jessica, a nurse practitioner, had been back at work for two and a half weeks, but despite what everyone said, it just wasn't getting any easier.

She'd drop her son off at daycare, force a smile for bye-bye, and then cry the whole drive to work. Every evening felt like a rush to cram in as much quality time as possible, and every weekend was lost to a major case of the Sunday scaries, to the point where she was losing sleep. Even her lunch breaks, when she had a moment to sit and think, became a trigger for fresh tears.

Working in healthcare was a constant worry too. Jessica cared deeply about her patients and had always loved working in her community, but the thought of bringing a virus home to her baby son made her stomach twist with dread. She washed her hands obsessively, sanitized everything, and still wondered if she was doing enough to keep him safe. She and her husband had spent years trying to conceive, and her baby felt so precious and precarious to her, like each time they snuggled might be the last time she'd hold him in her arms.

Jessica was dealing with postpartum anxiety (PPA), a very real and very debilitating condition that can start any time after giving birth. PPA can sometimes overlap with the related condition, postpartum depression (PPD), but it can also come on independently.

Symptoms That May Indicate PPA or PPD

- Depressed mood or severe mood swings
- Crying bouts
- Difficulty bonding with your baby
- Withdrawing from family and friends
- Loss of appetite or eating much more than usual
- Sleep problems (insomnia or excessive sleepiness)
- Overwhelming tiredness or loss of energy
- Less interest and pleasure in activities you used to enjoy
- Intense irritability and anger
- Fear that you're "not a good mother"
- Persistent worries about your baby's safety or health
- Feelings of worthlessness, shame, guilt, or inadequacy
- Reduced ability to think clearly, concentrate, or make decisions
- Panic attacks
- Thoughts of harming yourself or your baby
- Recurring thoughts of death or suicide

If you are experiencing a crisis, call or text 988 for your local mental health hotline.

The good news (such as it is) is that both PPA and PPD aren't just "hormones" or "baby blues" or "feeling out of it": They're medical conditions that can qualify you for accommodations, such as an extended leave under the Pregnant Workers Fairness Act (remember that from earlier?) so you have the time and spaciousness you need to get your mental health taken care of.

Fortunately for Jessica, she was a trained healthcare expert and was able to investigate her own symptoms. She knew she needed help. After seeing her own OB/GYN, Jessica was referred to a perinatal mental health specialist who agreed that she had PPA and offered to write a letter attesting to her condition. Jessica used that letter to request a leave extension of six weeks, during which time she also started therapy.

Returning to work after welcoming a baby to the family is hard, even when things go as smoothly as possible. If you are still physically disabled, or struggling with PPA, PPD, or another postpartum mood disorder, please know first that you are not alone. I've supported thousands of mothers who are in this exact place. Second, you don't have to tough it out. You may be able to take additional time off by using the PWFA, like Jessica did, to request a leave extension as an accommodation. And yes, this is a power move. No, you are not "failing" anyone if you need more time to address your anxiety or depression. In fact, it's exactly the most fierce and initiated mothers who will push to the maximum expansion and ultimate edge of their rights to protect their health and their babies. I would go as far as saying that PPA and PPD are natural responses to a culture that fails to support mothers. Being honest about your experience does not mean you can't handle the experience; it just means you have an excellent relationship with your body. There are many mothers who are actually experiencing PPA or PPD, but are too in denial, numb, or detached (I was one of them). It is so, so good to be in the truth of what is actually happening. It is a beautiful way to honor your body and model what it looks like to be an embodied mother.

As a refresher, the PWFA states that "It is an unlawful employment practice to . . . not make reasonable accommodations to the known limitations related to the pregnancy, childbirth, or related medical conditions of a qualified employee, unless [the employer] can demonstrate that the accommodation would impose an undue hardship."

This means that if you need an extended disability leave because you have mental and/or medical limitations, your employer has to grant it, so long as the request is reasonable and not an undue burden for the employer. If the temp in your position is doing a fine job, and you need a few more weeks to fully manage your PPA, then there is no burden on the employer to keep your job open for a few additional weeks. However, if the company is going down because you are an essential employee and they have been eagerly awaiting your return, they may not be able to keep your job open if you ask for six more months. I had a case where a mother maxed out her leave to recover from miscarriage, and asked for an extension. The company denied it, even though her work projects were "on hold" without any prejudice to the company. Again, "reasonable" and "undue burden" are vague, but using good judgment should make it easier to understand what's possible.

Transparently, it is easiest to get these accommodations in white-collar, office-type jobs, especially if most of the work is done on a computer. However, it is not impossible to get these accommodations if you provide manual labor, work in on-demand industries like food prep, janitorial services, healthcare, or education. In fact, the bulk of my clients through the course of my career have been blue-collar workers, and you'd be surprised how creative some traditionally inflexible workplaces can get when they need to accommodate mothers.

As with pregnancy-related accommodations, you'll need to be eligible for the PWFA (see page 97). When requesting a leave extension as a postpartum accommodation, it's best to give your employer notice in writing and as early as possible. Communicate with both your direct supervisor(s) and HR, cc'ing both on your emails, and bcc'ing your personal email address (just to be safe).

As for the request itself, there are no "magic words" you have to use to get your accommodation approved, but you do have to alert your employer of your postpartum-related needs (i.e., you can't just stop showing up and later inform them it was due to PPD) and then make a request for an accommodation. Make sure to explain your limitation in some detail and its connection to your postpartum conditions. Here's an example email:

> Hello [Name],
>
> The last date of my leave is [date]. Unfortunately, I am still disabled. It would be challenging for me to execute all of my job duties in light of my restrictions because the work would exacerbate my symptoms.
>
> [Include a brief explainer as to why/how the work would make your symptoms worse.]
>
> Upon the advice of my healthcare provider, I am attaching the requested leave extension as a reasonable accommodation under the PWFA. My return date would be [date].
>
> Please confirm whether you will approve these accommodations. I understand the company has to engage in the interactive process to investigate this request, and that it can only be denied if the

accommodation is an undue burden on the company, which I
understand to be a high bar.

   If you do intend on denying my request, please propose some
alternatives. In addition, please communicate with me before any
decision to deny is finalized so that I can determine my options.

   I'm happy to discuss these issues further.

Thank you,

[Your Name]

It's best not to go into too much detail about your baby. Often, I'll see mamas write pages and pages about how their baby doesn't sleep or doesn't take the bottle and, frankly, your boss doesn't really care. Your workplace is not the forum to submit your grievances about your baby (trust your mama crew with those). Your employer only needs to know how your limitations are impacting your job duties.

While a doctor's note isn't, strictly speaking, a legal requirement, it's my experience that you'll also have a much higher chance of success if you go in with one ready, like Jessica did. You can *try* to ask your employer for an accommodation without medical support, but more likely than not, your employer will just come back and ask you for a medical note anyway, so you might as well get one ready ahead of time (especially since it can be so hard to see a doctor on short notice).

Generally, an employer would expect a note from a provider who is authorized to write medical notes, so if you have already been having discussions about your needs with your OB, GP, or a psychiatrist, it would be a natural next step for your doctor to write a note for you to provide to your employer. BUT (!!!!) I have seen many employers accept therapy notes, midwife notes, even chiropractor notes as sufficient. If you want to cover all your bases, you can also ask your mental health providers to act as a team: Your (non-MD) therapist might be able to draft a memo for your primary care doctor with a specific list of your diagnoses, symptoms, and treatment plans, which your (MD) doc could then use to write the medical note.

Your Doctor Is Not a Lawyer

Just like you shouldn't trust me with medical advice, your doctor is not the ultimate authority when it comes to your employment rights. Doctors are important, busy people, but they are not lawyers.

Recently, I gave a presentation to NICU nurses and staff about postpartum rights, and I was given the following scenario, which I have heard SO MANY TIMES.

Mom: Doc, I am experiencing PPD / mastitis / pelvic pain / birth PTSD / pregnancy loss / other limitations and I cannot return to work just yet. I want to extend my disability leave or ask for disability accommodations.

Doctor: No, I don't think you're disabled. I can't write you a note for that. You'll need to go back to work.

Hold my breast pump, Doc. The law recognizes pregnancy- and birth-related medical issues as legal disabilities, including the ones listed above. The issue is that we may have a disagreement as to the scope of a medical disability and a legal disability, but for a worker to request accommodations, we only need to follow the employment rules. And you, dear doctor, do not *make* the employment rules, and you usually don't know them either.

So, what if this happens to you?

Bring the law to your doc. Highlight the portion that applies to you. This will usually be a section of the Pregnant Workers Fairness Act. (Seriously—I've had some of my clients do that and often the doctors feel embarrassed that they had it wrong on the law and immediately jumped to help, even going as far as calling other patients to educate them on potential accommodation options.)

Advocate with your doc. The way you feel about your own limitations should be taken into account. If you genuinely do not feel capable of working because of a physical or mental limitation, they should honor that.

Switch doctors. If your doctor puts the "OB" in "obstructionist," find a new provider. Some are more willing than others to work with their patients. If you need to find something quickly, you may need to book a one-off consult with a private psychiatrist.

In the note itself, your doctor should specify your limitations related to your postpartum condition and recommend an accommodation. *The note should specify the time frame needed. This should be a specific window, not a vague "when my condition improves." (Employers are not expected to accommodate an infinite window).* Keep in mind that you can always start with a request to extend your leave by a few weeks (I'd say about four weeks, max six), and then ask for another extension before that time is up, so providing a firm return-to-work date in the letter isn't necessarily the final word on the matter.

It can be a good idea to request one accommodation per medical need, but you can also propose a variety of accommodations as long as they are each reasonable. It's also best, but not necessary, to be specific about how your postpartum-related condition affects your experience at work so your employer can fully understand how to help you.

Finally, it's so, so important to know that you are protected from retaliation for making this request, *whether or not it is granted.* This is all part of the law.

I don't feel comfortable sharing private medical information with my employer. What do I do?

An employer cannot require a diagnosis from you if you are requesting a PWFA accommodation, as the focus is on your ability to perform your job duties, not the specific diagnosis. However, in my experience, it is very hard to speak about "the thing" without naming "the thing," because "the thing" and how it impacts your job is at issue.

I recommend disclosing medical information to the extent you feel comfortable, as it will put you in the strongest position to get accommodated.

Your employer may need to ask questions about your pregnancy-related limitations to be able to provide effective accommodations at work.

If your employer does not have enough information, the request can be denied. Ultimately you cannot have both complete privacy and accommodations. You have to choose.

Limited questions regarding a reasonable accommodation are okay, as long as the questions are tailored to assess your limitations in relation to your ability to carry out your job.

Will my medical information be kept confidential if I submit it along with my request?

Yes, your employer should keep the information confidential, but they may share the information with supervisors on a "need-to-know" basis. Your employer will also have to ask your immediate manager whether the request can actually be accommodated, so your manager will likely be notified of your request and limitations. No, you cannot keep this between you and HR. People often completely misinterpret HIPAA rules (notice the spelling; this is the correct spelling). It does not mean you just have blanket medical privacy rights. For example, a former client felt comfortable communicating with HR about her medical restrictions but was frustrated that her information was shared with her direct supervisor, as she was not ready for him to know. As part of the interactive process, it is actually your employer's obligation to ask your immediate supervisor questions about your job duties so they can see how you can be accommodated. So no, this is not a HIPAA violation. HIPAA protections are mainly an employer's responsibility to have measures in place to protect your data from unauthorized access (like a data breach).

What if I don't have a medical condition (and neither does my baby) but I still want to take more leave than I originally planned for?

In that case, a leave extension would be a privilege and not covered by accommodation regulations. If you are not ready to return to work upon the expiration of your leave, you can be terminated and it's legally fair and square.

However, while requesting extended leave could put you in the danger zone, it can be done successfully. Here's what I recommend.

If you want to continue your leave beyond what you're entitled to under the law, explain that you want to return, but that it's extremely difficult at this time, and you are actively working on the challenge.

> My baby is still very attached to me. Every time I give her to a
> caretaker, she will scream. We have been working on this every day,
> and while it is getting better, I am not ready. She will not take the

bottle at times, either, which causes me great anxiety. We are in the process of retaining an expert to help us figure this out, but in the meantime, I want you to have a productive employee and right now I will be too worried about my baby not eating and dropping to a dangerously low weight.

Please know I am committed to returning to work. I love my work and I have missed it, and it is genuinely important to me, as I believe my track record clearly shows. Right now, I simply request four more weeks of leave so that my baby and I can get used to being apart.

In the meantime, I will do everything I can to stay on track. You can send me updates on projects so I can start reviewing what I've missed while the baby is sleeping, and I will make myself available over email to get back in the loop with our team.

I am hoping for your compassion during this vulnerable stage in my life right now. I rely on this job for healthcare and my income to pay the bills. I have always done my best for you and made work a priority even over personal commitments. I now ask that you support my family during this difficult time. I promise that this is temporary, and that your investment will be returned through my long-term loyalty and dedicated commitment.

I will tell everyone in the community what you are doing for my family and how supportive you are of women and babies. We really need your support right now. Will you please help me?

Who could say no to that?

Telework and Flexibility Accommodations

Another way to make it easier for you during your postpartum period is by requesting an accommodation for telework or flexibility. In fact, that's exactly what I did after the infamous breastmilk-all-over-the-judge's-sandwich trial. A week after winning that trial, I approached my boss and said: "I need a postpartum accommodation. I want flexibility." He agreed and said, "You've earned it." I smiled and thanked him.

The challenging aspect of a flexibility or a teleworking accommodation is enforcing it. At first, I enjoyed my newfound relative freedom. I worked from home more, went to the occasional yoga class during lunchtime, and would take my time in the mornings, waiting out that Southern California traffic a bit (which had been such a stressor and time leak). It was a game changer for my family life and mental health. However, very quickly, junior staff started to moan that I wasn't there for meetings or trainings. After all, the others did not have a flexibility accommodation. So I started to feel guilty that I was offered privileges that others weren't, and it cut into my appetite to fully embrace the flexibility I was offered. Over the years, I cared less and less about what others thought, but it did cause a rift. I know they likely resented me, which is actually completely fair. Ideally, flexibility is a team-wide culture. Feeling singled out as "the mom" can sometimes exacerbate the isolation.

Getting an accommodation is only the beginning. Moving through your workplace doing "less" or being there "less" requires constant fine-tuning and boundary setting, including with yourself. It can feel like moving out of the left lane to take a few pit stops, except everyone is still in the left lane, so you're just sitting off the highway by yourself. So yes, it can sometimes make you feel guilty, and like you're "behind." And yet—it's worth it. I'm really glad I ended up standing firm in my flexibility needs, despite being the only one who was offered this privilege. It is an act of rebellion to say no to the pace at work. You may "miss out," but you will gain so so much more: You'll protect your body, your baby, your ability to say no and rely on your inner strength. These are skills and memories you will cherish (and use) for the rest of your life.

I'm not at the job anymore, I'm not in contact with that team anymore, but it made my early motherhood experience infinitely easier, and for that, I am grateful.

Docs can be uncooperative, but it is also risky when they are too generous. "Patient is not yet cleared to work, return date TBD" is how doctors accidentally get their patients (legally) fired. Docs can legitimize medical leave or accommodations, but your employer (or a lawyer like me) will review these requests based on workplace rights. These rights have multiple elements AND they have limits. Medical approval doesn't guarantee job approval.

10

Let's Get Pumped
Lactation and Work

My client Alyssa was already tired when she came back to work postpartum. She worked long shifts processing packages in a fast-paced, sprawling retail warehouse, and everything she did was timed down to the second: If she stepped away from her workstation, no matter the reason, the monitoring system would detect her absence, stop the time clock, and effectively pause her paid hours until she returned.

As if that weren't stressful enough, Alyssa was lactating and needed to pump her breastmilk regularly. Unfortunately, the designated pumping space provided by her employer was several floors and a *long* walk away from her workstation. Even worse, there were multiple lactating mothers working in that warehouse, which led to long lines to use the space even once she got there (or a bunch of topless women awkwardly sharing the room together). Alyssa was losing time, losing money, losing her dignity, losing her supply, and going through incredible discomfort the whole time.

Another client of mine, Jasmine, had her own issues with pumping at work. Jasmine was a mid-level manager in a big corporation, one that had given her a decent paid leave and was eager to have her back in the office, touting their new-and-improved private multi-purpose room she could use to pump in. But when Jasmine blocked off her calendar, packed up her pump, and dutifully went down the hall to use the designated room, one of her coworkers was in there . . . doing her "daily affirmations practice." When she reported to her boss that she had no private space to pump, the boss basically shrugged her off. "Well, I can't just kick them out. It's a multi-purpose quiet room. They also have a right to be there."

Then there was my client Romy, who was a barista at a major coffee shop chain. When she returned to her job as a lactating mother, her supervisor's solution was to have her pump in the bathroom. Romy, exhausted and frazzled on her first day back on the job, just went ahead and pumped there but made it clear to her supervisor that she knew her rights, and the bathroom could only be a temporary solution. Yet when she repeatedly raised the question of lactation space to her supervisor, promises were made . . . and nothing ever happened. Escalating to corporate HR just got her caught in a bureaucratic loop of "not my problem." And all the while, Romy had no choice but to pump somewhere explicitly prohibited as a pumping area by law. Romy called me and cried, "They want me to pour the milk, but I can't even pour my own milk! Imagine if I were pouring the customers' lattes from the bathroom. The business would go down the drain."

We read so much about conceiving successfully, staying healthy while pregnant, and preparing for birth, yet comparably little about breastfeeding: what it requires of you, what it looks like in a practical sense, and what you need in order to express breastmilk when away from your baby (like while you're at work). As a result, breastfeeding, lactation, and pumping are parts of motherhood that a lot of people don't truly understand until they go through it (at least, I didn't).

This chapter is designed to close that information gap: to introduce the reality of pumping and breastfeeding, to teach you the legal protections you have (because, yes, "lactating mother" is a protected class!), and, most importantly, to get you *pumped up*—pun very much intended. Because, information gap or no, to truly be successful in getting what you need, you need to know what you're legally entitled to, but you *also* need that inner, unshakable confidence that will see you through the process of getting there.

Alyssa the warehouse worker, Jasmine the corporate middle manager, and Romy the barista all had very different industries, careers, and workplace norms. Yet all of them were having their rights violated, and all of them had strong cases (that's why I took them on as clients). And once they got (yes) pumped up, they triumphed in the end.

Alyssa came to learn that taking a stand was not only an act of bravery for herself, but for all the other lactating mothers who needed that space to keep *their* babies fed and healthy. Jasmine needed to tap into her inner sense of righteous mama bear energy and fight back against her boss's wishy-washiness—because "wellness girlie" is not a protected class, and "lactating person" is. Romy needed to stay the course, even when the fight felt endless and she felt literally and emotionally drained, and ultimately triumphed, with a judgment in her favor and a new lactation pod installed at her worksite.

So allow me to pump you up the way I pumped them up: *Welcome* to the special club of pumping mamas. It takes tremendous grit, determination, and a sprinkle of luck to be a pumping mama.

On behalf of your child, thank you. Because of you, your child will have a kickass immune system and a deep bonding experience. These are gifts they will carry for the rest of their lives. They can't tell you yet, so allow me—I see your sacrifice. And we haven't even talked about work.

I know you may be worried about the impact of your pump sessions on your productivity. I also know that the thought of your baby will make your boobs and your heart hurt, and that tears will burst out of your eyes if you think about it for too long.

Dear Mama, your longing to be with your baby is so natural and so normal. Capitalism thrives on the separation of mother and baby. So, if you ever feel sad about not being with your baby, please know . . . *nothing about that is your fault.* Your guilt and your grief is just proof of your boundless love for your child. Your baby is so incredibly lucky to be the recipient of your milky love.

Remember, being a good mom also means providing for your child financially. Fathers have been branded as the "providers," and here you are: providing, in infinite ways.

See: lucky, lucky baby!

Pumping 101

We tend to think of breast pumps as something of a modern marvel, a nifty invention that makes it possible for moms to take off for the office in the morning and return home with plenty of nutritious milk for their baby (and no painful engorgement), all while never missing a beat of their workday. In reality, breast pumps have been around since ancient Egypt (when they were made of clay), with the more typical forms we're used to emerging around the time of the Industrial Revolution (thanks to the discovery of vulcanized rubber) and finally adding a mechanical component for the first time in the 1920s.

In other words, although you might think of a breast pump as a kind of optional, high-tech accessory for Today's Mom™, it's actually a device almost as old as breastfeeding itself—and given that 85 percent of lactating mothers will use a pump at some point during their breastfeeding journey, it's one you'll want to get familiar with.

At its most basic, a breast pump is a device that uses suction to express milk from your breast so that it can be stored (or frozen!) for later, fed immediately to your baby in a bottle, or simply extracted from your body to relieve the pressure of engorgement. (Ouch.) Breast pumps allow lactating mothers to feed their baby even while spending extended periods of time apart (such as at work), but they are also used by some breastfeeding mothers whose babies have trouble latching directly to the breast, who need to stimulate increased milk production when their supply is low, or who simply prefer to pump and bottle-feed expressed milk for a variety of reasons.

You'll likely be covered for a basic electric breast pump through your health insurance, with the option to upgrade to "fancier" models for an additional out-of-pocket cost. (I put "fancier" in quotes because some of the "upgrade" features are hardly luxury: Even things as simple as a battery pack or a quieter motor can be too ritzy for insurance to cover.) But just like no two boobs (even on the same person) are alike, no two pumps are identical—or likely to work for everyone. You should anticipate, and even expect, to test (and pay for) at least a few different sizes of flanges or cups (the part that goes on your boob), pumping bras (to hold the flanges in place), and even pumps themselves (different bodies respond to different pumps, well, differently, or you might prefer a portable pump, or a hands-free pump-and-flange combo or . . .).

Your pump-at-work kit will also need to include containers to store your expressed milk in (lots of people use plastic breastmilk storage bags, but there are plenty of options), and, because any part that touches milk needs to be washed and dried after use, either pump cleaning supplies (you *don't* want to be using the nasty office breakroom sponge, after all—there are lots of travel washing-up kits to be found for this exact purpose) or enough sets of accessories to last through all your daily pumps (so you can then wash at home).

Basic Pumping Setup

- Breast pump and power source
- Pump accessories (flanges, tubing, membranes, valves)
- Storage for expressed milk (bottles or plastic breastmilk bags)
- Washing-up supplies (sponge, soap, small basin, mini drying rack)
- A carrier + cooler bag for everything (include ice packs)
- Pumping bra + cover (it can feel weird to be topless in an office setting)
- A blanket (offices tend to run cold, set to the temp of men in suits)

As for when you'll be pumping, there are a few factors to consider. The typical advice for pumping moms is to pump as often as you would nurse your baby during the day, but plenty of moms deviate from that schedule once they go back to work. Personally, I did three pumps until the baby was six months, then two pumps until the baby was nine months, then one pump until the baby was twelve months, and then I stopped. But that's just me! Without knowing the ferocity and work ethic of your boobies, it's hard to predict—but basically, you'll want to pump often enough during the day for your own comfort and health (because going too long without expressing milk can be painful, and even dangerous, if engorgement turns into mastitis, an infection of the breast tissue). You'll want to spend enough time pumping to produce the amount of milk you need for your baby (which will vary from baby to baby, and whether you combination feed with formula or exclusively breastfeed). And, finally, you'll need to work your pumping breaks into your workday.

Ultimately—especially if you're a first-time mom—it's hard to know for sure what your pumping routine will look like, and a lot of this will come with trial and error. But what you *can* go in knowing for sure is what your legal rights are.

Legal Protections:
Your Rights as a Lactating Mother

Rachel, a dedicated admin assistant and new mom, faced an unexpected challenge during the pandemic. As a pumping mom, Rachel enjoyed the (small) silver lining of remote work: It was *way* easier to pump. She could work shirtless if she wanted—in the privacy of her own home office, who cared? Except Rachel never actually asked for pumping breaks and assumed she could just pump as needed, as she was in her own home. Rachel's job started to pick up its pace, and her boss started scheduling her for back-to-back Zoom meetings with clients. Still, Rachel did not ask for official pumping breaks because she felt that that was private information that her employer was not entitled to. After all, she was in her own house! Plus she was worried she would fall outside the graces of her employer if they knew she was doing "mommy things" during work hours. However, Rachel started to miss the beginnings of meetings and leave early, and her boss was not pleased. Rachel was spoken to about time management issues, and her boss threatened to revoke her remote work arrangement. Only then, on my urging, did she actually notify her boss of her pumping needs and get a clear schedule in writing.

If Rachel would have come to me earlier, I would have advised her to be more transparent. She had pumping rights but was scared and uncomfortable to use them. Unfortunately, you cannot have both complete privacy and also job protection.

In contrast, Alara, a teacher, was very vocal about her need to pump. She worked as a caretaker at a daycare. She asked her employer for pumping accommodations, and then her boss told her she could not provide these breaks because she was a salaried worker and fell outside the protections of pumping accommodations, and either way, they didn't have enough coverage for her to take the break. Alara was shocked. How could she be caring for babies all day, using the breastmilk of their mothers in their bottles, but she could not pump milk for her *own* baby? This felt cruel, and strange, like the wires got crossed for everyone.

As absurd as it may sound, this scenario used to be par for the course for pumping moms, and there was often nothing to be done.

Then, on December 29, 2022, we welcomed something beautiful into the world. No, not a baby—a piece of legislation.

With the passage of the Providing Urgent Maternal Protections (PUMP) Act—although, really, on its effective date of April 28, 2023— nine million more women of childbearing age gained critical protections for breastfeeding and pumping at work. (Previously, only hourly workers had rights to pump at work, leaving out many essential roles—teachers, nurses, and salaried professionals.) This law expanded lactation rights to all employees,* ensuring that women across professions have the legal space to care for their babies while they work.

It wasn't that lactating mothers had *zero* rights before this—they were just incredibly patchwork. Before there was any kind of federal act, many states had tried to fill in the gaps with their own laws, which really only added confusion to the mix, as companies and employees alike struggled to interpret a whole host of state-specific regulations. In the PUMP Act, we replaced the patchwork with a glorious banner: a consistent federal baseline to give us clarity and a universal set of rights.

However, as a lawyer, what excited me the most about this blessed event was the enforceability of these rights. Unlike previous laws, which didn't have much in the way of recourse for women whose rights were violated, the PUMP Act has *teeth*. Denied your pumping breaks? Treated unfairly because you asked for time to pump? Made—as Romy was—to pump in a disgusting *bathroom*?! Bam—you now have the right to seek justice through the courts. This baby allows you to seek compensation for stress and anxiety, lost wages, expenses like formula costs or unpaid leave, and even punitive damages to hold your employer accountable. Best of all, many attorneys will take these cases on a contingency basis, so you won't need to pay legal fees out of pocket.

---

* Except, unfortunately, those in airline roles.

To be sure, the PUMP Act isn't perfect. There are still a few gaps. But it's better than most mamas being forced to stop breastfeeding prematurely, which is what was happening previously. And that's a start.

Before we dive into the specifics, it's also important to know that the PUMP Act sets a baseline—meaning it's the *minimum* standard your employer must meet. Some states provide even more robust protections, and in those states, you're entitled to the federal standard plus any additional state rights. For instance, Illinois requires that employers pay employees while they're pumping, even if they're not actively working, while in California, the law mandates access to a refrigerator and a sink for milk storage, and there's no age limit for pumping accommodations—so you can still pump at work for your eighteen-month-old (or eighteen-year-old for the hippie mamas, jk, jk). There are a few more state expansions; I cover all these nuances in my program.

The PUMP Act says the following: "An employer shall provide a reasonable break time for an employee to express breastmilk for such employee's nursing child for 1 year after the child's birth each time such employee has need to express the milk; and a place, other than a bathroom, that is shielded from view and free from intrusion from coworkers and the public, which may be used by an employee to express breastmilk."

That means:

1. You have the right to pump each time you need to pump for a reasonable break time.
2. You have the right to pump for up to one year after your child's birth.
3. You have the right to pump in a private place that is *not* a bathroom.

The PUMP Act protects all employees: salaried and hourly, full-time and part-time, in-person and remote. And it protects all employees regardless of how long they've worked for an employer.

The PUMP Act does *not* protect the following:

- Employees in the airline industry.
- Employees working for businesses with fewer than fifty employees if the pumping breaks constitute an "undue burden." (This is a very high bar that few employers are able to meet.)
- Gig or contract workers.
- Prior to 2025, railway and motorcoach workers.

One of the most common sticking points here is what we saw with Romy earlier: Bosses hear "private" and think "bathroom." That doesn't cut it—so let's break down what does.

First, a pumping space must be clean—and I don't mean "tidy," but truly sanitary. You should feel confident that your milk won't get contaminated and you're not stewing around in other people's germs.

Then there's *usable*. "Usable" means functional. You'll need access to a nearby refrigerator to store your milk safely. Ideally, there's also a flat surface to set your supplies on—not the floor, of course. Running water is a bonus, making it easier to clean up afterward. The space doesn't have to be a permanent, dedicated room, but it must be available whenever you need it, no matter what.

And then there's private. Privacy means no interruptions or unexpected visitors. No one should be able to just walk in without your okay, there shouldn't be a camera or a peeking window in sight, and the space must be shielded from anyone trying to look in.

But what if you're in Romy's position, and the only option your workplace offers is a bathroom? Too bad—they have to do better. Legally, they're obligated to provide an alternative that isn't a bathroom. Don't hesitate to email the text of the law to point this out.

The solution here doesn't have to be fancy or even permanent. They could clean out the supply closet, put up a heavy curtain in an office, place a lock on a conference room door, set aside a changing room, or even use a portable lactation tent or pod.

OFFICE PUMPING SPACE CHECKLIST

- Space that is private (i.e., shielded from view), sanitary, and designated for pumping (bathrooms don't qualify—gross!)
- Door that locks
- Comfortable chair/seating, clean, flat surface for the pump itself, and adequate space to sit and pump
- Access to an electrical outlet
- Access to running water (to wash hands and pump parts—can be in a different room but must be easily accessible)
- Signage (e.g., a "Do Not Disturb" sign)

As for when you pump, the law here is supportive: You decide when and how often you need a break. (After all, you're the only one who knows your body's needs.) The law guarantees "reasonable time" for pumping, which means there's no rigid timer to dictate how long you should spend: You can set the pace and duration based on what works best for you.

While you can use your regular breaks if it's convenient, the PUMP Act also provides extra time for pumping, separate from your typical work breaks. Coordinating with your usual break schedule can sometimes minimize disruption (and help you avoid any loss in pay, since pumping breaks are protected *but* unpaid). Your employer may request alignment with existing breaks, but if you need more time, it has to be granted.

I'm Breastfeeding and Work Remotely: Can I Take Nursing Breaks?

Strictly speaking, the law only gives you the right to pump, not feed your baby.

A mistake I see a lot of women make is that they ask for accommodations based on their baby's needs. Remember, your baby doesn't work at your job, and therefore has no rights in your workplace. Your boss has no obligation to accommodate your baby, only to accommodate you. (Similarly, you are not protected to ask for accommodations because your baby doesn't have enough food. You actually have to rely on your own rights to get your supply back up.)

This means that remote workers do not have the right to feed their babies "right off the tap." Nor do you as an employee have the right to work remotely or go on leave because your baby is refusing the bottle. The only possible scenario where you could successfully advocate for breaks to nurse is with a note from your doctor about the medical consequences of not being able to feed directly (anxiety, mastitis, etc.) to get a lactation accommodation under the PWFA.

Of course, even though the law protects your right to pump, you still have to ask for those breaks. (And if you are hiding your needs and do not assert your pumping rights, you can be legally terminated for taking "unauthorized" breaks, so long as your employer had no knowledge you were taking these breaks to pump.)

And, as with all things motherhood and work, knowing your rights is one thing, but asserting them is another.

Can We Talk About My Boobs for a Sec? Educating Your Colleagues

In the workplace, you really have to assume a complete lack of understanding when it comes to lactation—on the legal *and* physiological front.

Male colleagues might be utterly clueless—or know only a scattered few things from their partners. Female colleagues might be more in the know, but many (especially from older generations) may have used formula and lack firsthand breastfeeding experience. And that's *before* accounting for edge cases—remote work logistics, off-site pumping challenges, or even sexual harassment around breastfeeding—where even well-intentioned managers can slip up due to ignorance.

Unfortunately, there's no unit in HR or management training on the beautiful process that is making milk out of blood. This means you have to do a lot of the educating yourself, both on what you need personally and on what you're legally required to.

And *that* means you have to actually talk to your boss about your boobs.

I know—eek. It's second only to the awkwardness of announcing your pregnancy (and therefore, I suppose, confirming you have in fact *Had Sex*. Gasp!). And, of course, you won't be using the phrase "my boobs," but, in essence, that's what you're doing, and yes, it can feel extremely uncomfortable. You're bridging two powerful frontiers of emotional reality: the awesome power you now have to keep another human being alive using only your body, and the humiliation of having to talk to your boss about, well, your boobs.

Fortunately, armed with legal knowledge and your own pumping schedule, there *are* ways to keep this conversation on a professional, need-to-know basis while still getting every single thing you're entitled to as a lactating mother.

This starts with stating your rights and establishing your intentions. During pregnancy, when you are figuring out your leave plan, let your employers know that you intend to return as a lactating mother. Then, when you're preparing to return, make sure to give notice of your state as a lactating mother *before* you return to work, and confidently ask for the breaks you need. I recommend doing this at least thirty days prior to returning to work (whether in-person or remotely). Send this email directly to HR and cc your immediate supervisor. (If there's no HR department, elevate it to the highest level of management, and cc your immediate supervisor.)

> Dear [Name],
>
> I am returning to work on [Date].
>
> When I return to work, I am seeking pumping accommodations according to the PUMP Act as well as 29 U.S.C. 207. I understand these laws allow me to take reasonable break time when I will need to express breastmilk.
>
> I also understand I should have access to a lactation space that is private, and not a bathroom.
>
> I also understand I may not be retaliated against for requesting these rights.

> [Optional, if applicable: As I can continue working while pumping, I
> understand my time spent pumping has to be counted as paid time.]
>
> Please respond to this email by confirming my rights. I am
> happy to discuss the best practices for setting up these breaks and
> this space. It's my intention to provide ample notice and minimize
> disruptions.
>
> I am excited to return to work. Your support is vital in allowing my
> baby to receive the nutrition needed, and will allow me to succeed as
> a working mother.
>
> Thank you,
>
> [Your Name]

In an ideal world, that will be that—HR confirms your rights, your supervisor is on board, you come to the office to find a beautifully appointed pumping space, and no one ever gives you so much as a weird look.

In reality . . . that might not happen. *Best* worst-case scenario, you get ghosted for a bit and have to be polite and persistent to get your needs acknowledged. Or your boss might be like Mona's, who said, quote, "Eww, gross! I don't need to know all of that!" (Uh, yes, yes, you do. Sorry, dude.) Or they might be like Leanne's, who told her, "Unfortunately, it's really not convenient for you to take breaks so often, but we can give you a solid hour in the middle of the afternoon—can't you just pump it all out then?" (Ma'am . . . no, no, I cannot.) Or like Nydea's, who asked for a *doctor's note* as "proof" (proof of . . . what, her baby needing to eat?!).

In instances like that, you've got to hold the line and do the educating.

First off, it really doesn't matter how your boss feels about it. Their feelings are not more important than your baby's RIGHT TO FOOD. We are talking about the survival of your baby, and everything else has to wait and everyone else has to bow to your baby's nutritional needs, #sorrynotsorry.

If your employer is giving you a hard time about the timing or frequency of breaks, explain that waiting to pump can result in infections (such as mastitis), which may cause an additional need for a medical leave and reduced productivity—which is your employer's nightmare. Medical language can be a huge help for these kinds of uncomfortable conversations. In fact: Employers are used to accommodating medical language, and are more comfortable with that language than "mommy issues." For example, don't say, "My boobs are exploding; I can't wait all day to pump!" Say, "To prevent infection, I have to express breastmilk at regular intervals." Be polite, and professional, but firm. These are your *rights*. Legally speaking, "expressing breastmilk" and "lactation accommodation" is the type of language we use in our cases.

As for a doctor's note—nope, not necessary or appropriate to ask for. The PUMP Act requires only that you inform your employer that you're a lactating mom. (That said, if you have complications and need protections beyond what the PUMP Act provides, you may need a doctor's note for additional help, as you'll be essentially asking for a PWFA lactation accommodation.)

Pumped-Up Mastery—
Using the PUMP Act with the PWFA

Most mothers don't know that the PWFA also protects lactation. This means you can request different forms of accommodations beyond what the PUMP Act allows. For example, I recently counseled a client who wanted to work from home instead of pumping at work. This is the template I wrote for her:

> I'm requesting a lactation accommodation under the PWFA to alleviate symptoms of anxiety. My body does not respond well to pumping and it has been very time-consuming to pump. As a result, I'm worried I will lose too much time pumping that I could spend working. I know I can be much more productive if I work remotely. In addition, because my body does not respond well to pumping, the expression of milk is usually impacted, which can result in infection. I want to avoid needing more time off as a result of infections. I propose we try this accommodation for four weeks and at that time we can reassess. I appreciate your support, which allows me to succeed as a working mother.

Her request was granted instantly, and she extended it two more times.

Even managers who think they're being supportive can need educating. Rosalie was a physical therapist preparing to head back to work after leave, and she was feeding her daughter through a combination of nursing and pumping, which she intended to keep up even after her return to work. Like so many of us, she wanted to be fully prepared, so a week before her return, she sent her boss a detailed, personable email about her day-to-day workflow plans, including a proposed pumping schedule and some follow-up questions about the designated space for pumping during the day.

After a bit of email tag, Rosalie's boss finally reached out by phone (their first chat since Rosalie went on leave), and when the topic of pumping breaks came up, her boss was eager to chime in. "You know, Anya has those wearable pumps—have you seen those? She just uses them while seeing patients," her boss said brightly. "I'll ask her what brand she uses!"

Now, Rosalie had already tried a whole host of wearable pumps, hands-free cups, and so-called discreet setups. They just didn't work for her—she didn't get enough output. She needed to use a traditional, hospital-grade pump, and she needed to do it during pumping breaks. Rosalie politely tried to explain this to her boss and just get back to concrete details about her schedule, but as soon as she did, the conversation became a bit vague. Finally, her boss wrapped things up with a nonspecific, "I'm sure we can just talk about all of that when you get back."

Rosalie hung up feeling uneasy. While her boss wasn't *un*supportive of pumping at work, Rosalie still didn't have a firm plan in place for scheduling her patients, which made her anxious. She was already worried about the adjustments to her patient load to make space for pumping breaks, and her manager—based on the blasé mention of wearable pumps—didn't seem to fully grasp that pumping breaks were a necessity (and a legal one, at that) for Rosalie.

Rosalie's boss may have genuinely believed she was being helpful, bringing up a convenient solution she assumed Rosalie just didn't know existed. But even assuming that good intent, the equivocation around pumping breaks that followed was problematic. Bottom line: It is not appropriate for your employer to suggest you skip pump breaks (which is really what wearable pumping is) instead of giving you the actual pump breaks. Pump rights are absolute—they aren't subject to any negotiation or back-and-forth—and what Rosalie's boss was doing, well-intended or not, was interfering in those rights.

In this case, I told Rosalie to stand firm in her pumping rights and continue the discussion in writing since her boss had already proven herself willing to skirt the law (even if by accident). Fortunately, after a clear follow-up email (with a not-so-subtle reminder that pumping breaks are legally required), Rosalie's boss capitulated, Rosalie had her pump breaks built into her schedule, and there was never a mention of wearable pumps again.

> Dear [Manager's Name],
>
> I hope you're doing well. I'm happy to let you know that I've been cleared to return to work on [Your Return Date], and I've attached the requested paperwork for your records.
>
> As we discussed previously, I wanted to remind you that as a lactating mother, I will be incorporating my pumping breaks into my workday starting on my first day back, following the schedule below. Ensuring we have this set up in advance will help ensure I can stay on top of my workload. I would appreciate confirmation that these breaks will be implemented and that a private space for pumping (as legally required by the PUMP Act) has been arranged.
>
> I'm looking forward to returning and getting back to work. Please don't hesitate to let me know if there's anything further you need from me to make this transition as smooth as possible.
>
> Best regards,
> [Your Name]

But let's say you've tried *alllll* this and your boss won't let you use your right to pump on the schedule your body and baby require.

Good news: You have options.

To reaffirm: Pumping rights are absolute rights, which means an employer cannot deny them as long as you are eligible. Unlike in the accommodation process, your employer also cannot offer alternatives or ideas they prefer, like sending you off-site to pump (thereby cutting into your pay), sending you to your car to pump, sending you to the bathroom to pump, asking you to "hold it" (like Leanne's boss), or insisting you use wearable pumps and keep working (like Rosalie's boss—though, to be sure, this is an option you may propose if *you* want to try it).

So, if your boss breaks the rules, here's what you do.

First, you have to give them notice. Do this in writing, cc HR, and bcc your personal email address.

> Dear [Name],
>
> As you know, I returned to work as a lactating mother on [Date]. However, since my return, I have been prevented from taking my legally protected reasonable break time to express breastmilk because of the following: [Your Issues].
>
> I made [Company] aware of my return as a lactating mother on [Date of Your Email] so that any preparations could be made, yet as of today, my right to pump as covered under the PUMP Act has not been adequately honored. If this situation is not remedied in a timely manner, I will be exploring my legal options.
>
> Sincerely,
> [Your Name]

If they fix the problem and you can pump, great! Keep an eye out, but keep doing your job. If they do not correct the violation within ten days, call a lawyer. With the help of an attorney, you can sue them in court.

Remember: It's your boss's responsibility to accommodate your breaks. It is not your job to make sure you can take your breaks. Yes, as the employee, you want to be proactive, but if your employer is not helping you, *they* are not compliant—it's *their* fault, in other words.

You are also protected from discrimination for exercising your right to pump. Breastfeeding discrimination is a thing, and it's very much illegal. This might look like:

- A potential boss rescinds a job offer once you disclose you are breastfeeding.
- Your boss uninvites you from a business trip after you tell them you'll need to pump on the road.

- A manager expresses discouragement when you say you need to go pump.
- Your boss says you might not be the best candidate for that promotion because you're a breastfeeding mom.
- Your boss asks you to move your pumping breaks around their meeting schedule.
- Your boss tries to convince you to quit after you report a PUMP Act violation because it would be "better for you and your baby."
- Any sort of harassment, including "jokes" or other comments about your status as a lactating mom or lactation plans and timeline. Breastfeeding harassment can sometimes rise to the level of sexual harassment, if it includes comments about your breasts, for example, which is separately and additionally illegal. One of the mothers I once supported experienced something quite disturbing: She had just finished pumping, her flanges and bottles and gear still exposed on her desk. Her boss walked in, licked his lips, picked up her bottle, and drank it while staring her in the face. "I'd love some more of that," he told her with a straight face.

If these things happen to you, report it immediately. And anything that your boss or colleagues are foolish enough to put in an email (like "honk honk, moo moo" in one of my cases, in response to my client's email that she had to take a pump break)—forward that shit to your personal email, stat. For conversations and comments, take notes as soon as possible after the incident, noting the date and time and as many details as you can. Email yourself these comments so you have a time stamp and there are no issues with authentication down the line. And if you feel even a tiny bit uncomfortable, you should report the incident up the chain (in writing) to HR as well.

If these comments and adverse actions add up over time, you can consult with a lawyer and explore your options for compensation for any way you may have suffered: lost wages, a promotion you were already due, additional money for emotional suffering, punitive damages to help make sure they don't do this again, and more.

Now, deep breath. All this is a worst-case scenario, and if your employer isn't a total pervy weirdo, they'll know better than to wander into these land mines. That said, while it is *their* job to be compliant with the law, you can be instrumental in making that easier for them—especially if you're the first go-round with pumping that your boss or company has had to handle. So let me close out this section with my expert advice on how to make pumping arrangements go smoothly.

Daphne's Pumping Pro Tips

Explain to your boss you will do your best to make your breaks and pumping efficient. Again, it's best to bring this up before you take your leave so they can prepare!

Buy multiple sets of bottles and tubes so you don't have to do a deep clean after every pump.

Come up with a regular schedule so everyone knows where you'll be and doesn't go looking for you.

Communicate to your colleagues that you can't be interrupted during these breaks. If they have a question, they can email.

Help! My Baby Is Not Taking the Bottle!

If your baby doesn't like the bottle, try to get a telework accommodation based on your postpartum anxiety (*not* your baby's needs—remember, you work for the company, not your baby!) before you stop breastfeeding.

Look, This Is Hard

I truly consider feeding my baby with my body my biggest accomplishment.

More than passing the bar in my third language, more than starting my own business, more than any case or award I've won, more than moving to America by myself with no money, more than paying off all my student debt. Breastfeeding gets the gold medal.

It may sound a little Earth Mama, but I am so very serious about it. Any amount of breastfeeding is an incredible achievement.

Because this is hard. If it weren't, I wouldn't have to write a whole damn book chapter about how to do it and keep your job.

True, I love breastfeeding—now. But my journey with breastfeeding has made me feel every emotion there is: pain, frustration, boredom, sadness, joy, gratitude . . . all for something I assumed would be "natural." Right after my baby was born, I tried breastfeeding—but he wouldn't latch, wouldn't settle, just fussed and turned away. A nurse named Carolyn, gentle and patient, showed me how to hand express, her hands squeezing and pressing and pushing until I could barely breathe through the pain, through the strangeness of a stranger's hands on my nipples. I tried again to get him to latch—nothing. I tried a lactation consultant next, who talked for what felt like hours, then put me on a pump—another round of pain, more squeezing, still nothing. Too long without a wet diaper, and they told me to supplement—formula or donor milk, my choice. So I tried donor milk, put a syringe and tube on my breast, hoping, praying he'd eat. He did. I was relieved but shattered. Then the consultant returned, called the nurse's suggestion to supplement a "panic" move. Maybe she was right. I obeyed blindly, afraid of jeopardizing his health, wanting so desperately to do it "right"—and now everything was off balance. He still wouldn't latch. I tried a nipple shield, the only way he'd feed. I tried to let it go, thought maybe this was just our path.

At home, it only got harder: I tried to nurse in front of visitors, tried not to feel awkward, tried to act like I had this together. I was exhausted; my baby was hungry, impatient, angry. Finally, after a few days without sleep, I slept, and when my baby was hungry, and my husband wanted to protect my sleep, he gave in and gave him a bottle. I woke to find the bottle empty and my heart breaking. I had failed—at being his mother—and I'd just started. No milk, a hungry baby, a tired husband. I tried everything: I took placenta pills; I nursed until my body ached. Slowly, my milk came, but it never felt like enough. I fed him; he cried. I tried more.

I tried more reading, tried to learn from books. I watched latching videos. I read about breastfeeding as an art, tried to manifest it. I put him to the breast every chance I got. It hurt; oh, it hurt. Some days I could get him to latch only if I was standing up; other days, only on the left side. I tried everything to keep my supply up, but it was never easy. I got milk blebs, clogged ducts, tried switching sides, tried the football hold, tried patience. He'd shake his head, frustrated, and I'd shake inside with despair, with exhaustion. I cried. Every day, I cried.

Each session dragged on, stretching my limits, my patience, my body. I was tired, thirsty, completely depleted. We both cried on top of each other, tears coalescing. I went upstairs, sweat beading on us both, the world outside my door waiting. And I tried to find a way to keep going, to keep trying, even though every inch of me wanted to rest, to quit, to just hold him.

Then, when I returned to work, my pump breaks were wildly incongruent with a litigator's life. I often had to ask to stop depositions and other processes to pump. Because legal processes often take place at the other party's offices, I ended up pumping in cold, sterile rooms all over the county. At a corporate defense firm where I had to go frequently, I asked for the lactation room. They did not have one, and they sent me to the bathroom. I responded, "Only if you join me to have lunch in the bathroom. I'll order sushi. You can sit on the toilet and eat it." (I'm cheeky like that.) They ended up sending me to the "war room," which is where they plot their "war strategy" to try to defeat "the enemy" (me). So I sat there, boobies out, filling bottles of milky love smack-dab in the middle of their battle plans. How's that for a micro-rebellion?

And I did keep going. And I'm so damn proud of myself for doing so.

So, if you are breastfeeding and pumping, I want you to own this sense of life-giving power. I want you to bask in that sense of pride and achievement that comes from nourishing your baby.

But what I do not want is for breastfeeding to feel like another thing for you to fail at, another "must-do" on your endless "yes girl" task list, another accomplishment you have to achieve no matter how much it compromises your physical, mental, or emotional health.

That's why, even though I'm proud of my breastfeeding experience, I'm also a strong advocate for formula feeding. Back in village times, there would be other lactating mothers around who could feed our baby while we rested. This is not where we are. Many breastmilk advocates can be a bit too aggressive and unforgiving about their "breast is best" stance, without taking into account the truth of motherhood in modernity, including how mothers are isolated and overworked and constantly shamed for doing it wrong, whatever it is. Yes, I know that the large formula companies engage in predatory marketing, but I trust your wisdom in discerning what is helpful and what is harmful.

In fact, the pressure to exclusively breastfeed can also be incredibly unhelpful to mothers, and the judgment that mothers face for using formula is not only unfair but harmful—the stress and the shame makes the body go haywire, which is terrible for milk production. And formula *saves lives.*

If you find yourself considering formula at any point, I support you fully. I've been there myself. Feeding choices aren't black and white, and we shouldn't pretend they are: Many mothers, including myself, use a combination of breastfeeding and formula. Formula is an incredible gift for our species' survival. What your baby needs most of all is a present, mentally and physically healthy mother, not simply breastmilk. Trust your instincts.

11

Resignations and Job Transitions in Motherhood

You Climbed the Ladder and Turns Out the View Sucks

I didn't have an easy time coming back to work after my second baby. It was much harder than the transition after my first baby. At this stage of my career, I was a senior attorney, managing a large caseload, managing staff, and marketing the firm to build a book of business. I had a pandemic miscarriage, followed by a pandemic pregnancy (plus a toddler at home due to school closures).

During my pandemic pregnancy, I spearheaded and managed an extremely complex case, representing a group of Mexican women who had been trafficked and essentially enslaved. They were kept to work in an elderly care facility, where they were made to tend to the patients all day (including cooking, cleaning, and lifting them to bathe them and provide medical care). The women also had to sleep there, and were woken up every two to three times whenever one of the patients rang a buzzer. A bell would go off in their room (where they slept on mats on the floor) and they'd be woken up to attend to their needs, only to wake up at 5:00 a.m. to start their workday. They were paid for only a few hours per day and were prevented from seeing their families. (One of the mothers had a baby in the hospital she was prevented from seeing.)

The case became a class action, but it had a tricky component because the women were undocumented. When we filed suit, the employer hired three defense firms, with large teams of expensive attorneys, while I was doing the case with just one paralegal and one other lawyer. The defense lawyers were mean, insulting, and threatening, filing motion after motion, burying us with work. They hired private investigators to follow the clients, and us, too, all to dig up "dirt" to blackmail us into giving up the case (luckily for me, I lived a very boring life).

Then my fear came true—they called ICE in retaliation, and the women had to flee. One of the women was caught and detained. Together with an immigration lawyer, I pleaded in front of the immigration judge, explaining that we required her presence in the United States because she was a party to a civil lawsuit, and that we were investigating the employer for unfair business practices. I explained that allowing the employer to escape justice would result in an unfair advantage over employers who were dutifully following the law. The "I'm trying to protect 'Merican businesses, Your Honor" line worked with this ultra-conservative judge, and he allowed her to stay. The problem? She was already on her way back on a bus to Mexico (where she hadn't lived for two decades). I asked the judge to call the bus driver. The clerk found the number, and the judge called the driver and made him turn around. They were only five miles from the border.

It gets better—through the work on the immigration side, we were able to get all the women legal residence, so they could come out of hiding and get honorable jobs. We also got all these women paid for their many years of unpaid labor and emotional distress, essentially lifting entire families out of generational poverty. Most of them were able to buy houses and settle down in peace. This will always be the case I'm most proud of. I took on ICE, and won. And also, the case had dominated my entire pregnancy (which, again, also fell during the pandemic). So your girl was *TI*-RED.

We'd also just gone through so much staff turnover. They'd get hired, I'd train them, we'd give them cases, they'd get overwhelmed, they'd leave, we'd have to absorb their work. It was years of this cycle. When I returned from leave, I found myself without any foundation—I did not have a junior attorney team, and my paralegal was constantly at the brink of burnout as she was also doing the office manager role and acting as my boss's assistant. I ended up doing a lot of my own paralegal work too. No one was doing anything wrong during those final years at the firm. In fact, I know everyone was working as hard as possible and trying their best, but all of us at that juncture were spread so thin. We just needed more (wo)manpower, and no one was up for the task—it was a tough job, after all.

So, when I was on leave with my second baby, I felt so uncomfortable. Things were falling apart left and right.

The firm brought in interns, but they weren't paid, weren't experienced, and weren't much help, so I ended up redoing practically everything they touched while nursing a newborn baby. One of the interns made a mistake that resulted in a state bar complaint against me personally, except I was on leave when the mistake was made, and no one had checked his work. I started to feel like I was punished for having a baby—not by anyone personally, but just by the nature of being a senior litigator with a lot of high-stakes responsibilities. Responsibilities that—if left unchecked—could result in a malpractice lawsuit, getting sanctioned, or slapped with a state bar complaint.

Eventually, I started to just come back to work to prevent further disasters. My baby was only eight weeks old. It's a decision I regret to this day, yet, I felt like I just did not have a choice, in light of my professional caliber at the time. I was at such a senior level that it was also just hard to cover for me, and it's generally hard to take over someone else's case (years of work goes into them, after all). On top of all that, I was also hustling and doing entrepreneurial work, bringing in my own cases to increase my earnings and improve the profits and profile of the firm (including garnering extensive media coverage). I started to feel this pang of, *Hmm, I feel like I have all the stressors of being a business owner, without all the benefits.*

Then came the last straw. I had given notice of illness and our team had an urgent brief due. My boss, well aware that I was *not well*, called me to ask, "Could you work with Steve the intern on this real quick? Just explain it to him."

Actually, no—I couldn't "just explain it," because Steve didn't know anything about this brief or this case and didn't have the expertise to understand it. So, I ended up working on it for hours myself, late at night, and I was absolutely fuming the whole time.

It was at that moment that I realized: I don't need to do this. I'm bringing in cases, I'm experienced, I know how to manage a team. I knew I could live very comfortably with a much smaller caseload (and cases I actually enjoyed and was interested in) and take home all the profit, which would net me more than what I was making at the firm. Suddenly, it just all felt like a terrible bargain. The math wasn't mathing.

It was clear: I'd outgrown my job. It was time to move on.

If you get back from your leave and feel overwhelmed, exhausted, and ready to quit: I know how you feel. You've climbed that career ladder and suddenly see that the view sucks. What I want you to do—and what this chapter will *help* you do—is to scrutinize your motives and figure out the right next step so that you can achieve the right balance for you.

Granted, this sense of balance in your new life as a working parent isn't always easy to achieve; it often takes time, risk, and some really tough conversations and decisions. But I genuinely believe that, as a mother, you deserve a career that truly excites you and fills you up—and I want to help you get there.

Why Are You Working?

Deciding whether to make significant career moves after having a baby depends on so many factors. Beyond the immediate "I'm miserable and need to get out of here" feeling that's very much a hallmark of returning to work, there's the long-term effects to consider, on both your own career and the mothers' movement as a whole. There's money and benefits and childcare and partners' careers and just so, so many things that swirl around this decision.

All these are important to consider—and we will. But the best place to start is with a simple question: Why are you working?

At the heart of it all, this is what you need to ask yourself, what you maybe are *already* asking yourself. And your answers will reveal a lot about the best way forward for *you*.

"I pretty much had to force myself to go back to work," Jenna, a thirty-four-year-old engineer at a tech company, recalled. "I was really dreading it. But now I'm incredibly glad I did."

Jenna's top answer to the question of "why are you working?" was probably what most of ours is: money. Sure, she'd love to spend more time at home with her baby, but she and her husband need her income. They can cover all their bills, plan family vacations without financial stress, "and honestly, we just fight a lot less when the bills are taken care of," Jenna added.

Of course, money is no small consideration here. We don't work for free, and we deserve to be paid what we're worth. So it's a good place to start investigating your "why" around work.

Your turn: Think of all the financial benefits you get from your job (income as well as perks like insurance). How important are those to you?

That said, we don't work for free, but we don't work *just* for money, either. Work engages us, challenges us, gives us problems to solve. The truth is, once you have a baby, you're either parenting or you're working; there's very little in between. Time at home used to be your break from work, but as a parent, working becomes your break from parenting. Ideally, you get that sense of "Oh, I get to do some grown-up tasks today! That is going to be a blast. Such a welcome escape from the crying dictators."

Indeed, for Jenna, money's not the *only* answer. Over her four months of leave, Jenna had come to love the domestic bliss of the baby bubble, but she'd also gone a little nuts. Stir-crazy, cabin fever, whatever you want to call it—the repetitive cycle of days with an infant and the lack of intellectual stimulation had left her itching to do something, anything else—a fact that she didn't fully appreciate until she was back in the office. Being able to step out of "parent mode" during the day gives her a chance to recharge, as it does for her husband. "I realized that when both parents have jobs, they each get a mental break from parenting, and that's so important for us and our marriage," she shared. She needed her own identity and agency, outside of the domestic realm. I would argue that this is the most natural thing. We are humans with multiple needs and desires, and expecting mothers to just care about their babies is akin to dehumanizing them and reducing them to just baby-making machines. We are wildly creative creatures. We can make babies and make business plans and sometimes those dreams converge and clash, but all of it is part of who you are. What's important is how you integrate all of it.

Personally, I always want to return to my baby in a better state than when I left, instead of coming back exhausted, drained, with nothing left to give. So I ask myself: Why am I doing *this* instead of spending time with my baby, resting, or doing anything else that restores me? And if I don't have a good answer, then I need to rethink my professional life.

Your turn: Is your work something that excites you and fulfills your need to exercise your intelligence and imagination? Do you relish the chance to switch out of "mom mode" for a bit and get some socialization/interaction that isn't purely baby-related?

Work can be selfless too—and not just in the sense of "providing for my tiny baby with no means of earning an income on their own." In fact, dads are called good "providers" for working hard and taking care of their family financially. Yet we don't call mothers "providers" when they deploy child-care to earn income for their families. We call them bad mothers. This is a trap. You are providing for your baby by working, and providing is *part* of being a good mother. Animal mothers regularly leave their cubs to go hunt too. Because if they don't leave, the cubs don't survive. Being a working mother is primal and it is natural. In fact, being alone with a baby, without a village, is actually a new construct and a symptom of modernity. It is less natural than going to work and using your chosen village (childcare and your workplace) to collectively care for your child's needs. In addition, working toward a better world for our children, all children, benefits your child too. And it's exactly this sense of service that was ignited through motherhood. I was committed to leaving the world a better place for them.

Most of us gravitate toward those lines of work and professional roles that don't merely leverage our skills and interests (or provide a nice pay-check) but also contribute something to the greater good. I know that even when I struggled with the day-to-day of my law firm office politics and frustrations, I did feel good that I was working in the name of justice, broadly speaking (and even more so when I was able to set up my own shop).

That's not to say you have to be in a "do-gooder" career to feel that way, either. Jenna isn't—her firm oversees specialized budgeting software for architectural firms—but she's a leader of the Asian-American and Pacific Islander (AAPI) affinity group at her employer and also mentors two up-and-coming women engineers. Coming back after giving birth and going through the leave experience, she felt even more motivated to keep up those roles within her workplace, knowing specifically "how fucking hard it can be" and wanting to share support and insights to those who don't always have the same institutional access to power and knowledge.

Your turn: How do you feel about the impact your work makes on the world and the people in it? Small or large, symbolic or concrete.

Finally, there's the fact that many of us work because we've devoted a lot of time and effort *to* our work. I don't mean that in a grim kind of hamster-wheel way: What I mean is that we've poured hours of our attention and effort and intelligence into learning our trade, honing our skills, and becoming the professional that we are today. Continuing to work affirms and uplifts and celebrates that effort and experience. This doesn't mean we have to resign ourselves to an idea like, "Well, I got that accounting degree, so I'm going to be a CPA forever, I guess," but more that we have built ourselves into a person with so much to offer, regardless of what our specific job is. In fact, from that standpoint, it's actually quite liberating: We *don't* have to stay in this role to keep working (and, in fact, many women do find that their post-baby lives call for a change of industry or position), but we can still make use of the brilliance that we've cultivated within ourselves over all the years of our adult life.

Jenna emphatically agrees that this is a big reason why she works. "I am really, really good at what I do, and I'm proud of that," she said. "I am naturally a 'numbers person,' so the fact that I now work successfully with huge tranches of customer data is really meaningful to me. I love seeing all my years of education and job experience start to take shape into this real career narrative for myself."

Your turn: What is your career narrative, and how does that affect your "why" at work?

Stay, Switch, or Quit?

Once you have a clearer picture of why you personally work, you can tackle the next question. No matter the specific details, every new mom who starts to question her career choices is really just asking the same thing: *Should I stay here? Should I switch jobs? Or should I quit the workforce entirely?*

STAY

A few weeks after Priya returned from her first leave, her firm announced layoffs. The laid-off workers all got a chunky severance and were able to recover unemployment benefits as well.

Priya wasn't one of them. She knew she should feel relieved. Oddly, though, she found herself . . . envious.

Prior to having a baby, Priya had never imagined leaving work. She had proudly paid her way through college and her master's program, loved her job as a financial analyst, and had received a generous (by US standards) maternity leave.

But those first few weeks back in the office were disorienting, to say the least. She was physically exhausted, overwhelmed by the backlog, and had a short fuse with her direct reports. It was harder than it had ever been to do her job—and she wasn't really sure why she was doing it anymore.

Priya knew being a stay-at-home mom wasn't financially realistic—her salary was nearly double her partner's, and one income would mean they'd have to scale back to the point of selling their house and moving to a different area, for starters. She also felt reluctant to even so much as pause her career path, let alone step off it entirely: She was genuinely proud of her work and accomplishments.

That was a few years ago. Priya's now a mother of three, and she didn't end up leaving her job. "The fact is, with every kid, it takes me a good six months to feel steady at work again. It's much easier knowing for myself that it's just temporary."

Much like there's a major cultural expectation for women to "bounce back" to their former body after pregnancy, there's this idea that returning to work is as simple as just pressing play and moving forward. In reality, the transition is long, tricky, and not always a linear path back to "full speed ahead."

It's perfectly normal, almost textbook, to struggle with these mixed emotions like Priya did. The early days at work postpartum are a *liminal state*, where you're between a past version of your work self that's now firmly gone, and navigating toward a new employee-and-mom identity that hasn't fully formed yet. Studies have found that it takes anywhere from three months to a year to settle into a new job, and I'd argue the same thing is true of settling back in after maternity leave: The job might be the same, but *you're* not, and that's going to simply take time. With the benefit of hindsight, Priya's advice to her first-time postpartum self is simple, and I think it's worth sharing with *every* new mom: Take it slow, don't make any big decisions too quickly, and prioritize your mental health.

Questions to Ask Yourself

- How long have I been back at work? Do I feel capable of giving myself a ninety-day "probation period" to test the waters before making any big decisions?
- Am I sleeping, eating, moving my body enough to feel good? Could how I'm feeling be the result of physical exhaustion? How can I help myself get more rest and restoration?
- Do I think there's something else in play here, like postpartum anxiety or depression? What would it look like to get an accommodation for that?
- Do I/we have the financial bandwidth to absorb more unpaid time off?

In some cases, it really can be just a matter of time—for your new rhythm of life to settle in, for your hormones to keep leveling out, for you to finally get some freaking *sleep*—before you can properly take stock of how you feel about your job and working in general. If you're struggling with self-care (and I mean the basics here, like hygiene, nutrition, and sleep, not bubble baths and massages), *ask for help.* Your partner or parent or BFF can't *do* your job for you, but they can take on a baby shift or two during your off-hours so you can get a nap, stretch, or cook yourself something nourishing.

In some cases, however—like Jessica's, from chapter 9—the problems you're experiencing when back to work are the result of lingering postpartum anxiety and/or depression. In those cases, there's no medal for powering through. Remember you can use the PWFA to assert your right to get the additional time off you need to take care of your mental health.

That said, those leave extensions may be unpaid (though, depending on your situation, you may be able to get additional disability payments, but that's not a given). But just because you need a paycheck doesn't mean you have to continue doing something that makes you miserable. If it's possible, seek out a therapist or other mental health professional—even without a clinically diagnosable condition, therapy can help you contend with your life as a mom and an employee and give you tools to help you that are more personalized to yourself and your situation than any book can. If cost is an issue, you can look into therapists who provide a sliding scale or are members of groups like the Open Path Collective, or you can look up peer postpartum support groups, many of which are free to attend (and some of which meet virtually). Just having a sense of community and a listening ear can make all the difference when you otherwise feel like screaming into the void.

You can also "stay" while making some changes to your work schedule that help you navigate your new reality. That's what Priya did after her first pregnancy. "We couldn't afford for me to take more unpaid leave, not without saving more," she said. "I knew there were accommodations for PPD, but I didn't feel 'depressed' so I didn't think that mattered for me. But when I started seeing a therapist, she pointed out that the moodiness and insomnia and general sense of doom I was feeling were actually PPD symptoms." In the end, Priya used this information to request telework accommodations, and she worked remotely for four weeks before returning to the office. During that time, she was also able to make a meaningful dent in her work, so that by the time she was back in-person, the whole work environment felt less overwhelming to her.

Staying, but working remotely, is possible, with some caveats. There is no straightforward, universal teleworking right. You cannot simply ask your boss if it would be okay to keep working from home because it has been proven that the job can be done entirely from home. Your boss may say yes, but if the answer is no, you would need to return back to work, or risk job loss. However, teleworking rights *are* routinely granted in accommodation cases if you are "legally disabled," and the law has recognized mental health limitations, including depression and anxiety, as disabilities. As such, these conditions could be a legal justification to telework, as long as your doctor agrees.

Obviously, there are exceptions. Telework accommodations are not a reasonable request in jobs that cannot be performed from home, such as nursing, food service, retail, or anything that requires you to be on-site. However, in those cases, other accommodation rights exist, such as a flex schedule, additional breaks, reduced hours, extra time off, ramp-on options, etc. The accommodation process is job-specific and disability-specific, and there is no exhaustive list.

To request teleworking rights, you'll follow the same process for requesting an accommodation under PWFA, detailed in the previous chapter. As with leave extensions, you'll need to specify an end date (although you can always try to request an extension) and you should ideally come prepared with a note from your doctor.

Now that her first "baby" is entering second grade, Priya's glad that she stayed in her job. "It was rough at the beginning, for sure—for each kid," she reflected. "But ultimately, I love what I do, I enjoy my colleagues, and staying here was honestly good for my soul. Plus, that cute baby very quickly turned into a rambunctious toddler, and during peak tantrum season I was so relieved that we had access to our nature-based preschool because his boundless energy surpassed what I could give. He needed trained educators and other kids." She's now a VP in her department.

SWITCH

Sometimes, it's not working in general that's getting you down postpartum. It's just *this job.*

Let's get back to post-second-baby Daphne, who was overloaded with work and being asked to "just explain" a complicated case to the rookie.

When I got that request from my boss, I couldn't help but mentally seethe at him: *Why can't you fucking do this?* I sent him a late evening email telling him that was not okay. The following day, my boss sent me a text that the firm was going through "growing pains," and urged me to "please put the frustration behind you."

But I couldn't. One stormy day in the backyard, after requesting sick time, I had a panic attack. I was hyperventilating, feeling overwhelmed, and in that very moment, I made a decision. I wasn't going to let myself suffer any longer. I couldn't sleep, I had a newborn at home, I had endless motions to deal with, and I was stuck handling these dominating yet mind-numbing firm cases I did not want to do, all while bringing my own cases in, too, because I had to provide for a growing family. It felt like I was drowning, and I'd had enough. And the painful truth is, there is no one I could blame but myself. I cannot fault anyone for treating me like the all-capable Wonder Woman when I was presenting myself as the all-capable Wonder Woman. But it was all too much, and it was time to be honest, first with myself, and then with everyone else.

The next day, I handed in my resignation.

If you find yourself in a situation where you're being treated poorly, in a lousy work environment with no support, you should absolutely go ahead and leave that job behind. Your life is precious, and your employment relationship should be a positive one. You should feel protected, inspired, and genuinely appreciated for your work. If that's not happening—whether you've recently had a baby or not—it's time to leave.

But leaving *a* job doesn't mean leaving work entirely. So often, new moms go back to work and finally have the scales fall from their eyes—the "family friendly" environment and "support" they were promised never materializes. The "natively distributed team" gets an abrupt RTO order. The much-hinted-at bonuses aren't awarded; the micromanaging boss gets on your last nerve. That's what happened to me: I was fed up with *this place*, but not with *being at work* in the abstract.

Becoming a mom makes you value your time differently. Suddenly, everything you do is seen through the lens of "you asked me to leave my baby for *this* bullshit?" You may find that, even if your workplace isn't discriminatory or harmful in a legally actionable sense, your newfound appreciation for the value of your time makes all the old frustrations you've suffered for years suddenly *in*tolerable. (Or, now that you're supporting a family, you're simply not willing to work for a stingy paycheck anymore.)

Whatever the specifics for you, you should honor your feelings of frustration—and *act* on them. You need to switch it up and find a new, better job for the person you are now. In fact, I'd recommend doing some industry research as soon as you feel that first twinge of *ugh, this again?* (It's just window-shopping, after all.)

Questions to Ask

- If I imagine myself at this job a year from now, do I feel a sense of fulfillment, or am I already dreading the idea of more of the same frustrations?
- How have my values shifted since becoming a mom? Where does this job not meet them? What would a job that *does* meet them look like (e.g., remote work, flex hours, better benefits for childcare/healthcare, shorter/no commute, etc.)?
- How would a job change impact my family's finances, and am I prepared for any potential gaps in income during the transition?
- Am I willing and able to invest time in updating my resume, networking, and interviewing right now? Or would I rather just spend that energy powering through for the time being?
- Who in my network can I start asking about opportunities? Is there someone I can reach out to for informational interviews, informal mentorship, etc.?

The first step is getting your resume up to date, which I know can be a chore . . . but the good news is, thanks to your leave coverage plan, you've already got an up-to-date, comprehensive list of exactly what you do at your job.

From there, you can start to scope the job market for roles that appeal to you and you'd be a good fit for. And really—dream big, here. If you've always imagined pivoting into another industry, or working for a start-up, or going from government to the private sector (or vice versa), now's the time. Be bold and be fearless—it's so true that the easiest time to find a job is when you already have one, and that's you right now.

If you feel guilt over "disloyalty" starting to gnaw at you, take a step back for some perspective. Remember, employers don't hesitate to make massive layoffs, even when people are on leave, right? Why should you reward them in kind with a loyalty they'd never show you? And the fundamental truth still holds: *They* are lucky to have *you*. You've always known that, but sometimes it takes you leaving for another job for your *employer* to realize that.

That was what happened to me. Do you know what my boss did when I started reading my resignation letter? He said "put that away," and started promising me the world: "Daphne, you've earned the right to demand anything you need here. So what do you need? More money? An entire team? Heck, I can create a whole department around you."

That only solidified my decision. In that moment, I finally saw my true worth. It was at once validating and *incredibly* frustrating, to say the least. I was mainly frustrated with myself. I did not demand to be treated in accordance with my value, and in the end, it was just too late.

But I knew I had made the right decision (not least because it eventually led to me becoming The Mamattorney and writing this book). I ended up telling him very clearly that I had made my decision, and I wanted to do the work under my own name. I also explained the math part of it, that I knew I could make more on my own. He understood. We both cried a little. We'd been working side by side for a decade. That's a big deal. We knew each other so well, and were really attuned to each other. We had a dynamic way of working that was extremely powerful and complementary.

I am so grateful for that firm. It was a boot camp, an initiation. I went from a wee law clerk to a top dog in the industry. After some bumps, I found a way to integrate and center motherhood in this workplace, however awkward it sometimes was. The pressure and pace ended up being too intense, yes, and there were also so many sweet moments I look back on fondly. My boss holding my baby while I worked on jury instructions. My paralegal held him quite often when I was in a crunch. She even kept a box of snacks on her desk, just for him. My colleagues (including some sweet, kind men) also bonded with him. In a culture that tends to alienate and exclude children and mothers, it was a revolutionary act to embed my new identity into my workplace.

I'm proud that I centered motherhood at this workplace (and not just motherhood, my actual baby), that I advocated for motherhood, that I celebrated motherhood, and that I set policy for motherhood, policy that still stands today. I was able to do this mainly by bringing in a shit-ton of mother clients, essentially capitalizing on my new identity, and building a bridge to this market. If you bring that kind of value to a business, you better center motherhood too.

I've never felt more of a sense of belonging than at that firm. We were close. What I gained in agency and sovereignty after I left, I lost in community and camaraderie. And honestly, I still feel a pang of grief writing this, because I actually miss working there. And this may happen for you too. The decision may never be fully clear, and will always be bittersweet, but sometimes, you just gotta jump and bet fully on yourself. Your time is so limited, after all.

You might also want to channel some energy into sharpening some key skills or getting some new qualifications under your belt. Even if you're not actively job searching, just throwing that iron in the fire—starting to stack the bullet points that'll eventually get you that new job—can help you feel like you're moving forward instead of spinning your wheels. So many trainings and certifications are available online, too, even from name-brand universities.

Another option for skill-building and resume-boosting is to find some nonprofits or volunteer organizations and donate your time there—which I fully recognize is a bonkers suggestion for a new mom already overwhelmed with too much to do. If that's you, then don't, full stop. But if part of what you're struggling with at your current job is *boredom* and *no sense of purpose* (or worse, the realization that your job might be actively adding to the crappiness of the world), then finding a group with a mission that lights you up can actually make you feel better even though, technically speaking, it's more work. Nonprofits aren't going to be as picky about qualifications (they need all the help they can get!) so they're a great way to flex some skills that might be rusty (or new entirely). (And if you're stuck for a group to work with, might I humbly suggest your local Chamber of Mothers chapter?)

Interviewing Like a Mother

When you do start landing interviews for new jobs, you've got a golden opportunity to lay your boundaries down from the start. Instead of the gradual whittling away of promises you may have seen at your current position, as a potential new hire, you get to ask the point-blankiest questions to size up whether or not this new organization is a fit for what you value now as a mom.

However—and big caveat here—asking too many questions (or the wrong ones) can raise subtle alarm bells. And that's where things get tricky. Legally speaking, employers are not allowed to discriminate against applicants on the basis of gender (including pregnancy status), race, religion, marital status, disability, and so on. In practice, though? Hiring managers and recruiters aren't stupid, and they know which side their bread is buttered on. Though technically simply *asking* these sorts of questions might be perfectly acceptable, they'll probably want to steer clear of it just so they can plead ignorance in the case of any discrimination claim. Nevertheless, if their prerogative is finding people who'll live and breathe this job, never take time off, and use as few benefits as possible, then you can bet they're going to be cold-reading you for any whiff of, well, humanity.

Often, they go about finding these things in sneaky ways . . . by basically making you offer the information up. The simple opener "tell us about yourself" followed by a friendly smile and a pause? That's them rolling out the red carpet to talk about your spouse, your kids, your pets . . . whatever. It's up to you to resist the urge to be, honestly, friendly and human (because in any other context those are perfectly reasonable things to share!) and to keep your answer to need-to-know, professional-level things. (If you want to humanize your answer a bit, try mentioning things like hobbies, sports fandoms, or random "fun facts" to lighten things up.)

If they do ask you any inappropriate questions outright ("Are you married? Do you have kids?"), just politely deflect. "I'd like to keep my interview about my qualifications for the job" with a smile is always a good one, as is (in a neutral/polite tone), "Why do you ask?" If they're halfway competent, they'll take either of these as a neon sign to change course (or, sometimes, they'll have a good reason for asking—I know of at least one woman who was told, "Oh, because we have an on-site childcare center that our employees love, but I didn't want to waste time telling you about it unless you were interested!" Sweet, but still . . . not an appropriate question, dude). If they persist in asking them, you can always fall back on, "I'm surprised by this question. I was under the impression that these questions are not allowed during a job interview."

Most moms will then tell me, "Well, I would not want to work for a company like that anyway," to which I say, most recruiters don't work for your company either. Usually recruiters are third-party vendors, and they are using a ton of AI these days. You have to get through the robots before you can actually discern whether this is the right company for you. So please be careful during the initial stages.

When it comes to the questions *you* ask *them*, you also want to tread somewhat carefully. Again, they can't *legally* discriminate against you as an applicant because they find out you're a lactating mother (when you ask about pumping space) or married (when you ask about flex schedules and mention your spouse), but it's in your best interest not to show your hand on any of these issues, just in case.

You know how sometimes when you go to the drugstore for tampons, you also throw in some skincare items, a bag of chips, and some allergy medicine so that the checkout clerk doesn't stare at you and think, *Wow, this lady is menstruating!* The same principle applies here. When you ask about benefits specific to your being a mom with a job (e.g., remote work, flexible hours, dependent care FSAs, health plans, paid leave), ask them as part of a big bundle of questions, even if those other questions are things that don't matter to you or you already figured out. Having a complete list of benefits questions across things like retirement plans, PTO, *and* parental leave will come off more as "this woman is really prepared!" and less as "this is obviously A Mom fishing for Mom Things." I recommend sending these as a numbered list (in writing!) so that if HR conveniently "forgets" to answer some of your questions, all you have to say is, "Thank you so much. I don't believe I got an answer to numbers 2 and 5 above—could you address those as well?"

You can also ask them to provide you with a company handbook by explaining, "I'd like to understand the company mission and ethos better so that I can anticipate how to weave in my skill set." Lastly, you can ask them if the company organizes extracurricular events. If the only off-site event is golf-related, it's probably a boys' club. But if they do family picnics and baby showers, then motherhood seems to be more integrated.

As part of the benefits and compensation discussion, you're also going to want to negotiate. Odds are, even if the company has a platinum package compared to your current position, there might be one or two things they could improve. And *everything* is negotiable. Plus, if you already *have* a job, you couldn't be in a stronger position to ask. So ask.

My general advice is this: When mothers need to set professional goals, my recommendation is to do so without extensive details about the children and their needs. Instead, focus on how motherhood has ignited you to seek opportunities to maximize your income as you have a family to support. (This is what men do, after all!) I would keep goals aligned with how you've always set them too—otherwise you are either "mommy tracking" yourself or inviting being mommy tracked.

First, do not provide your prior salary history. (In some states, a prospective employer is prohibited from asking job applicants about their salary history, but there is currently no federal law prohibiting this question.) Giving away prior salary information may only perpetuate pay discrimination from job to job because employers will use your prior pay as a starting point to determine their offer. It's already hard enough to avoid pay discrimination, so don't give them easy ammo to rely on. Remember, you've earned the spot because of your worth, so you should be paid for it.

How to Answer the Salary History Question

- "I don't feel comfortable answering that question." (If you are in a state with a salary history ban, you can add, "especially with the laws regarding prior salary.")

- "I am a little uncomfortable answering that question. I'd love to focus further on the value I can bring to the company and I still have some questions about . . ."

- "I'm not comfortable answering that question, and I think what's important is what value I can provide to the company in this position. I would love to talk about the specific responsibilities of the position, and how I can add value . . ."

- "This position is not exactly the same as my last job. I'd love to discuss what my specific responsibilities would be here to help me respond to any offers provided."

- "It sounds like I may be the right fit for you. If you have an offer, I would love to consider it. I do still have some questions about . . ."

What if they ask you for your salary *expectations?* Same idea: Don't provide a number before they do. Instead, focus on whether you and the potential employer would be a mutual fit, whether you fill a need. In any case, you always want to get the offer first before you provide them with a desired number. (In some states, there's another legal right that will help in this scenario.)

As always, do your homework. Ahead of time, research your target salary/range. You can start with comparable job titles by comparing job descriptions, job duties, and required education and experience. Then find the matching salaries by using the job titles you've identified and review salary ranges for those titles on websites/resources, such as Glassdoor, Indeed, or PayScale. (Or you can ask peers and colleagues, even if you currently work with them—it's illegal for an employer to ban employees from discussing salary!)

How to Answer the "Salary Expectations" Question

- "If we're a good fit for each other, I'm sure we can come to an agreement on salary."
- "Before we talk about salary, I'd like to learn more about the role. Could you tell me more about . . ."
- "I expect to be paid for the value I bring to the company, so I would love to hear more about the role and responsibilities (and the typical pay scale for the position)."
- "I don't necessarily have a specific salary in mind, but would love to hear more about the role and responsibilities of the position so I can understand the value I can bring to the position and better assess whether and how I could be a good fit, and go from there."

> - "I don't have an expected salary set in stone in my mind, and would rather at this point focus on whether this position could be a mutual good fit, and then go from there. I would love to hear more about . . ."
>
> If they continue to press, you can always deflect by just asking for the pay scale: It's now your legal right in some states. "What do you usually pay someone in this position? Can you provide the pay scale?" Some state laws make it much easier to deflect on any conversations about your salary expectations before you receive an offer.

Ultimately, you just need to keep deflecting and flip the script. Keep asking questions to learn more about the position, the expectations, and how the company values your background and skill set. Then, once you get the offer, try to find out how they arrived at their number within the pay scale. How did they rate your background and skills? Get it in writing.

That said, when it comes to salary, you can be bold. If they try to low-ball you and won't budge, be explicit and tell them that you're paying for childcare now and that this low salary would literally mean paying to work there. If that's the base comp, then you need something else to make this worth your while: a guaranteed bonus structure, additional paid time off, a waiver on minimum tenure for paid leave, or whatever would genuinely help you. If you use your spouse's healthcare coverage, ask if they can bump your pay to reflect the fact that they're not covering any premiums for you.

If you need to negotiate something like flexibility or more time off, I would add those items to a long list of projects and goals you intend to complete in your new role, and not as a stand-alone request. I also would not go into excessive detail as to why you need it (i.e., "my husband gets out at 3:00 p.m. but he has a long drive and daycare closes at 4:00 p.m. and there's a late policy of $1 a minute, etc. etc. etc."), but just add it in there. Overexplaining at work is what makes employers spiral and worry that it's the start of a never-ending issue of availability.

Remember: Everything is negotiable, and they are lucky to have you.

QUIT

When Tabia and I sat down for a consultation, she'd been through a lot.

As one of the only Black people at her company, and the only Black woman, she was subjected to egregious racial and sexual harassment almost every time she showed up to work. To be clear, this behavior went beyond awkward questions and unfortunate slipups; her coworkers were doing truly awful things like making racist "jokes" and calling Tabia slurs right to her face. Understandably, Tabia was stressed out, anxious, and upset on a daily basis, which eventually culminated in what was essentially a nervous breakdown. Tabia gave her notice, quit the job, and took some time off from work entirely to recover mentally and emotionally. Once she was in a better place, she came to me.

After telling me her story, she posed the question that I knew was coming. "So, do I have a case?"

I gave a very lawyerly answer: "That depends." What had happened to her was unacceptable, but to know whether we could successfully sue, I needed more information. Had she reported any of this behavior to her HR department, her supervisor?

Tabia shook her head. "No. I was scared to say anything. I thought I'd lose my job if I spoke up."

I then asked her, "Did you tell them you were quitting because of racism?"

She responded, "No, I told them I left to focus on personal matters."

She gave me the answers I was dreading, and I hated what I had to tell her next. "I'm sorry, Tabia. What happened to you is not right. It's unjust. But without anything documented to your managers, this is very hard to prove. There's no evidence that you quit because of what they did to you. The odds of you prevailing in court are very low." My heart ached for her as I broke the news, and all I could do was apologize. "I'm really, really sorry."

Unfortunately, this is something I see a lot—with women generally, like Tabia, and with mothers in particular. We just don't want to rock the boat. We don't feel like we can speak up. We're so tapped out by life and the struggles at work that we don't have it in us. So we bite our tongues and try to power through until the situation becomes untenable and we simply *can't* work in that environment anymore—and then, like Tabia, we have no choice but to quit, for our own sanity and health.

Compare this scenario with the story of my client Sage. Sage, a new mom, came to me after experiencing discrimination after she went back to the office. She, like Tabia, was *done* with this place: really and truly fed up and itching to hit send on the resignation email she'd already drafted.

But after we talked through what happened to her, and I'd seen that what she'd been subjected to clearly crossed a legal line, Sage agreed that she could hold out long enough to report the discrimination, in writing, to HR—which she did. Through my support, we were able to negotiate her exit. Her employer ended up offering her a generous severance to part ways amicably—basically a buyout if she promised not to sue.

For Sage, who wanted out anyway, this was a checkmate moment. Because she'd spoken up, and articulated her protected rights, she ended up with a half-million-dollar package that jump-started the next stage of her career. She bought a house, started a business, and is thriving. And, after that expensive lesson, I have to think that her former employer was a *lot* more careful about what they permitted to happen on company time.

To be clear: I fully support a mom's right to quit. Life's too fucking short and kids grow up too fast to keep you chained to work if you hate it.

But there are nuances to quitting. Quitting your job because you don't find value in your job anymore and gradually realized your life needs to change course? Amen. If it's right for you and for your family, go spend time with that baby. Quitting because you're experiencing harassment, retaliation, or anything punishable by law? Sadly, that only sabotages ourselves and our careers in the long run: We risk forfeiting any recourse to make ourselves whole, and the toxic workplace isn't going to change its ways after we leave because they weren't forced to learn a lesson. If this is you, and you really can't take another day, consider going on a mental health leave first. This may give you some time to rest, recover, and strategize.

And quitting because you've always known that you want to be a full-time mom, dedicated to caring for your kids, and just haven't gotten around to telling your employer? I am really, strongly sensitive to what that does for moms in the workplace as a whole. In the cases I represent, the most common reason for firing pregnant women or women on leave is that employers assume those women will quit anyway: "She just had a baby, so she must not care about work as much now. Why should we bother keeping her on payroll?"

So let's take these scenarios one at a time.

Having a baby changes your priorities. That's normal—but it can *feel* unexpected. You may never have seen yourself as a stay-at-home parent, but with an actual, physical baby to cuddle and play with, the vision comes into sharp focus. Again—that's okay. Part of that priority upheaval might be you realizing that you don't want to stay in the workforce right now. Your job might be "just fine" or it might be actively stressful and frustrating (though not discriminatory) or it might actually be *great,* but just not *as* great as spending time with your little one. You don't need any more justification than that to quit.

But it's still worth reflecting on what this decision means over the long term. It's true that many women leave their jobs when their children are small and return to the workforce once they're school-age, but that doesn't mean that doing so is always simple. Beyond that, the years when you are having babies are also (cruelly) the years that ultimately influence your lifetime earnings. It's so unfair that the window that we start to gain professional momentum overlaps with our baby-making years. It's like some kind of cosmic joke.

Future salaries are always based on previous salaries, for one thing, so you may be starting from a bit behind when you do start working again. But there's also the power of compound interest: The money you earn early in your career is more "valuable" in the sense that it has more time to grow. The bottom line is that even short breaks from working can lead to massive disparities in how much money you'll have in your later years: According to the Center for American Progress, a twenty-eight-year-old pregnant woman making $75,000 a year who takes five years off following the birth of her child would be forfeiting over *$1 million of earnings* before she reaches retirement age: $386,049 to lost wages, $357,390 to lost wage growth, and $281,222 to lost retirement assets and benefits. I personally believe stay-at-home mothers should be paid for their labor, but that is not our reality.

So I invite you: When you ask, "Can I afford to leave the workforce?" don't *just* look at your income and expenses now. Consider the effect that staying home (temporarily or long-term) will have on the money you'll be able to give your family over the course of your life.

Questions to Ask

- Can our family afford for me not to be taking a paycheck right now? Are we able to cover our bills and savings goals?
- How will me not working affect our benefits like health insurance? What about retirement savings?
- How long do I intend to stay home? What would different lengths of time look like over the long term?

Now, if you're in a situation like Tabia's or Sage's, you're either feeling like you want to quit or you are sensing that you may get fired, so you might as *well* quit.

And I understand wanting to quit. A lot of people who are experiencing challenges at work want to quit. That makes sense. Why would you want to stay in a workplace that doesn't respect you?

I'm sharing this because I've talked to *too* many people who told me, "I wish I knew this before I quit."

If you feel like you might get fired, a lot of people will quit to "save their dignity." Employers love when employees do this. When you quit, it is almost impossible to enforce your rights against them. It's only through *firing* employees that companies put themselves at risk, so when you leave voluntarily, you eliminate that risk for them. In other words, quitting reduces your leverage for a potential case or a severance negotiation. You will have essentially removed the problem for them. Resigning voluntarily also means you won't be eligible for unemployment benefits—another thing your employer loves, because they don't have to deal with paperwork *or* take the hit on their unemployment insurance premium. (As a general rule, you can only receive these benefits if you are fired and haven't committed gross misconduct.)

Questions to Ask

- Are the things I'm dealing with at work grounded in discrimination against me as a protected class (lactating mom, person who took protected leave, etc.)?
- If so, how can I document what's happening to me (writing down records of conversations, saving email conversations, etc.)?
- What kind of recourse am I seeking beyond not having to work here anymore?

Again, this does not mean you shouldn't quit—it's your life! But please make sure you understand the factors involved. If you have faced discrimination, it's *hard* to summon the will to fight back and leverage your rights. But the law is there to ensure fairness, and what you're going through *is not fair.* An employment attorney can help force out problematic colleagues, negotiate your exit through a separation package, or even take your employer to court.

Severance Agreements: A Deal with the Devil

Something employers *love*—and I *hate*—is a quick and hush-hush severance agreement. You leave the company, you sign away a few rights, and pocket a check. Except not! These agreements do so much to protect the employer.

Here is what you give up when you agree to sign a severance agreement:

Your rights. Fired illegally? You can no longer assert your rights in court.

Your story. You will be bound by confidentiality, and there will be some restrictions involved.

Potentially, unemployment benefits. Often these employers will classify the termination as a resignation, and you will not be eligible for benefits. They will work really hard to convince you that resigning is in your best interest because it will make it easier to find another job.

What you get? Money. It's hush money, really. In my humble professional opinion, a severance amount is always a fairly small, nominal amount. You get it quickly, but in the pursuit of immediacy, you sacrifice a much larger, and deserved, payout that you could get by pursuing legal recourse. I'd frame it more as, would you rather have $5,000 today or $50,000 in a month? What about $500,000 next year?

Yes, *that much money* is what some of my cases go for. That's the power of your rights. You get those numbers only through an attorney—never through a severance agreement (or the EEOC).

When termination is hanging over your head, these employers know that you need money and will convince you that signing the agreement is in your best interest. They will give you a deadline to make it feel urgent. This deadline is arbitrary and only serves to pressure you. You don't need to sign it. Once they fire you, they can no longer tell you what to do.

When you receive a severance agreement, you need to call a lawyer right away. It probably means your employer did something illegal; otherwise, they would just fire you and send you home (because employers are not obligated to provide severance). Most of us employment lawyers will review these for free (because if you have a good case, we will recover our fee through the contingency structure, where your employer pays us if you win, so it's a win-win). If you don't want to file a case, a lawyer can often negotiate better terms for you, like a clause protecting your professional reputation, more cash, or your employer's commitment not to contest unemployment benefits, or better tax allocation.

It's pained me how many people have forfeited good cases because their employers took advantage of their vulnerability. Know your rights and use your power!

Which brings me to the last scenario of moms who quit. It's one thing to leave because you don't want to be working at this stage of life, or because your employer is actively harming you. But it's another to fudge the truth about your intentions.

What I find particularly troubling is when a pregnant woman knows she wants to be a stay-at-home mom but waits until the end of her leave to announce it. After all, the company is holding her job open, and that's not an easy feat operationally. They could have found someone to fill the position if she had been up front about her plans. When that doesn't happen, it's almost like the company goes through a sort of "teachable moment," and they might become hesitant to hire or promote other moms—which harms everyone in the company and beyond.

So what should you do if you know, or even strongly suspect, that you don't want to come back from your leave? Be honest that you are not sure in what capacity you want to return (keep it open-ended), and try to negotiate with your employer. If you are concerned about your healthcare, offer to pay for the premium. This should not be too much. The mothers I have worked with have maintained their professional relationship with their prior employers through this transparency. In fact, many of them were able to transition from an employee to a contractor role with the same company. They explained that they are not sure whether they will want to return as a full-time employee, but they do want to keep working with the company. This can actually be advantageous to the company, as they would not have to pay for payroll taxes and other deductions on your income. It also removes any legal protections, so it eliminates any risk for the employer. You can offer to support certain projects for a specific time frame and a specific amount of money, or you can offer to work on a retainer basis as a contractor. If you are going this route, create a proposal that is cheaper than your current salary, and be very transparent about your time commitments. That way, you will stay in control of your hours, which would give you more time freedom on the home front. It also means you don't leave your employer hanging, and you also give them ample time to shift their organizational needs. But please, if you have a well-intended, generous, and supportive employer, don't shoot off a quick email at the conclusion of your leave that you are not coming back, after having received the benefits of your leave protections. Not only can it harm your reputation if you decide to reenter in a few years, it may result in resentment and fear of the next mother in that workplace.

Closing Argument

We made all of 'em . . . Yeah, do you remember? Truly remember that we made all of them? All the humans. Including those managers you're so scared of. A mother roared him into the world. Treat them accordingly. I know *they* are your boss under employment law, but under natural law, *you* are the boss. Childbirth remains the most biologically important function to our society, securing the survival of our species.

There's this myth in capitalism that mothers are distracted and less committed employees, but mothers travel to the realm of the souls and bring one to Earth from this dimension, creating a whole new human with her body, so I'm sure she can handle your stupid spreadsheets, Bob. If you are a mother and you are at the same professional level as men without kids, then don't you dare have impostor syndrome. You got there despite lack of sleep and family responsibilities. You are actually more qualified.

Remember that you are a Mother. You are the source. Walk into those meetings as the Divine creator of all that you are. I know that society does not always treat us as such, but start treating yourself as such. Women can simultaneously manage teams, grow new humans, launch businesses, run a household, use their bodies as a FOOD SOURCE, and society is still all "nah, women can't lead." So lead, woman. Lead the way. And let the men do more. If we expect women to work like men, we need to expect fathers to parent like mothers.

It has been a beautiful journey for me to integrate motherhood into my work and my work into my motherhood. Motherhood used to exist in the margins of my work and it felt imbalanced and unnatural. Now, mother-hood is integral to my life and my work.

I also invite you to center motherhood in the workplace and to build a world where we don't have to hide our motherhood at work but celebrate it as the superpower that it is.

Motherhood at the center of life truly is the way of both the past and the future. I'm a student of prehistoric history, and this inspires my work. Indigenous and pagan cultures all bowed to childbirth as the ultimate act of creation, and God was a Mother. Motherhood at the center of life is not a new concept; in fact, it is our origins. When you feel disre-spected as a mother, it's not all in your head and, no, you're not being "difficult." This inner rumbling is your ancestors reminding you that all of them, even that snarky manager, came from the Mother. It's time to remind them where they came from. I want you to walk into your HR meetings knowing in your bones that you are Divine, that we carry the whispers of foremothers who bowed to the goddess, and that ancient societies centered and celebrated mothers. I want you to feel your own sacredness when you ask for that time off for your baby, because growing and birthing and nursing and nurturing babies is life-giving work, and despite being so universal, it is magical and a miracle. No one gets to rob that experience from you. And if no one has told you before, on behalf of all of us, thank you.

And on behalf of your baby, too, thank you. Thank you, my powerful and strong mama. Thank you for protecting me. Thank you for setting me up with this great life.

You will tell them this story one day, my dear friend. You will tell them how you embraced motherhood as an opportunity to advocate for them and protect them in this beautiful way, and maybe even protecting the organization and the collective. Keep track of your accomplishments. You're over here creating humans and meeting expectations and it's something to be so proud of. Just because motherhood is universal does not make it really easy. Own that when you're still doing great work and offering that to the organization, you should be rewarded for that time and loyalty. Leaving your baby to work (and essentially paying so you can work there) is the ultimate act of loyalty. This is an incredible gift to your employer, by con-tinuing to offer your assets, your time, and your talents. And this should be honored and respected—and also centered, really put at the center of decision-making power in meetings. Claim that space completely. You are a Mother.

In celebration of your motherhood, and in a deep bow to the power of your womb,

Daphne

Appendix

Where We Go from Here

I hope this book gave you a road map and some peace of mind. I recognize that one book can't cover every situation, and some things fall *just* outside of the scope of this book while still being relevant to some readers. If that's you, this short appendix will cover where to go next.

If you fall between the gaps of the law: I acknowledge that some of you may still fall between the gaps of the laws and protections, and I want to share some words here as to where to go next.

First, recognize that even if you do not have a legal right protecting your request, you can still ask your employer to support you. Requests that are not protected by legal rights are essentially policy requests, based on your employer's generosity. (Technically, these requests are actually a form of DEI—more on that in a bit.)

The best framing for these requests is to use similar language as the legal requests. In addition, be overgenerous with the royal we and explain how the request will benefit the company, whether through increased retention or public goodwill. Data helps here too. It may be possible that your employer would prefer to follow the law regardless, because the exemptions are confusing and, therefore, risky. Plus, by following the law, it will be easier for them when the eligibility barriers are eliminated (for example, when they hire their fifteenth employee and have to abide by the PWFA).

So try the tools regardless, and you may end up setting policy.

If you want to create family-friendly policy at your workplace: If you are a trailblazer, and you feel secure in your job, consider improving policies at your workplace. The best way to do this is to make the business case, and to bring in a ton of data about how it will actually help the company (i.e., speak money). Clarify that it is an experiment (i.e., something you want to try out, as opposed to a permanent plan). This is much easier for a company to say yes to.

A script for a ramp-up policy:

> I really enjoy working here and I have a few ideas to increase visibility for our company. As you may have seen, a lot of companies are creating family-friendly workplaces in an effort to retain talent and reduce turnover. Here are a few of our competitors and their policies [link]. To prevent us losing our competitive edge, I've created a ramp-up plan for parents returning from parental leave. This plan would be a temporary accommodation for new parents where they could perform part of the work from home. I propose we try it out for six months. If it doesn't work, we can still return to the original policies of 100 percent on-site attendance. If it does work and we receive positive feedback and improved production, I intend to share these stories in local professional networks, and I intend to submit articles about the success of this plan to local business groups. This will allow us to gain goodwill and attract the best employees.

If you want to learn more about your (state) rights and stay up to date: Some of you may benefit from more information on your state rights, as well as more email templates to make specific requests to your employer. I have general advocacy tools and state specifics in my membership program. I also provide 1:1 coaching there. You can join us at themamattorney.com.

If you are a mama, but your baby is no longer a baby: When our children are babies, we have access to disability, bonding, and lactation rights. However, when our babies become older, our rights dwindle. But our children still need us! Kids don't stop needing their parents when they are no longer babies. They may get injured at school or wake up with a fever.

So what can we do at work if something happens at home? The FMLA allows eligible employees to take up to twelve weeks of unpaid leave for caretaking for your child's medical condition. States and towns also have sick leave laws. These are highly localized. In addition, many states have specific paid leave laws for school-aged children, including enrollment, orientation, disciplinary issues, and natural disasters (including fires and floods). (These local laws are also covered in my membership.)

If you're concerned that your rights will end up on the chopping block as DEI initiatives are canceled: Beginning in 2025, executive orders and other legal initiatives to terminate grants and contracts related to DEI (diversity, equity, and inclusion) began to rain down hard and fast from Washington. While (as of this writing) the upshot of these efforts is still in flux and not yet enforced (a US district judge issued a preliminary injunction, ruling that parts of the order likely violate free speech rights, among other things), it is important to know how this affects you and your rights.

At their core, DEI policies are just that—policies. While they may receive government funding (which, as we're now seeing, can come and go at the discretion of elected officials) to stay operational, they are not in and of themselves government programs, nor legal rights you are entitled to.

This means that even while DEI policies are at risk, your legal rights remain intact. This includes the provisions of the FMLA (twelve weeks of job-protected, unpaid leave), the PWFA (pregnancy and postpartum accommodations are required), the PDA (illegal to fire or discriminate against pregnant employees), the PUMP Act (the right to pump at work in a private space that is *not* a bathroom), the Equal Pay Act (women must be paid equally for equal work), the Fair Labor Standards Act (ensures overtime pay for eligible workers and protects breaks), the ADA (covers reasonable accommodations for pregnancy-related disabilities and conditions), and the ACA (insurance must cover maternity care and breast pumps).

That said, if you think DEI has nothing to do with motherhood? Honey, you got played. Mothers are a historically excluded and penalized group in the workplace, and any motherhood initiative or program that is not *legally mandated* is a form of DEI. Self-excluding your identity as a mother from "that whole DEI thing" is a betrayal. Our foremothers fought too hard, *we* fought too hard, we sacrificed too much to be silenced and isolated and pregnant with no support and no autonomy and no financial freedom. That only reduces us to serve and center men's needs and ignore our own.

This is a temporary moment. And it is in this moment in history that we as mothers will gather strength and become a truly united power block.

If you'd like to join the fight for mothers' rights: If you would like to advocate for improved maternal rights, please consider joining the Chamber of Mothers, an organization I cofounded.

When I was a young and hungry lawyer, I spent a lot of time on extracurricular volunteer activities. One of those activities included speaking to politicians and representatives to advocate for improved labor laws. This is when I learned that our work was consistently blocked by the chamber of commerce. We think of the chamber of commerce as a group that champions the local mom-and-pop shop, but it is actually an extremely powerful player in the political scene, working aggressively to block any labor-friendly initiative, including most maternal rights. They will place these pending bills on their "job killer" list and lobby against them. What they do so well is pooling resources, as well as clever branding.

So when the federal paid leave proposal (as part of the BBB package) failed in 2021, the top leading motherhood advocates joined forces and we created the Chamber of Mothers. While breastfeeding, I shared the vision with Erin Erenberg (my friend and current CEO): *Unite all the mothers into one power block, in a chamber of commerce–model template.* Mothers were scattered, divided, stuck in mommy wars. Mothers were stuck between an economy that told them the work came first and a society that told them the kids came first, but no one was advocating for the mothers' needs. The result was an entire generation of burned-out women. We said, "No more. Let's unite. Together, we are so powerful."

Join us in one of the local chapters, where we share stories and write letters while centering and celebrating motherhood. Find your local chapter at themamattorney.com.

If you are a boss mama: Whether you are a team lead, shift leader, in the C-suite, or a small business owner managing a team of hand-picked hires, being a boss mama is a whole 'nother (mother) level. And when you're a boss, a mother, *and* an empathetic person who's been through the wringer of arranging accommodations, leave, and childcare, the temptation to create the perfect mother-friendly team and be the Most Understanding Boss Ever is completely understandable . . . and can lead to your own burnout.

Remember: Don't set yourself on fire to keep someone else warm. You can advocate for systems and policies that support working parents—including clear expectations for parental leave, flexible hours, and remote work—but also make sure these arrangements work for both your team's objectives *and* your own well-being. Being a leader is a lot like being a parent: If you're constantly sacrificing your *own* needs, everyone suffers.

Remember, too, that being empathetic doesn't mean sacrificing sound management judgment. Make decisions based on data and performance *as well as* compassion and connection to someone else as a fellow parent—if you're constantly doing the work of two people because one of your team members is unreliable, that merits a conversation.

Finally, set the example. I talked to a judge once and she was one of the first moms on the bench in the whole state of California. She told me that she saw the dad judges be *so* bold about their family responsibilities. They'd just leave midday and say, "Sorry, I have to go coach a game." Just full on sending people away, even when they weren't done with their court calendar. We just don't see moms do that . . . but what if we did?

As an entrepreneur, my motherhood experience exists at the center of the work of my own business. I am exceptionally transparent about motherhood with my own team, to overcorrect the cultural norm. So much of motherhood is still happening behind closed doors, so placing it front and center in our workplaces is how we embrace and model a mother-friendly world. (There's so much to say here, really—it could fill another book! ☺)

Acknowledgments

To mothers everywhere, I bow to the power of your womb, the quiet altar where creation begins. You are the sacred, regenerative, and fruitful land upon which your children are planted.

To my mother, Greet De Wolf, raising us three children with endless resourcefulness and strength. You made something from nothing, again and again. Thank you for my life.

To my sons, Matteo and Lorenzo Zummo. My muses. My wildest teachers. You boys are my most daring creation, the prism through which I see the divine. I am boundlessly proud to be your mother.

My partner, Daniel Zummo. You are the sturdy haven where my dynamic spirit can rest. You help me find equilibrium. Our partnership is unglamorous work, but it is sacred. I am grateful every day.

My publisher, Tim Burgard. It was such an easy yes to work with you. You move with kindness, gentleness, and a calm protectiveness. The mothers owe you their gratitude.

My agents, Steve Troha and Jan Baumer. Steadfast, deeply trustable companions. Thank you for carrying this work with such care.

Misty Copeland, the creative capital M Mother embodied. Thank you for making space for this work. Thank you for showing us what grace looks like when it is rooted in power.

Blair Thornburgh, Meghan Stevenson, my collaborators. Your sharp attunement gave structure and cadence to my musings. Together we midwifed a book with a strong heartbeat.

Mel Judson, whose deep well of skill and devotion infuses and gives shape to everything we do. Creative firekeeper, strategist, and soul sister in one.

Jennifer Young, my ops manager. Thank you for your intuitive tenderness, for tending the invisible threads.

Anisha Banerjee, my comms manager. Your consistent rhythm is our drumbeat. So wise, so smart, so funny. You bring clarity and joy to every exchange.

To my dear friend Ji-In Houck, thank you for your generous peer review and discerning eye.

To my mother-in-law, Pamela Kravitz, for your consistent love.

To the women who have mothered me: Jacqueline Uytterhoeven, Mia Delvaux, Kris Delvaux, Hilde De Wolf, Stefany Reed, Sofie Verhoelst. Thank you.

Thank you to my brothers Matthias and Timothy Delvaux, my father Johan Delvaux, and my godfather Koen Delvaux.

My friends: Suraya Alkebulan, Karina Bennett, Ellen Bollion, Raena Boston, Monisha Chandanani, Erin Erenberg, Kelsey Lucas, Juliana Luna, Nisha Moodley, Emily Nachazel, Sarah Wildeman, Tine Wyseure, Summer Zaffino—your sisterhood sustains me.

Pooja Lakshmin, Eve Rodsky, Lauren Smith Brody. You helped me anchor this book into grounded legitimacy.

Josh Gruenberg. I would not be where I am now without the initiation. I look back with nothing but gratitude. Thank you for teaching me about loyalty, gravitas, and stamina.

Adding Ben Silver, Josh Pang, Jesse Collmann, and Gerardo Galaviz. Thank you for accommodating the mothers. Thank you for standing guard and covering so many times. It never went unseen.

Kiley Shai, my photographer, you saw me in a way I have never seen myself before.

All the Founding Mothers of Chamber of Mothers, including Alexis Barad-Cutler, Cait Zogby, Cassie Shortsleeve. We created something beautiful together.

Nuit Camacho and Sienna Medina, thank you for mothering my children while I worked. Without you, none of this would exist.

To all who mother, whether in body, in spirit, in work, may we keep weaving the world back into harmony, one act of love at a time.

May this work stand as a small offering to the great lineage of mothers.

May we all remember that the womb is holy ground.

May we all remember where we came from.

Index

About the Author

When attorney **Daphne Delvaux** became a mother, she realized that the work of justice extends far beyond the courtroom. It lives in the pumping room, the HR office, and the hours spent in meetings that could have been an email.

As a senior trial attorney, she'd long defended women facing pregnancy discrimination, representing mothers doing the life-affirming work of creating babies, while also meeting professional objectives.

When motherhood came to Daphne, any tension between her work and her truth dissolved. She was no longer speaking *for* mothers; she was speaking from them. In those moments, she understood that advocacy is a survival skill that anyone can learn.

If you are longing for more support or flexibility without losing yourself or your calling, you're in the right place. Daphne has stood at that same intersection (between devotion and ambition), armed with a briefcase and breast pump. She knows the ache of rushing between the courtroom and the pumping room, the guilt of wanting more agency, and the fear of asking for what you need.

She embodied these experiences, and they emboldened her. In walking through these initiations, she became a wayfinder for mothers reclaiming both their voice and their worth.

Motherhood sharpened her instincts and deepened her empathy. She began sharing what she learned publicly. She translated complex concepts into straightforward language so that every woman could understand her own power. What began with sharing her maternity leave templates grew into a larger movement where mothers could learn, rejoice, and rise together.

Through her work, Daphne has helped women negotiate better schedules, secure paid leave, and challenge unfairness with grace and gravitas. She is part advocate, part storyteller, part wise woman guiding others through the terrain she once navigated alone.

She has lived the contradictions of modern motherhood: drafting motions while nursing, taking depositions through nausea, and arguing cases while defending her own rights. Each moment rooted her more deeply in her purpose. Her approach merges clarity with care, without taking it all too seriously.

This book is her torch, offered to every mother who wonders if she can protect her family without losing her paycheck, professional advancement, or sanity in the process.

Daphne's work carries a rare blend of courtroom mastery, sharp insight, and communal healing. What began as a legal mission has become a living revolution, proving that justice, at its best, is reverent, regenerative, and deeply human.

Her work continues to build a collective force of people who know that justice for mothers is justice for everyone, as we all come from the Mother.